2.98

GARBO

Other books by John Bainbridge

Little Wonder, or The Reader's Digest and How It Grew
The Super-Americans
Like a Homesick Angel
Another Way of Living

The
famous
biography,
lavishly
illustrated

GARBO

by
John
Bainbridge

GALAHAD BOOKS · NEW YORK

Grateful acknowledgment is made to the following individuals and organizations for permission to use their photographs.

National Film Archive, pgs. 3; 10 (upper right); 10 (lower right); 10 (lower left); 101 (top); 116; 139 (top); 142 (top); 214; 253 (upper left).

Portrait study by Cecil Beaton, pgs. 6; 7; 261; 299 (top).

Culver Pictures, pgs. 10 (upper left); 71; 72; 78–9; 85; 98; 101 (bottom); 103; 109; 110–11; 126; 127 (top); 127 (bottom); 134 (top); 134 (bottom); 139 (bottom); 142 (bottom); 149 (top); 149 (bottom); 151; 154 (upper left); 154 (upper right); 178 (top); 180; 183 (top); 183 (bottom); 186; 187 (top); 187 (lower left); 187 (lower right); 199; 203; 207 (bottom); 207 (top); 210; 218 (bottom); 219; 222; 223; 225 (top); 227 (upper right); 227 (bottom); 276 (bottom).

Vivienne, London for the photograph by Anthony Beauchamp, p. 13.

Filmhistoriska Samlingarna, pgs. 16; 17; 21; 26; 29; 30 (top); 30 (bottom); 32; 36 (top); 36 (bottom).

International Magazine Service, p. 44.

G. Norman, pgs. 52 (bottom); 55.

Svensk Filmindustri, p. 52 (top).

Brown Brothers, pgs. 66; 88; 202 (lower right); 265 (top); 265 (bottom); 270 (top); 270 (bottom); 274; 276 (top); 285 (top); 288.

The Museum of Modern Art Film Stills Archive, pgs. 69; 91 (top); 95; 118; 132; 147 (top); 169; 171; 177; 178 (bottom); 195 (top); 195 (bottom); 202 (top); 212 (bottom); 215; 218 (top); 225 (bottom); 243; 244 (top); 253 (upper right).

Conde Nast Publications, Inc., for the Arnold Genthe photograph for *Vanity Fair,* p. 83; Copyright © 1925. Edward Steichen photograph for *Vanity Fair,* p. 147 (bottom); Copyright © 1928, 1956. From *Vanity Fair,* p. 206; Copyright © 1934, 1962. *Vogue* photograph by Baron Philippe de Rothschild, p. 299 (bottom); Copyright © 1970.

Kiers Photo, pgs. 91 (bottom left); 209; 212 (top).

Penguin Photo Collection, pgs. 91 (bottom right); 108; 144; 154 (bottom); 160; 201; 216; 237; 244 (bottom); 253 (lower right).

The Collection of the Memory Shop, pgs. 202 (lower left); 227 (upper left); 253 (lower left).

Wide World Photo, pgs. 259 (top); 280; 291; 294; 297.

Acme, p. 259 (bottom).

Collection of the Museum of Modern Art, Edward Steichen, Photographer, p. iv.

To Dorothy

with Reason

Chapter One

"She was gifted with genius, and led one of those exceptional existences which cannot be judged by ordinary standards." So wrote Balzac of George Sand, the French novelist. So, also, might one write of Greta Garbo, the Swedish-born actress, for these two remarkable women, though separated in time by a century, are alike in many ways. Garbo is aware of this, and more than once, during the thirty years she has been in retirement, has considered leaving it to portray Sand on the screen. There is small chance that she will ever make that or any other film, though the Sand role would suit her well. Like Sand, Garbo is a child of the earth who has become one of the great ornaments and excitements of her age. She has also, like Sand, dared to live her life according to standards of her own devising and quietly accepted the penalties imposed for failing to follow the conventions of the herd. Her life has been frustrated, like Sand's and every other artist's, but hers perhaps more so than most, because she is Greta Garbo, a woman who has become a legend in her own lifetime.

One of the ironies of Garbo's life is that she became a legend against her will, though possibly that is the only way one becomes a legend. Those who deliberately set out to invest themselves with legendary qualities are usually shown up as counterfeits. Garbo is the real thing, everything a legend should be. She is an idea, a dream, shadow, substance and mystery. Yet none of this did she wish upon herself. As a child, she wanted to be an actress, like thousands of other girls before her and since, and she also wished to escape being poor, another desire that is not uncommon. In the course of satisfying these two ambitions she became the most celebrated actress the screen has ever seen as well as one of the wealthiest, and, perhaps as an inevitable concomitance, one of the loneliest. "I never said, 'I want to be alone,' " Garbo once told a friend. "I only said, 'I want to be *let* alone.' There is all the difference."

Mystery intrigues, and it is not in human nature to leave it alone, especially when the mystery appears in the form of a beautiful woman. Whether by accident or design, Garbo has made herself the most enchantingly mysterious woman of her time. By the expedient of almost never talking about her private affairs, even to her friends, she has managed to keep her origins as obscure as her present activities and future plans. In Hollywood, which expects its leading citizens to share their lives and loves and sorrows unsparingly with the public, Garbo remained a mystery by breaking all the rules. Except at the very outset of her career, she granted no interviews, signed no autographs, attended no premieres, answered no fan mail, endorsed no products, and for a long period kept her address and telephone number a secret from Metro-Goldwyn-Mayer, the studio that employed her. To keep in touch with their elusive star, M-G-M found it necessary to put one of Garbo's friends, who was privy to her whereabouts, on the payroll at two hundred and fifty dollars a week.

As the legendary woman of mystery, Greta Garbo has baffled journalists at home and abroad. She has eluded them in both body and spirit. Groping for the revealing phrase that would provide a clue to the unguessed mystery, they have had to settle for something rather commonplace, such as "the Swedish Sphinx," "the Hollywood Sphinx," "the unapproachable Sphinx," "the bashful Baltic beauty," "the shy Valkyrie," "the dazzling enigma," "the Swedish Swan," "the Arctic Mystery," "the million-dollar hermit," and so on. Instead of dispelling any of the mystery, these efforts have, if anything, only deepened it. What remains hidden is the cause of the strange, unquenchable drive that has propelled Garbo in her perpetual and agonized flight from the eyes of the world. "Being in the newspapers is awfully silly to me," she once said in a rare interview. "It is all right for important people who have something to contribute to talk. I have nothing to contribute." These remarks, though admirably modest, are oddly misleading, for privately Garbo has a very keen sense of her importance, as everybody who knows her well is aware. The mystery is why she denies it, why she has never been able to accept being Greta Garbo.

She prefers, instead, to masquerade as Miss Harriet Brown, Miss Karin Lund, Miss Jane Emerson, Miss Emily Clark, Miss Mary Holmquist or Miss Gussie Berger—all pseudonyms that she has used in an effort to lose her public identity. Her favorite is Miss Harriet Brown. Hiding behind that drab and faceless fiction, she strolls the streets of New York, Paris, London and Vienna, often stopping to browse in antique shops, where, if she asks that some piece be set aside for her (she almost never buys), she reluctantly gives her name as Miss Harriet Brown, fooling nobody, perhaps not even herself. But her desire to avoid playing the role of Greta Garbo before strangers is overpowering. She has never fully understood the part.

The character of Garbo, to its creator, is an image that exists only on the screen. In that form she regards herself with the interest and affection that she might have for a rather good friend. Occasionally, when she feels like renewing this friendship, she goes to the Museum of Modern Art, in New York, which has a large film library, and in the company of a museum official with whom she is well acquainted looks at a private showing of one of her pictures. As the film unfolds she comments to her companion on her actions on the screen, always referring to herself in the third person. "Watch her now," she may remark, "she's going to ask for money. Then she'll go outdoors and smoke a cigarette. Oh my, look at the way she's done her hair." While the film is showing she is at ease, animated and gay. When it is over and her image has vanished from the screen, she again becomes the woman of legend, pensive and uneasy. Turning up her coat collar and pulling down the brim of her floppy hat, she strides out of the museum, looking neither to right nor left, and back into a world that is not as real to her as the one she has just left. In her view of herself, Garbo resembles the actress-heroine of Henry James's novel *The Tragic Muse.* "Her character," James said of his heroine, "was simply to hold you by the particular spell; any other—the good nature of home, the relation to her mother, her friends, her lovers, her debts, the practice of virtues or industries or vices—was not worth speaking of. They were the fictions and shows; the representation was the deep substance."

For more than four decades, Garbo's admirers on six continents have contended with one another in trying to describe her particular spell. Their prolonged and enchanting verbal skirmish has been trippingly fought on the field of superlatives. Garbo has been called "The Divine" in several languages and not a few dialects. To some of her worshipers she is only "The Incomparable One," while to others she is simply "poetry, sunrise and great music." In England she has been characterized as "a super-human symbol of The Other Woman," and in Germany as "the supreme symbol of inscrutable tragedy." Other European gallants, blowing hot and cold simultaneously, have described her as "the flaming icicle" and "the frozen torch." In America she has been hailed with majestic dizziness as "the mysterious, inscrutable, available but untouchable essence of the indefinable." At the peak of her film career, when she had just turned thirty, she was "every man's harmless fantasy mistress," in the words of Alistair Cooke, the erudite American correspondent of *The Guardian*. "By being worshiped by the entire world," Cooke said, "she gives you the feeling that if your imagination has to sin, it can at least congratulate itself on its impeccable taste." Today, at sixty-five, Garbo has lost none of her power to evoke the superlative phrase. Once "the First Lady of Hollywood," she can now rejoice in her position as "the world's most alluring spinster." Age cannot wither a legend.

Whatever else Garbo may represent, she is undeniably the classic symbol of womanly beauty in our time. Other women may be more beautiful, as even some of Garbo's most ardent admirers have acknowledged, but she alone has been universally accepted as the latter-day Helen of Troy. To be the fairest woman in the world, in any age, is no small responsibility. Just as Helen's good looks drove thousands of Greeks to take up the sword, so Garbo's singular features have moved a sizable army of her contemporaries to take up the pen. In prose as rich as whipped cream they have extolled her beauty with loving meticulousness. It is not her figure they have so much praised, because that, at least by American standards, is quite plain; nor her legs, for she has the thick, awkward legs of a statue; nor her feet, which despite the tiresome jokes, are neither large nor dainty (she wears a 7 AA shoe); nor her hands, which she herself modestly describes as "kitchenette hands." About these

features her idolators have sung small. The cause of their rhapsody is her face.

As a rule, those who have celebrated what has been called "the face of this century" begin their tributes with a considered and rather general statement, such as "To watch her face is like contemplating a masterwork—it becomes an experience that strikes both heart and mind," or "She is as beautiful as the aurora borealis," or "It needs a work of fiction to invent a face to approach hers, a Hardy and a Eustacia Vye," or "Garbo manages, because she is a supremely beautiful woman, to make beauty look like a mark of religion." After that come the particulars, beginning with her hair, which is "biscuit colored and of the finest spun silk and clear and sweetly smelling as a baby's after its bath," proceeding to "the flawless structure of the brow and cheek and chin," and taking into account her skin, which is "smooth as marble, generally burnt to an apricot honey color." Her nose, depending on the way it is observed, either "has the pristine sensitivity of some timid creature of the forest," or else it is "so delicate and sensitive that she seems to be conscious of perfumes too subtle for others to enjoy—the perfumes perhaps of her own beauty." In any event, Garbo's nose is clearly one of her good features.

Even more arresting are her eyes. They are blue, or, more precisely, of an "unforgettable blue." The adjective most often used to describe them is "haunting," though they have also been characterized as "haunted," "sad," "quizzical," "languorous," "melancholy" and "omniscient," none of which would seem to be adequate in view of their extraordinary power. "They effect in amorous scenes sensual transport and, at the same time, the adumbration of the end of love," an American writer once recorded, after getting a grip on himself. "Her eyes," Cecil Beaton, the fashionable British photographer and man about the arts, has written, "seem to offer a special compassion for each of us. Inexhaustible spiritual assets highlight the sensitivity and delicacy of these features, continually hinting at every nuance of all that she is feeling, and giving the spectator the tenuous and remarkable impression that he is witnessing the remotest depths in a human face." As for her eyelashes, they are so long and luxurious that, when lowered, they remind the poetic spectator of a "veil," or a "heavy canopy," or "a pair of miniature fans," or a "peacock's tail." Her mouth is generous and "delicately controlled" or "vainly disciplined toward severity"; furthermore, it "combines, in a wistful, childlike ambivalence, the Greek masks of comedy and tragedy," and her teeth are "large and more glistening than pearls." When she smiles, "she makes the Mona Lisa look like a D.A.R. president receiving at tea," and when she laughs, "she proves that things metallic have a soul."

Such is the likeness of Garbo, the legendary beauty, as far as words reveal it. It is, of course, no likeness at all, nor could it be, for Garbo, like any other thing of beauty, is indescribable. Yet the effect of her magic looks is everywhere evident, because Garbo has probably had a greater influence on the appearance of women today than any other person. The change she brought about was dramatically illustrated in the early thirties, when *Vanity Fair* published, under the heading, "Then Came Garbo," a set of photographs of Joan Crawford, Tallulah Bankhead, Katharine Hepburn, Marlene Dietrich and several other stage and screen actresses, showing how they had looked before Garbo began her reign in Hollywood and how they looked a couple of years afterward. The pre-Garbo portraits show a collection of rather plump and perky young women with short, fuzzy bobbed hair, thick eyebrows, fussy make-up and wearing expressions that were either fatuous or coy. In their post-Garbo portraits the same young women look startlingly alike—their hair is now worn in the long, plain page-boy style, their eyebrows are mere pencil lines, their eyelashes have been artificially lengthened, their cheeks look as if they are being determinedly sucked in, their make-up is of the simplest, and their expressions are uniformly languorous and inscrutable, as if they were brooding over some abiding sorrow. Perhaps they are only brooding over their inability to look even more like Garbo.

The studied imitation of Garbo was practiced not only by actresses but by shopgirls and ladies of quality as well. Her classic features became the standard in fashion drawings, and even the mannequins in store windows began to bear an arresting resemblance to the enigmatic actress. Unwittingly, she set the style for the wearing of slacks, low-

heeled shoes and wide-brimmed hats that hide the face. These things were more easily copied than the so-called Garbo manner—the slow, quiet, graceful motions combined with an air of weary and melancholy dignity—but that, too, was widely aped. The imitations, however skill-fully contrived, were bound to be nothing but pale carbon copies, for the Garbo manner, like its creator, is *sui generis.*

As an actress, Garbo is also unique. Since her departure from the screen, nobody has taken her place, or seriously tried to, or could. "She stood alone—there was no one like her," Lewis Stone, who appeared with her in *Queen Christina,* once remarked. "She was Greta Garbo, and that said it all. No one ever created such an impression." Searching for a possible comparison, critics have often likened her to two of the greatest actresses of another day, Sarah Bernhardt and Eleonora Duse. Such accolades Garbo finds embarrassing. Shortly after completing one of her most memorable films, *Camille,* a work in which both Bernhardt and Duse won world-wide acclaim on the stage, Garbo was present at a small party attended by close friends. One of the elder of them enthusiastically remarked that her performance of the role was superb, even finer than Duse's. Without saying a word, Garbo sprang from her chair and rushed from the room. "Her face was white as chalk," one of the guests has since recalled. "She went home alone right after-ward. It broke up the party, but she couldn't help herself. She valued the compliment, of course, but her very great modesty made hearing it unendurable agony."

However Garbo may compare professionally with Duse and Bern-hardt—and that can never be truly known because Garbo will not appear on the stage—she is personally in their tradition. Like Duse, she leads a curious, seclusive life, and seems to belong to no time or place. "I am a vagabond, a nomad," Duse used to say of herself. And Garbo has said of herself, "I am a wanderer, just a wanderer." Like Bernhardt, who kept in her bedroom a complete human skeleton as well as a pearwood coffin that she occasionally slept in, Garbo is a woman of many idiosyncrasies, but they are not, as the Divine Sarah's often were, consciously calculated to attract attention.

Unlike both Duse and Bernhardt, Garbo has never married, but her attachments, like theirs, have been many and often widely publicized. Her extended European vacation with the colorful maestro Leopold Stokowski, for example, created at least as much international interest as the holiday in Egypt that Duse once took with the flamboyant Gabriele D'Annunzio. Garbo is quite as aware of her irresistible magnetism as Duse and Bernhardt were of theirs. One of Sarah Bernhardt's greatest admirers was Theodore Roosevelt, who always made a point of seeing her when he went abroad. "I could not come to Paris," he once wrote in a letter to her, "and miss seeing my oldest and best friend there." When Bernhardt showed this letter to friends, she used to murmur in her golden voice, "Ah! but that man and I, we could rule the world!" Though Garbo has never shown any aspiration to rule the world, she once had an idea for trying to save it from ruin. One evening during the early stages of World War II, she was talking in the home of a friend with a man who had recently returned from Europe. He told her that her films were Hitler's favorites, that the Fuehrer had them shown for his private enjoyment over and over again and that his adoration was so overwhelming that he had personally intervened to permit one of her later films, which had been directed by a Jew, to be shown publicly throughout the Reich. After listening to this intelligence with rapt interest, Garbo said that she thought she should arrange some way to meet with Hitler, so she could talk to him about the awful things he was doing and try to make him change his mind about continuing the war. "At least," she said after some reflection, "if I couldn't make him change his mind, I could shoot him." Though she spoke with seriousness, she was not, her friend from Europe gradually discovered as the conversation went on, keenly aware of all the practical difficulties that lay in the way of assassinating the Fuehrer.

In at least one respect, Garbo departs radically from the tradition of Duse and Bernhardt, who were so mercilessly driven by the urge to act that they carried on in their profession, despite all manner of reverses, almost to the moment they died, when they were both very far along in years. By contrast, Garbo gave up acting without a struggle when she was in her middle thirties, at the peak of her powers. Her life as a star had extended over a period of fifteen years, more than twice the average

Hollywood span, and she had become firmly established as the most famous screen actress in the world. Since her retirement, in 1941, she has turned down hundreds of offers to return to the films. She prefers to rest on her laurels, and they are considerable.

"Garbo brought to films," the novelist and playwright Truman Capote has written, "a sense of poetry approached by no one else except, perhaps, Charles Chaplin. In even her earliest pictures, if seen now, she illuminates all that surrounds her, however dated or ludicrous, for she is a classic actress controlled by an artistic truthfulness that seldom permits a spurious moment." This opinion is shared by Clarence Brown, who directed seven of her pictures. "Garbo is the kind of actress who simply cannot ever play a part wrong, who never makes a mistake," Brown said recently. "She was not only a great star with a rare power to charm. She had an intuition that no one else in films has possessed." Lionel Barrymore, who appeared in four films with Garbo and was never known as a man given to flattery, once paid tribute to her as "the greatest actress ever seen on the screen."

During her long and illustrious Hollywood career, Garbo starred in twenty-four films, several of which have come to be regarded by critics and film scholars alike as permanent classics of the screen, and yet she never won an Oscar. It is ironic, but that's the way it is with legends.

Chapter Two

It is customary in telling the story of a person's life to begin by examining the subject's family tree. This procedure can be quite a bore, unless the forebears under consideration happen to be either unusually distinguished or bizarre. Garbo's ancestors were neither. They were farmers. According to an investigation made by the Scandinavian Family Study Association, Garbo's ancestors as far back as the early 1700s were all tillers of the soil. Some owned their own land, others were tenants on one of the great Swedish estates. Surveying the family tree, one finds an occasional progenitor who lifted his head briefly above the crowd by serving as a deacon in the church or as a juryman in a provincial court, but nothing more. All the others, as the musty records disclose, were plain, rugged, law-abiding country folk whose lives were as dull as their common occupation.

The fact that Garbo is descended from six generations of farmers cannot, of course, be dismissed as a matter of slight importance. On the contrary, her genealogy is of great significance, for her myriad ancestors had a profound influence in shaping her physical and mental being. If she is a peasant at heart, as her friends have often said, there is a reason.

Of perhaps even more importance in shaping her character were her early years. What a man is at twelve years old, a philosopher long ago observed, so will he be all the rest of his life. Garbo has said very little in public about her life at twelve or at any other age. Soon after her arrival in Hollywood she was asked in an interview the usual questions about her childhood. "Some people were born in red brick houses, others in plain white board ones," she said. "We were all born in houses. I do not want it printed that I was born in this house or that— that my mother is this or my father was that. They were my mother and father. That is enough. Why should the world talk about them?" Garbo was then nineteen. Her public character as the enigmatic woman of the world was yet to be established. Her private personality had already been irrevocably shaped.

Garbo was born in neither a red brick house nor in a white board one but rather in the Southern Maternity Hospital in Stockholm, Sweden. The date was September 18, 1905. She was the third child born to Karl Alfred Gustafsson and his wife Anna Lovisa. The baby was christened Greta Lovisa Gustafsson, the name that she bore for the first eighteen years of her life. She had been preceded in the family by a sister, Alva, and a brother, Sven. "I was the youngest," she recalled many years later, "but they always treated me as the oldest. Nobody ever thought of me as a little girl."

Her father, Karl Gustafsson, had been born and raised on a farm in southern Sweden. In 1896, when he was twenty-five, he quit the rural life and moved to Stockholm, where he was married the same year to a

Garbo's father

With her mother on a visit to Stockholm in 1928

plump young woman named Anna Karlsson, who had also been brought up in the country. By the time Greta was born, nine years later, her mother had become a stout, round-faced woman with heavy arms and a thick neck. Her father was still a youthful-looking man with a countenance that was almost feminine in its refinement. Tall and slender, with finely chiseled, ascetic features, classically shaped nose and generous, sensitive mouth, he was a specimen of Nordic handsomeness.

Though a man of exceptional appearance, Karl Gustafsson had few other attributes to help him make his way in the city. He was by nature quiet, reserved and lacking in enterprise. Furthermore, his health was not robust. Having had very little formal education and no technical training, he earned a meager living as an unskilled laborer, taking work wherever he could find it. As a result, making ends meet was always a problem in the Gustafsson household.

From the time she was born until she left Sweden, Greta lived with her family in a four-room, cold-water flat on the fourth floor of a five-story, walk-up apartment situated at Blekingegatan 32. Blekingegatan is a street on Stockholm's South Side, a district that Stockholmers regarded in those days as the city's slums. By American standards the area would hardly have been considered a slum; the streets were clean, and the apartment buildings that lined them, though old and drab, were kept tidy and in fairly good repair. But it was a neighborhood of low-income, working-class families, and there was nothing cheerful about it. There were neither lawns, trees nor flowers. On the ground floor of several of the apartment buildings along Blekingegatan were grocery stores, meat markets, tobacco and stationery shops and a couple of dingy workingmen's restaurants that sold beer, coffee and sandwiches at cheap prices. The apartment buildings themselves rose straight up from the sidewalk to form an unbroken façade of monotonous gray. The view from the apartment that Greta grew up in was one of the least pleasing prospects in Stockholm, a city that generally abounds in beauty. Across the street from Blekingegatan 32 was a square block filled with a jumble of low, metal-roofed wooden sheds, piles of sand and cement, pieces of building construction equipment and other unsightly odds and ends. That lot, the sidewalk and the street were Greta's playgrounds.

As a child, Greta was plump, towheaded, healthy and tractable. Her nickname was "Keta," derived from the way she pronounced her name when she was very small. Her life as a little girl was in no way unusual, except that she had few dolls or other toys, but neither did the majority of her playmates. Many years later, when she could afford to indulge a whim, she bought herself a collection of dolls. She kept them for a few years, and then sold them at auction in Stockholm along with a considerable amount of other personal property. Following her instructions, the firm that auctioned the goods did not advertise them as hers. The dolls, which filled a crate, were knocked down for thirty kronor, the equivalent of something less than eight dollars. Had the identity of their owner been known, they would, of course, have brought many times that sum.

Like the other children in the neighborhood, Greta learned to ski and skate, and did her share of household chores, though she never took with enthusiasm to housework and never developed much interest in cooking or sewing. Her sister Alva was a much closer companion to her mother than Greta was. Together Alva and her mother did the marketing and cooking, while Greta was assigned the simpler chores, such as washing dishes. Mrs. Gustafsson had to pinch pennies, but she was handy with the needle, made most of her daughters' clothes, and saw to it that all her children, though not dressed in any finery, were comfortably and cleanly clothed. A good housewife and mother, she was also a popular woman in the community, and had the reputation of always being willing to lend a hand whenever a neighbor needed help.

One of Mrs. Gustafsson's close friends was a widow named Agnes Lind, who ran a stationery and tobacco shop down the block on Blekinge-gatan. Like so many Swedes, Mrs. Lind was fond of the theatre and had one wall of her shop covered with picture postcards of Sweden's leading actors and actresses. Greta spent a good deal of her time around the shop and often ran errands and did other chores for Mrs. Lind, who usually gave her as a reward one of the theatrical postcards. Greta's favorites at that time, Mrs. Lind once recalled, were Naima Wifstrand, a star of light opera, and especially Carl Brisson, the handsome, curly-haired Danish singer who was the reigning matinee idol of the day.

Owing to their straitened circumstances, Greta's family could not afford the luxury of going to the theatre, taking summer vacations away from the city or any similar pleasures. Like many other people in their neighborhood, the Gustafssons had a garden plot similar to the American wartime Victory gardens, only larger, on the outskirts of Stockholm. On most Sundays during the spring and summer, Greta and her family, carrying a picnic lunch, took the trolley to the end of the line and then walked a mile or so to their garden, where they spent the day hoeing and weeding and enjoying the fresh air. The produce from the garden, a large part of which Mrs. Gustafsson put up for the winter, was not the least of its attractions.

In late August of 1912, two weeks before her seventh birthday, Greta began attending school. She enrolled in the Katarina grammar school, in her neighborhood, and continued her attendance there for the next seven years. According to her report cards, she was absent, during that entire period, a total of sixteen days on account of illness; she played hooky only once.

Greta was a better than average student, obedient and industrious. In Behavior and Application she was marked "Perfect" on her report cards for all seven years. Generally speaking, she was a slow starter in her studies. During her first two years she was judged "Fair" in Intellectual Growth, but throughout the next five she was marked "Quite Good." That was the mark she also consistently received, after her first two years, in Bible, Reading, Writing, Geography and History. Her grades in Arithmetic varied from "Passing" to "Fair"; in Handwriting from "Passing" to "Good"; and in Singing from "Fair" to "Quite Good." Her poorest subjects were Gymnastics and Drawing. In the former, she was given the grade of "Passing," next to the lowest mark on the scale, for five years, finally improving to "Fair" in the last two. In the latter, she was never able to rise above "Passing." Her final year in school was her best. Her grades in all subjects, save the unconquerable Drawing, ranged from "Quite Good" to "Perfect," and she promised to develop into a first-rate student.

However, her formal education ended abruptly after seven years. She was obliged to drop out of school in 1919, when her father was taken seriously ill. His illness was prolonged. The family, left without a breadwinner, was soon penniless. Greta's mother, sister and brother all went to work to provide an income, while Greta stayed at home to take care of her father.

On one of the few occasions when she has talked to friends about her childhood she recalled that it was among her duties to take her father once a week to a charity clinic for treatment, and she spoke of the humiliation and sadness she felt in having to watch him, suffering

Garbo in her confirmation costume

great pain, wait for what seemed an endless time for attention. She decided then, she said, that she would order her own life so that she would never be financially dependent on anybody. In later years her friends and acquaintances were often impressed, and sometimes slightly annoyed, by her exceedingly close management of her purse. The scars of childhood are slow to heal.

Chapter Three

After her father's death, which occurred early in 1920, Greta made up her mind not to return to school. She told her mother she planned to go to work instead. Though Mrs. Gustafsson was not in sympathy with this move, the family was having a hard time paying its bills, so Greta's decision was not seriously opposed. Now fourteen, she had grown rapidly; her mature appearance and manner belied her age. She was already five feet, six inches tall, only an inch shorter than she is today. Her height, combined with the responsibilities she had shouldered, had forced her prematurely to take on grown-up ways. She looked and acted like a young woman. She had been denied, along with many other things, the luxury of girlhood.

Greta obtained her first job in a neighborhood barbershop, operated by a man named Einer Widebäck, where she was employed as a *tvålflicka,* or "soaplather girl." This was not, at the time, an uncommon occupation in Sweden. Even today, many Swedes consider women more expert at barbering than men, and there are several shops staffed entirely by so-called lady barbers in Stockholm and in other Scandinavian cities. A lady barber normally learns her trade by working first as a soaplather girl. This was the kind of apprenticeship that Greta served. Wearing a white smock, she deftly performed her job, which consisted of mixing lather, patting it on the customers' faces, laying out razors, scissors and clean towels and tidying up after the barber had finished his operations. The work was not excessively stimulating, nor was it well paid, but Greta dutifully stayed at it for nearly half a year.

After two months at Widebäck's shop, she left to take the same kind of job in a much larger establishment situated on Götegatan, about a mile from her home. Her second employer was Arthur F. Ekengren, whose wife worked in the shop as cashier; she also hired and supervised the soaplather girls. According to Mrs. Ekengren's recollection, Greta was paid a weekly wage of four kronor, or approximately one dollar, and made an almost equal amount in tips. "She could do anything she set her hand to," Mrs. Ekengren once recalled. "None of her customers ever complained, but they probably wouldn't have, even if she had scalded them. She was really one of the most beautiful creatures I have ever seen. She was more filled-out in those days, almost buxom, and she simply radiated happiness. I remember she was wild about Carl Brisson. She used to sing his songs—she knew them all—and she had her locker, where she kept her smock and wraps, covered with pictures of him. We were all very fond of her. She was a sunbeam."

While working as a soaplather girl, Greta was dreaming of something quite different from making good as a lady barber. She was stage-struck. She had set her mind on becoming an actress.

This ambition, considering her circumstances and background, might seem on the surface a whimsical one. There was no theatrical tradition in her family, no aunt who had run away from home to go on the stage, no uncle who had done anything more daring than milk cows and walk behind a plow. She had never been fired by interest in the drama while in school, had never met an actor or actress, and had, in fact, been inside a theatre not more than four or five times in her life. But none. of those things, as the careers of theatrical people so often demonstrate, is important. In the biological sense, actors and actresses are apt to be sports. What secret demon drives them to embrace the world of make-believe is their private mystery. However, to Greta, as no doubt to many other aspiring actresses, almost any other world looked more inviting than the one she lived in.

Furthermore, it is not so rare for a good-looking Swedish girl to have theatrical ambitions. The theatre is a great deal more popular in Sweden, very much closer to the everyday life of the people, than it is in America. Swedes go to the theatre more or less the way Americans go to the movies. A Swedish family will gladly give up many other pleasures to be able to spend an evening attending a play or a revue. "The theatre, to the Swedes, is much more than a means of entertainment," a student of the Swedish theatre has written. "It is a necessary adjunct to their daily life." This was as true when Greta was growing up as it is today. In 1920, when she was still working in the Ekengren barbershop, Stockholm, then a city of slightly more than four hundred thousand people, had twelve legitimate theatres in operation. Few American cities of similar size, then or now, can boast even one. As people who cherish the theatre, Swedes have a high regard for the acting profession. Parents encourage their children to enter it.

Greta needed no encouragement, of a parental nature or any other kind. She had resolved to go on the stage. She had no clear notion of how she was going to realize her ambition, but she had known for some time that the theatre and theatrical people were all that interested her. The two most popular theatres within walking distance of Stockholm's South Side were the Sodra and the Mosebacke. Those were Greta's shrines. Though she couldn't afford to enter them, she began, when she was nine years old, to stand around the stage doors, watching the actors and actresses arrive and depart. That continued to be her favorite recreation for many years. She had a preference for the Mosebacke because Carl Brisson frequently played there. She made friends with the Mosebacke's doorman, who once said that she was around the building so much that he came to regard her as part of the place, "like the theatre's cat," as he put it.

Once, during the time she was working for the Ekengrens, Greta got inside the Mosebacke to see her idol Brisson. Mrs. Ekengren's daughter had been given two tickets to the theatre, and she invited Greta to go with her. When Brisson took his curtain calls, Greta, flushed with excitement, jumped to her feet. Applauding vigorously, she cried, "Bravo, Kalle, bravo!" again and again. She was so singularly demonstrative, the Ekengren girl later reported to her mother, that the rest of the audience showed more interest in the wildly appreciative spectator than in the somewhat bewildered star.

However sunny Greta's disposition may have been around the Ekengren barbershop, she found the work there unrewarding in many ways, and began looking for a better job. Her sister Alva, who worked as a stenographer in the office of an insurance company, had two friends who were clerks in Paul U. Bergström's department store, an emporium customarily referred to in Stockholm as PUB, after the founder's initials. It was, and is, one of the city's two largest department stores, and at that

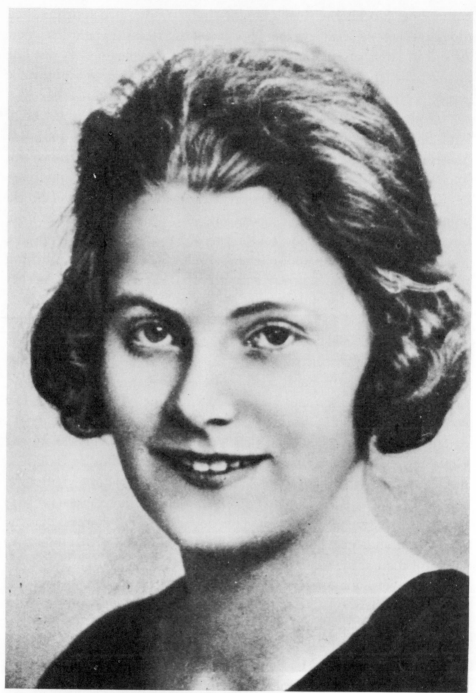

In 1920, shortly before turning fifteen

time had about six hundred employees. Alva's friends suggested that Greta apply for work at PUB. Toward the end of July, 1920, she filled out an application, and on the twenty-sixth of that month was hired as a trainee in the millinery department. After a couple of months, she became a full-fledged clerk. Her salary, according to the store's personnel records, was a hundred and twenty-five kronor a month, or about twenty-five dollars. This was a respectable sum at that time, when the krona had more than twice the purchasing power that it has nowadays. For the first time in her life Greta had a little spare money of her own. Once in a while she was able to go to the theatre or the movies.

Even if it wanted to, PUB could not forget the fact that it once numbered among its employees the girl who became the screen's foremost actress. So many tourists from all parts of the world, especially women from America, make a Garbo pilgrimage to PUB every year that the attendants at the ground-floor information booths do not bat an eye when they are asked the question, "Whereabouts in the store did Greta Garbo work?" The pilgrims are directed to the fourth floor. There is a great deal of merchandise to be seen there, but that is all. Nevertheless, the clerks on the fourth floor say, the visiting Garbo devotees usually walk around the premises in an interested and rather reverent way, as if they were inspecting a cathedral. To accommodate visitors who have a special interest in its celebrated ex-employee PUB has on hand a supply of prints of a photograph made for the store's personnel department soon after she was hired. The picture shows a full-faced, placid-looking young woman—she had just turned fifteen— with thick, long hair casually combed into loose puffs over her ears. Her tentative smile reveals teeth that are slightly gapped. Her expression is wistful.

The first discovery of Greta's photogenic qualities was made at PUB early in 1921. The store was preparing its spring catalogue, and Greta helped the head of the millinery department pick out the hats to be featured in it. When the advertising manager appeared to look over the selections, he asked Greta to try them on. She looked so attractive to the manager that he suggested she also model the hats for the catalogue. Greta was more than pleased to do so. The face that was to launch a thousand sighs was accordingly first presented to the public, under an assortment of five fussy straws and felts, in a department store catalogue.

Greta enjoyed the modeling assignment. The chance to appear before a camera and pretend to be an actress had been a welcome diversion from her daily duties. But even these, as far as her friends of that period could observe, she enjoyed. She often said that clerking was more fun than work. She liked meeting people and made friends easily. She had a lively temperament and an infectious laugh. She never seemed spiteful or jealous. She was popular with her associates at the store, both men and women.

On Sundays, the only day that PUB employees had off, Greta often went skating in winter with some of her friends from the store; in summer they rose early and spent the whole day at the beach, sunning themselves, cooking their lunch and swimming. Greta was an excellent swimmer. Like most Swedes, she enjoyed walking; she had a rapid, easy-swinging stride. Often in good weather she walked home from work, a distance of about four miles, with other girls who lived in her section of the city. On the way she talked about the theatre and the movies and about actors and actresses. It was her favorite subject. She seemed to know all the current theatrical gossip. And she was forever talking about how she was going to be an actress. Her friends listened patiently, but they were not greatly impressed. After all, as they remarked among themselves, she wasn't doing anything about it—she hadn't even joined the amateur theatrical group at the store. Greta's working companions thought she was a gay and generally sensible girl, but on the matter of becoming an actress they decided she was just a little moony.

It was true that Greta was long on talk and short on action. It was also true that she didn't know what action to take. A working girl of modest education who moved in a very small world, she was unlikely to encounter anyone with theatrical connections who could advise or help her. Then, by one of those happenstances that have occurred so often, at least in this country, that they have become a cliché of the movie business, Greta was given her first opportunity to appear before

AVDELNING
för
Dam-,
Flick-
och
Barn-
Hattar

"CLARY"

Damhatt av tagal-
fläta m. bandgarne-
ring. Finnes i marin,
svart, vitt, rött, beige
eller brunt
Kr. **18**.—

"ETHEL"

Damhatt av tagal-
fläta m. bandgarne-
ring. Finnes i marin,
svart, rosa, gråblått,
beige eller brunt
Kr. **26**.—

"JANE"

Damhatt av liséré-fläta.
Finnes i svart, marin el.
brunt .... Kr. **22**.—

Slöjor i svart, marin
el. brunt, med mönster i
olika färger ... Kr. **10**.—

"HELNY"

Damhatt av tagal-fläta, monterad med
blommor. Finnes i svart, marin, rött,
brunt, beige eller vitt ..... Kr. **25**.—

"SOLVEIG"

Damhatt av liséré-fläta med bandgar-
nering. Finnes i gråblått, marin, ljus-
brunt eller mörkbrunt ..... Kr. **21**.—

73

Ur Paul U. Bergströms Aktiebolags Vår- och sommarkatalog
1921.

Modeling hats for Stockholm department store

Two stills from Garbo's first film, an advertising short

a moving picture camera while she was still in ladies' millinery. Her discovery was not as dramatic as that of many American movie actresses who have been tapped for better things while running elevators, demonstrating cosmetics or turning flapjacks. Still, it was a start.

As part of its advertising program, PUB had engaged a producer of commercial films, Captain Ragnar Ring, to turn out a short film to promote their women's apparel. When Ring and the store officials in charge of the project visited the millinery department to look over hats for the film, Greta again acted as the model. Ring observed her with interest but didn't, to Greta's disappointment, suggest that she appear in the picture, for which he had engaged professional actresses. However, the following day he returned to talk to Greta. For light relief in the film, he told her, he had decided to include a short sequence showing how women should *not* dress, and offered her the chance to do the comedy bit. She instantly accepted. What had seemed evident to Ring—that Greta could play comedy—didn't dawn on the perceptive producers in Hollywood until after she had been in their midst for thirteen years and was at last allowed to show her comic talent in a brilliant film called *Ninotchka*.

A print of the PUB movie in which Greta made her debut on celluloid is in the possession of the Filmhistorical Archives, in Stockholm. Greta makes her first appearance in the picture wearing high button shoes and a curious-looking outfit that is clearly a couple of sizes too big for her; at first glance, it seems to consist of a three-quarter-length cloth coat with wide gingham cuffs, a voluminous checkered skirt, a long scarf of the same material and a kind of visored dust cap also trimmed with gingham. As if this weren't funny enough, it develops, as Greta smilingly models the gig, that by unbuttoning the skirt and doing a couple of other tricks the outfit can be transformed into, of all things, a riding habit. Additional hilarity is provided when Greta models another ludicrous garment that serves a similar dual purpose. In a straight bit she then models a knee-length fur coat. Throughout the film she appears gay and somewhat self-conscious, the way most people do in home movies.

Greta's good looks and willingness to follow directions led Captain

Garbo (white blouse) in her second commercial film, advertising bakery products

Ring to engage her for another production a few months later. This was a film to advertise the bakery products of the Consumers' Cooperative Association of Stockholm. The first part of the picture was shot on the roof garden of the fashionable Strand Hotel. Sitting at a table with two other young women, Greta is seen delightedly devouring a cream puff. To judge from her plump, pretty face, the fare agrees with her. As she finishes the last bite of pastry and daintily takes a sip of coffee from her demitasse, the camera turns to diners at other tables and settles briefly on Lars Hanson, Sweden's most noted young actor. This is one of those coincidences that delight the archivist, since Greta later played opposite Hanson in two of her most successful early films.

Leaving the Strand Hotel, the second half of the bakery epic shows Greta and three other girls, all in long, white dresses, enjoying a picnic on an island. Greta and two of her companions are playing at the water's edge when the fourth girl calls them to lunch. Dashing to the spot where the refreshments are being served, Greta grabs a big bag of cookies, sits down on the ground and begins eating them with the abandon of a starved child. When she takes too big a bite and some of the cooky is about to fall from her mouth, she stuffs it back in with her hand. She next picks up a glass of fruit juice, and without bothering to remove the spoon, takes a quick draught. Then she goes after the cookies again, and there the film ends. Since the camera is kept on Greta almost all the time, she can rightfully be considered the star of the film. Whatever her acting may have lacked in finesse was more than made up for in enthusiasm.

After working in the commercial films, for which she was paid the equivalent of three dollars a day, Greta understandably found clerking a dull occupation. She had been transferred to the women's dress department at no increase in salary. Twice Captain Ring offered her work; both times she was obliged to refuse because the pictures were being made outside of Stockholm, and she couldn't get sufficient time off from the store. Her budding career as an actress had for the moment come to a standstill.

One day in the summer of 1922, however, a Swedish film director and producer named Erik Petschler walked into Greta's department with two of his popular actresses, Tyra Ryman and Gucken Cederborg. Petschler, a Swedish counterpart of Mack Sennett, had brought the actresses to the store to buy them dresses to wear in a forthcoming film. Greta recognized the interesting customers and contrived to wait on them. While talking to Miss Ryman, Greta asked her advice on how she might go about getting work in one of Petschler's films. The thing to do, Miss Ryman said, was simply to go ahead and ask him, but Greta couldn't work up the courage to approach him then. Later that day, however, she telephoned Petschler at his office and secured an appointment to see him the following day during her lunch hour.

In the course of the interview, Petschler inquired about her experience and asked her to read some lines or do a scene. Greta responded by reciting a short poem she had learned in school. Her performance, Petschler later recalled, was quite touching. More impressed by her good looks and bouncy figure, Petschler offered her a part in a comedy he was getting ready to produce. Accepting the part and hurrying back to PUB, Greta tried to make arrangements to have her vacation changed so that she could make the picture and still keep her job. That effort failing, she was faced with the decision of taking the part and losing her job or of passing up her first opportunity to be a bona fide actress. She quit her job. On her employment card at PUB there is a space headed "Reason for leaving." The reason Greta gave was both clear and confident: "To enter the films."

Chapter Four

In her first legitimate screen role Greta was cast as a bathing beauty in a picture called *Luffar-Petter,* or *Peter the Tramp.* The film was written, produced and directed by Erik Petschler, who also played two of the leading parts, the tramp and a dude. It was a low-budget picture, very low. Besides Greta and Petschler, only four other players received screen credit; the film was shot entirely out of doors and in a period of a few days. Petschler's debt to Mack Sennett is evident. No custard pies sail through the air in *Peter the Tramp,* but it contains some of the same kind of fine nonsense and spontaneity that distinguished Sennett's masterworks.

The plot of *Peter the Tramp* is woven as loosely as a fish net. As the picture opens, a tramp arrives in a small town and promptly tries to seduce the policeman's wife. He is chased away and joins the local regiment of the army. He had met the regiment's captain before under adverse circumstances, so, to settle an old score, he puts itching powder under the captain's coat just before he sets out for an amorous meeting with one of the mayor's daughters, the role played by Greta Gustafsson. The mayor also has two other daughters. All three are enrolled in a girls' gymnastic academy. This provides an opportunity to show Greta and the two other girls practicing their calisthenics while uniformly clad in black sateen track pants, black jerseys, black half socks, white sneakers and black straw hats trimmed with white. Their gym teacher is a hatchet-faced old woman. The girls make life hard for the teacher by slyly tripping her and kicking her in the seat. The mayor's eldest daughter is engaged to the local fire chief, a dudish fellow. He sets out with the three girls on a trip to Stockholm. On the way they all stop for a swim. Greta and the other two beauties now appear in identical black bathing suits and exhibit their well-rounded charms by prancing about. The tramp comes by and sees them and the fire chief. He notices that he looks like the chief, so he steals his uniform and goes to Stockholm.

Peter the Tramp *1922. Garbo at left (above), at right (below)*

When the real chief arrives in the city with the mayor's daughters, they spot the bogus chief and chase him all over town in a dilapidated touring car. They finally tree him and turn fire hoses on him. The tramp goes back to the little town and marries an unattractive but wealthy widow.

As the synopsis indicates, Greta's part was somewhat limited. Her performance had the primary distinction of being energetic. Petschler was satisfied with her work. "She was a very determined girl and very willing and anxious to please," he said later. "She was a bit shy and uneasy at the beginning, which is natural, but when we started shooting she really came to life. She had had no training, of course, and her movements were quite awkward, but I think she showed signs of having a knack for acting. At least, she had the desire, which is not the least important thing."

Peter the Tramp, which opened at the Odeon Theatre in Stockholm, did not make Greta a star overnight, as movie stars are so often created in fiction and occasionally even in fact. Her work in the film did, however, result in giving Greta her first press notice as an actress. Soon after the picture had been released the Swedish magazine *Swing* led off its department devoted to motion pictures with a short item calling attention to Greta's debut. "Since Miss Gustafsson has so far had only the dubious pleasure of having to play a 'Bathing Beauty' for Mr. Erik Petschler in his fire department film," the item read in part, "we have received no impression whatever of her capacity. It pleases us, though, to have the opportunity of noting a new name in Swedish films, and we hope to have a chance to mention it again." In an adjoining column *Swing* published the newcomer's picture. It bore the caption: "Greta Gustafsson. May perhaps become a Swedish film star. Reason—her Anglo-Saxon appearance."

However accurate this prophecy eventually proved, neither *Swing* nor any other publication had a chance for some time to mention the name of the young actress again. After completing *Peter the Tramp* Greta was, in the euphemistic theatrical phrase, at liberty. Petschler, it developed, had no other films scheduled for early production. Greta looked up her only other motion picture acquaintance, Captain Ring, who said he might be able to use her later on as a Valkyrie in a commercial film he planned to do for a shoe polish firm, but he had nothing to offer at the time. She made the rounds of the other film producers, who gave her no encouragement. The possibility of having to return to clerking was becoming more likely by the day.

While in downtown Stockholm one afternoon in the summer of 1922, Greta met Petschler on the street. He invited her into a nearby *konditori* to have a pastry and a cup of coffee, which, Petschler once said, seemed to be all that she lived on in those days. As they chatted Greta spoke of the efforts she had been making to continue her acting career and of the generally dismal results. Petschler, a man of benign disposition who had had wide experience in the theatre before turning to motion pictures, listened sympathetically to this not unfamiliar tale. Though he had not influenced Greta to give up her steady job to take a flier in the films and had, in fact, cautioned her about the risk involved, he nevertheless felt an indirect responsibility for her situation. Added to this was his belief that she had talent, and he wanted to help her.

Petschler told his disconsolate companion that he thought she had marked native ability as an actress but that her chances of going far would be slim indeed until she had received dramatic training. The best place in the world to get such training, he continued, was at the Royal Dramatic Theatre Academy. He asked Greta why she didn't try to secure an Academy scholarship. Greta knew about the Academy, of course; to study there was the dream of every aspiring Swedish actress. As she modestly told Petschler, however, she had never thought she would stand a chance in the stiff competition. Petschler was encouraging. Furthermore, he said that if she wanted to try for a scholarship he would arrange for her to talk the idea over with a friend of his, Frans Enwall, who could tell her what steps to take and might even be willing to help her prepare for the examination. Greta said that she would like to see Enwall right away.

Frans Enwall, a former director of the Academy, was then a well-known private dramatic coach. He was very elderly. When Greta called at the Enwall residence, she was courteously received by her aging host but quickly informed that because of his health and previous commitments he would be unable himself to give her instruction. However, he introduced her to his daughter Signe, who was also an experienced dramatic tutor. Greta made an instantly favorable impression on Signe Enwall. "She had such a charming personality and such warm radiance, and her sincerity was very affecting," Miss Enwall has recalled. She agreed, after talking with Greta at some length, to give her private dramatic lessons in preparation for a tryout at the Academy. Greta asked about the fee for the instruction. Miss Enwall said not to worry about that.

The Academy, at the time Greta became seriously interested in it, had been turning out first-rate actors and actresses for more than a hundred years. It was recognized as the seedbed of practically all important Swedish theatrical talent. The Academy, like the Royal Dramatic Theatre of which it is a part, has always been supported by the government; the young people lucky enough to be accepted receive their training free. The number of new students annually admitted is limited to a dozen or less. Once a year a jury composed of officials of the Academy and of the Royal Dramatic Theatre meets to audition applicants. They must be prepared to perform three scenes, each lasting not more than five minutes, from plays of their own choosing. The jury, Greta learned during her first interview with Miss Enwall, convened that year in August. Since it was then July, Greta had less than a month to make her preparations.

Having only a sketchy knowledge of the drama, Greta naturally had to place great reliance on Miss Enwall in selecting material for the audition. "Don't forget that she was only sixteen years old," Miss Enwall has remarked, "and she was not from a theatrical family. But she was so anxious to succeed that she was completely receptive to assistance. We picked out the parts for the audition together after discussion. They were things I felt she was able to do." The first selection that Greta undertook was a monologue from the third act of *Dunungen,* a Scandinavian classic by Selma Lagerlöf. The second was the scene from the first act of Sardou's *Madame Sans-Gêne,* in which Catherine, the washerwoman turned duchess, tells off the other ladies of the court, and finally, a shorter excerpt from Ibsen's *Lady from the Sea.*

Miss Enwall was very pleased, though not especially surprised, by the rapidity with which Greta learned her lines and by her apparent instinctive understanding of the characters she was portraying. "It was obvious from the start that she had a very convincing dramatic talent," Miss Enwall has said. "The fact that her knowledge of the drama was not wide didn't matter. What really counts in an actress is contact with real, everyday life and an ability to feel and understand it. In that sense Greta Garbo, or Greta Gustafsson as she was then, was extremely well equipped. She was very mature for her age."

Greta had never performed on the stage of a theatre when she arrived, with several dozen other applicants, at the Royal Dramatic on the day of the auditions. While waiting her turn, she told a friend afterward, she was so nervous that she would have risen and fled, but her feet, like pieces of iron, held her in her seat. Her name was called at last. She performed the scene from *Dunungen* and the one from *Madame Sans-Gêne.* She was then interrupted and told that she could leave; the members of the jury would inform her by mail of their decision. Three days later she received a letter saying she had been accepted. She was one of seven who got that good news.

Greta's first semester at the Academy began in September, 1922. As a student she was obliged to put in a working day lasting from nine until five and frequently longer. With her six classmates she received instruction in acting, voice culture and diction, the history of the theatre, dancing, rhythmics, posture, fencing and make-up. Her teachers, who were mostly professional actors and actresses attached to the Royal Dramatic Theatre, were exacting. Greta and the other newcomers were keenly aware that any student who failed to measure up to the Academy's uncompromising standards would be dropped after the first year. Those who succeeded would be invited to return for another nine months' course; in addition they would receive, during the second year, a small monthly salary and the opportunity to appear in regular productions at the Royal Dramatic. Except for a tendency to be tardy to class ("I had the disgusting habit of always arriving late," she once recalled), Greta kept her work up to the mark.

During her first few weeks at the Academy she was a puzzle to her classmates. About all they knew about her was that she came to school by streetcar from somewhere on the South Side. At lunch and between classes she kept mostly to herself and made little attempt to join in the general conversation. The three other girls and the three boys in her class included Lena Cederström and Karl-Magnus Thulstrup, who became well-known players on the Swedish stage, as well as Alf Sjöberg, who became one of Sweden's most successful film directors. The student with whom Greta first became well acquainted was a small, dark-haired, vivacious girl named Mimi Pollack. A popular member of the Royal Dramatic repertory company as well as one of its regular directors, Miss Pollack was Greta's best friend at the Academy. The reason for Greta's early aloofness, Miss Pollack believes, was simply that she was very unsure of herself. The other students had had more formal education, some had been exposed to a smattering of dramatic training, and they took the neophyte's pride in talking about their work in rather highbrow terms. By keeping silent, Greta kept her classmates guessing as to whether she knew more than they did or less. "She shied away until she had learned enough to be able to join in the discussions," Miss Pollack has remarked. "Then she became one of the gang. She was always gay and good-humored, always full of fun and ready for mischief."

Some of her instructors remember her differently. "In the classroom she was very quiet," her speech teacher, Karl Nygren, has said. "Sometimes I wished she would show more initiative. I remember that now and again she seemed very depressed and troubled. She often blushed, especially when we were discussing things that she wasn't acquainted with. I think that this was probably due to the fact that her schooling had been meager, and she was acutely conscious of that. I was often sorry for her in the classroom. But when I would meet her by chance in the halls or in the theatre she was not at all bashful. Once, during class, I remember I was trying to explain the way to make certain tones—I wanted to show how to speak with a kind of nasal twang. In trying to get this across I imitated the popular cabaret stars, Hansi and Jean Moreau. Always after that, whenever I met Greta outside the classroom she would greet me in those nasal tones, saying, 'Good morning, Director Nygren. Is this the right way to say it?' She had a very pleasing personality, very attractive."

None of Greta's classmates, including Mimi Pollack, ever learned much about Greta's family. She didn't talk about them and her attitude was not one that encouraged her fellow students to ask questions on the subject. Miss Pollack knew that Greta had a brother and sister and was under the impression that her father had been a taxi driver, but she knew little else about the Gustafssons. Greta had already developed a talent for keeping part of herself a mystery. With the other Academy pupils she was admitted free to the productions at the Royal Dramatic. Her friends of that period remember that she usually appeared at the theatre wearing an evening cloak of black velvet. "In that," one of her classmates has said, "she looked like such an elegant lady you'd never have suspected she was a South Sider."

One afternoon in the late spring of 1923, a couple of weeks before the end of her first term at the dramatic school, Greta was unexpectedly summoned to the office of the Academy's director, Gustaf Molander. Already there when she arrived was another student named Mona Mårtenson, a beautiful young woman who had entered the Academy a year before Greta. The reason he wanted to speak to them, Molander explained, was that he had received a request from Mauritz Stiller, the film director, to select two actresses from the Academy to be tested for parts in a picture he was casting. Working with Stiller would provide a splendid opportunity for practical training, Molander continued, and added that if they were successful in getting the parts the Academy would grant them a leave of absence while the picture was being made. If they were interested, he said, they should report the following morning at ten o'clock at the studios of Svensk Filmindustri. Greta and Mona Mårtenson, making no effort to conceal their excitement, said they would be there. Stiller, as they were both well aware, was then the foremost figure in Swedish films and easily the most colorful.

Chapter Five

It is always rash to designate any single event in a person's life as the most fateful one; the turning points of lives are usually too hard to discern. More often than not it is the seemingly trivial incident—the chance meeting, the road not taken—that turns out to have momentous consequences. Occasionally, though, the great moment can be spotted. In some lives there is the single critical occurrence that stands out boldly as the one that made all the difference. Such an event was the meeting of Greta Gustafsson and Mauritz Stiller.

When they met, Stiller was forty, worldly and famous; Greta was seventeen, innocent, unknown and still in the larval stage. At this point Stiller took command of her destiny. He gave her a name, taught her, bullied her, encouraged her, fought for her and made her into a world-famous actress. But he was far more than her professional mentor. He was an intimate friend who exerted more influence than anyone else in shaping her character and personality. He told her how to dress, what to think, how to behave—there was almost nothing he didn't tell her. She listened and obeyed. The relationship was Svengali and Trilby all over again.

Mauritz Stiller, a Russian Jew, was an arresting figure in many ways. In appearance he was curiously imposing. Over six feet tall and thickly built, he had an abnormally large head, the feet of a giant and hamlike hands. A vain man, he usually kept his hands in his pockets when he was photographed. His hair was iron gray and closely cropped, and his eyes, under thick, black eyebrows, were gray and brooding. He had a prominent, bulbous nose and a long upper lip on which he wore a full mustache.

Stiller was such a fancy dresser that he was often referred to as "The Grand Duke," a term he did not resent. He wore diamond studs in his shirt front and had his evening clothes, jaunty Norfolk jackets and much of his other apparel tailored in London. In winter he customarily strode around in a yellow fur coat that reached almost to his ankles and

Mauritz Stiller

was adorned with a collar and belt of contrasting black fur. He collected old, richly embroidered waistcoats, which he had made into ties; on them he wore a gold tiepin encrusted with oriental pearls. Stiller could not check his passion for jewelry. He habitually wore rings (though they called attention to his ungainly hands) of a dazzling variety; they included one of gold set with sapphires, two of platinum set with diamonds and another of platinum set with both pearls and diamonds. Stiller had a number of superstitions, among which was his conceit that it was bad luck to change his suit during the course of making a film; whatever suit he was wearing the day production began was the one he wore throughout. But he had it pressed every night.

It was not only by his distinctive dress that Stiller made a striking impression. His manner was attractive, though his temperament was mercurial. He was intense, ambitious, talented, noisy, egotistical, troubled, cultured and brutally outspoken. "He never shirked or hesitated to call a spade a spade, to tell people straight from the shoulder what he thought," Stiller's closest friend, Victor Seastrom, the venerable Swedish actor and director, remarked. "While directing he often lost his temper. He couldn't help it, but then he could say things that hurt, could hurt badly, and at the same time could be strikingly funny. Although not so funny for the poor victim. But he was quick to make amends, and I don't think anybody was angry with him at heart."

Stiller, to use the phrase his colleagues have most often applied to him, was a born director. He enjoyed telling people what to do, and he had taste, a rich imagination and a love of beauty. "He'd get physically sick when he saw anything ugly," Victor Seastrom has said. If Stiller's friends or acquaintances were wearing clothes he thought unbecoming, he would gratuitously tell them so. When he walked into a room, he couldn't restrain himself from suggesting how the furniture should be rearranged to produce what he considered a better effect. When he got ready to build his own house, he engaged his friend Vilhelm Bryde, an architect who also designed the sets for many of Stiller's films, to draw the plans. "What he had in mind was a cross between a Russian villa and a Swedish cottage," Bryde has said. "It was a novel idea and a rather hard assignment, but he eventually got what he wanted. He almost always did."

A man who habitually lived beyond his means, Stiller was fond of good food and drink and considered himself something of an epicure. He was an easy spender, though inclined toward stinginess in small ways. He liked to save money by not buying his own cigarettes. His command, "Give me a cigarette!" was as closely associated with him as his embroidered foulards. If anyone hesitated in responding, Stiller always said, "I'll give you a whole pack for Christmas," but he never did. On the other hand he was given to impulsively generous gestures. Once, shortly before Christmas, he met on the street in Stockholm an actress who, he learned on stopping to speak to her, had been out of work for some time. "I was on my way to send you some flowers for Christmas," Stiller said. "But here, why don't you pick them out yourself?" He put a hundred-kronor bill in her hand and walked on.

As a rule Stiller didn't do much walking. He preferred instead to drive his powerful sports roadster, the most distinctive and generally feared passenger conveyance in Stockholm. It was a Kissel Kar, custom-made and painted a shimmering canary yellow. Among its other attractions Stiller's machine had two auxiliary seats, one on either side of the rear fenders, that could be let down to accommodate passengers who enjoyed riding out in the open and motoring dangerously. "He drove that car like a flying machine," Vilhelm Bryde has said. Decked out in snappy sports attire, Stiller roared through the streets of Stockholm at such speeds that his flashy roadster came to be referred to locally as "The Yellow Peril."

Like most people who go in for ostentation, Stiller was trying to make up for something he had missed. Until he was twenty-eight, he had never had more than enough money to exist. Born in Helsinki, Finland, when the country was a Russian grand duchy, he was the fifth of six children in the family of a musician in the Russian Army. His given name was Moses; though he later changed it, his close friends usually called him "Moje." He was orphaned at four, when, within a month, his father died and his mother committed suicide. Adopted into the family of a Jewish merchant who made caps, young Stiller received eight years of schooling before he quit to go to work for his foster father. A conspicuous failure in business, he drifted into the theatre, where he managed to make out for five years playing bit parts.

When he was twenty-one and being hunted by the police for failure, as a Russian citizen, to report for compulsory military training, he fled from Helsinki and reached the Swedish border. Using a false passport and confidently speaking Swedish, which he had learned in school and perfected on the stage, he talked his way into the country. Stiller had the reputation of never being afraid to take great risks— in fact, of never being afraid of anything except rats. He performed a little ritual, when the need arose, to give himself extra courage. With both hands he seized the lapels of his coat and gave them a quick, hard jerk, snapping back his head and giving a defiant thrust to his chin. He recommended this trick to his friends, saying, "Do like Moje Stiller and you become a new and a braver man."

Arriving in Sweden penniless, Stiller needed all the courage he could muster to survive the next six years, the leanest period of his life. He held a number of menial jobs, played small parts with a threadbare theatrical company that toured the provinces and took a short, unsuccessful fling at vaudeville. Often destitute, he became accustomed to taking his night's lodging on a park bench. His fortunes improved somewhat when he made the acquaintance of a celebrated light opera star who let him move into her home. For days at a stretch he didn't go out of the house. "I would rather not go out at all if I have to appear in a dirty collar," he explained to his hostess. Eventually he joined a group of young actors who scraped together some money, rented a small theatre and formed a company called The Little Theatre. With Stiller as its director The Little Theatre developed into an avant-garde stage. He received some critical attention for his directorial work, especially for his production of Tolstoy's *The Power of Darkness,* but the theatrical enterprise failed after a few months.

Meanwhile Stiller had seen his first movies, a French film with Sacha Guitry and a couple of American two-reelers, and his interest in the new medium was aroused. He applied for work as an actor with Swedish Biograph, a motion picture company which had recently opened studios in Stockholm. Julius Jaenzon, the firm's first cameraman, has recalled that Stiller showed up for his screen test wearing an elegant suit with silk lapels, which he had borrowed for the occasion, spats and white gloves. He didn't make the grade as an actor, but he talked himself into a job as a director. It was soon apparent that films were his métier.

Between 1911, when he went to work as a movie director, and 1923, when he encountered Greta Gustafsson, Stiller turned out some forty motion pictures, a number of which gave him an international reputation. Having learned his craft directing two-reel thrillers, Stiller, in company with his colleague Victor Seastrom, who had experienced a kind of religious conversion in coming to the belief that films could serve a high artistic purpose, turned his attention to more serious undertakings. It was then that Swedish films, dominated by Stiller and Seastrom, entered what has been called their golden age. The motion pictures that came out of Sweden during this period have been recognized by critical filmgoers in both Europe and America as the most advanced of any that had been produced on either continent up to that time. "It was the Swedish film that first depicted individual human character with amplitude and truth, and taught the screen how to suggest motive and mood," the distinguished film historian Iris Barry has written. "Both Seastrom and Stiller consciously and in original ways sought to make the film a vehicle for expressing by purely pictorial means subtleties hitherto unknown to it."

Stiller's contribution to the golden age of Swedish films consisted of several pictures based on Scandinavian literary classics, most of which had as their theme the conflict of man with society and nature. His most widely praised work, prior to the film in which Greta Gustafsson appeared, was a cinematic tale of crime and punishment called *Sir Arne's Treasure.* Unlike Seastrom, who preferred to handle only somber themes, Stiller also distinguished himself as a master of sophisticated comedy with his film *Erotikon,* produced in 1920. Until then light fare on the screen had been limited to slapstick comedies and gross farces. *Erotikon,* which has been called "the first modern comedy in film history—brilliant and witty in a way that was acceptable even among educated and

48

cultivated people," had a significant influence on the development of other directors, particularly Ernst Lubitsch.

In 1923, Victor Seastrom was lured to Hollywood, leaving Stiller the undisputed headman of Swedish films, a role he had no trouble playing. In both his business and social life Stiller's flamboyant manner, ready talk and generally outgiving character brought him a wide circle of friends, but he remained in some ways a mystery even to the closest of them. "We were great, very great friends," Seastrom once remarked. "But in spite of our sincere friendship, I am not sure that I knew him profoundly, got deep in under his skin. I don't think anybody did. So many different kinds of men were gathered within him."

Stiller never married. "He liked to have beautiful women around him," Vilhelm Bryde has said, "and he was interested in· them, but he was never in love with them." Though Stiller was not, as another of his friends has put it, "normally attracted to women," he had a mental image of what he regarded as the perfect female. The ideal woman he was seeking, as he described her to intimate friends, would be not only beautiful but "supersensual, spiritual and mystic." He made an effort to fashion a young Swedish actress named Mary Johnson, who played a leading role in *Sir Arne's Treasure,* into a realization of his dream woman, but she did not prove malleable, and Stiller continued his restless search.

Being an egotist, he became dedicated to the fancy that if he could find a woman who fitted his dreamlike specifications he could mold her into an actress such as the world had never seen. "Stiller, like Eisenstein, dreamt of capturing the world, but by choosing other paths," Stiller's friend and Sweden's leading film critic, Dr. Bengt Idestam-Almquist, has written. "If he only could find a suitable female type, he would make her a 'star' for whom the world would irresistibly fall. After the luxurious comedy *Erotikon,* he was possessed with this thought. 'The Star' should be sophisticated, scornful, superior, but under the shining surface humanely warm and womanly, like Tora Teje in *Erotikon.* She should also have something of the soulfulness and mysticism encompassed in Mary Johnson in *Sir Arne's Treasure.* Stiller asked his manuscript assistant, the future doctor of philosophy and professor of history,

Mr. Arthur Nordén, to find a suitable name for this visualized international star. Nordén came to think of the Hungarian king, Gábor Bethlen, and suggested the name Mona Gabor. Stiller was delighted and tried the pronunciation in different languages—Gábor, Gabór, Gabro, Garbo . . ."

For the actress who was to fulfill his fanciful dream Stiller now had a name and a plan. When Greta Gustafsson answered his summons to appear for a screen test, he had the woman.

Chapter Six

Although Stiller had never met Greta Gustafsson, he had heard favorable word about her from Carl Brisson, the handsome revue artist and former prize fighter, for whom both Stiller and Greta felt the warmest regard. In neither case could it be said that the feeling was reciprocated by Brisson, who was a happily married man. He had found Miss Gustafsson something of a nuisance. She still had a schoolgirl crush on him, continued to dog his footsteps and, according to Brisson, had attempted to convey her admiration by carving the legend "GG loves CB" within a heart on the door of his dressing room at the Mosebacke Theatre. Hoping to direct her attentions elsewhere, he had, unbeknownst to Greta, suggested to Stiller that this ambitious and good-looking young actress might be suitable for a part in his film, *Gösta Berling's Saga,* which Stiller was casting in the spring of 1923. Consequently, when Stiller telephoned the director of the Academy to ask that he send him two pretty students—"not necessarily the best but the prettiest," as he put it—he specified that one of them should be Greta Gustafsson.

On the morning they were to report for their tests Greta and Mona Mårtenson together took the streetcar to the studios of Svensk Filmindustri, situated in the suburb of Råsunda. One of Stiller's assistants who met the nervous young hopefuls and took them to have their make-up applied has recalled the appearance they made: "Mona was rather short and plump and very attractive. Greta was plump, too, but also gawky, with unkempt hair and gaps between her front teeth. Mona was said to be the most beautiful girl in the dramatic school. Greta was by no means as pretty, but she had a lovely figure, though tending to plumpness." After she had been made up, Greta, who was wearing a plain, tailored suit, was conducted to a set, where Stiller and a couple of his colleagues were waiting. When she was introduced to the director, she curtsied.

Gösta Berling's Saga

"If you want the part," Stiller said, uttering his first words to her, "you'll have to lose at least twenty pounds." Greta blushed. "But look," Stiller went on, turning her around and talking partly to her and partly to his associates, "isn't she beautiful? . . . Did you ever see such eyelashes? . . . But, miss, you are much too fat. . . . Yes, she is very pretty. . . . Notice her feet—such beautiful heels, one straight, fine line." As Stiller continued in this enthusiastic vein, one of those present has since remarked, his colleagues exchanged looks of amazement.

"Now, miss," Stiller said, indicating a divan, "lie down and be sick." Greta hesitated, but as Stiller began to frown, she walked over to the sofa and lay down. Confused and self-conscious, she was able to register no emotion except fright. Stiller strode over to the divan. "For God's sake," he shouted, "don't you know what it is to be sick? Have you no feelings? Do you know nothing of sadness and misery? Have you never been inside a dramatic school? Act, miss, act!" On the verge of tears, Greta tried again. Whether satisfied or not, Stiller at length told her to get up and directed the cameraman to take some close-ups and long and medium shots as she walked about the set. Again he spoke favorably of her movements and figure. Then, without any further word, Stiller told her she could go home.

With childlike eagerness Greta rode out to the studios the following day, looked up the cameraman, Julius Jaenzon, who had photographed her test, and shyly asked how she had made out. Jaenzon gently warned her that he didn't think she had done too well. Greta thanked him and left. Jaenzon wasn't alone in holding this unfavorable opinion; it was shared by almost everybody else at the studio, except Stiller. The writer, Ragnar Hyltén-Cavallius, who was working with Stiller on the script of *Gösta Berling,* was not impressed by Greta's personality and risked incurring Stiller's displeasure by telling him so. "She is shy," Stiller replied. "She has no technique, so she can't show what she is feeling. But she will be all right. I'll see to that." Stiller exercised complete authority over his productions. He alone made the decision to cast Greta as Elisabeth Dohna, the second female lead in *Gösta Berling.*

Why did Stiller select this inexperienced, naïve, seventeen-year-old student for such an important role? To this question there are two answers. The first is that he sensed in her, by what intuitive processes nobody knows, the raw material out of which he could refine "The Star" he had so long visualized. The second is that whenever possible Stiller used amateurs instead of professional actors in his films. In this respect he was a pioneer. If he saw on the street a person who looked like an interesting type, he would briskly approach the stranger and invite him or her to make a screen test. It made no difference to Stiller whether the person he picked for a part was a blacksmith, bank president or seamstress, provided his or her appearance fitted Stiller's conception of the way the character should look. He selected Greta's friend Mona Mårtenson, who had never made a movie, for an important role in *Gösta Berling* because he liked her eyes. Among the amateurs he cast in smaller parts were a fishmonger, an office manager and a fur dealer. He even tried to find an amateur to play the difficult role of the hero of the film. His first choice was the well-known Swedish poet, Sten Selander. Though Selander had neither the training nor the ambition to be an actor, Stiller convinced him that he had the perfect face for the part and finally succeeded in persuading the reluctant poet to come out to the studios. Arriving at Stiller's office, he was invited to sit down. "For several minutes," Selander, who became a member of the Swedish Academy, has said, "Stiller just looked at me as if I were a stick of furniture, saying not a word. Then he waved his hand in a gesture of dismissal. 'No,' he said, 'a person would go crazy if he had to watch that face for five minutes.' Thus ended my career as a movie actor." After testing a number of other candidates, including Carl Brisson and a Russian novelist, Stiller decided at last to give the hero's role to Lars Hanson, Sweden's most popular young actor.

The casting completed, Stiller was ready to begin shooting the film that he hoped would not only crown his own career but also make an international star of his shy protégée. The picture was based on a novel loved by all Swedes. Written by Selma Lagerlöf and awarded the Nobel Prize, the novel recites the adventures of the Byronic hero Gösta Berling, a minister with a well-developed thirst for hard liquor and the inclinations of a Casanova, who is fired from the pulpit, sinks to the depths and is redeemed by the love of a pure and beautiful

With Lars Hanson in Gösta Berling's Saga

woman, Elisabeth Dohna—the role assigned to Greta Gustafsson. Trans-
ferring this melodramatic tale to the screen was the most ambitious
undertaking of Stiller's life. Sparing no expense, he had forty-eight
separate sets built for the film and, among other extravagant gestures,
engaged Stockholm's leading couturier to design the gowns that Greta
wore in the picture. (Two of these are preserved in the Filmhistorical
Archives.) Stiller not only approved sketches for the gowns but personally accompanied Greta to the couturier's establishment for the
fittings.

The sum that Stiller paid Greta for her work in the film was
respectable but not excessive, considering that her role was to require
her presence at the studios off and on over a period of six months.
According to the contract she signed with Svensk Filmindustri on July

23, 1923, her total payment for the picture was three thousand kronor, or approximately six hundred dollars. It is not surprising, as things go in the movie world, that later on in Hollywood she was paid at the rate of six hundred dollars for one hour's work.

Once the shooting had begun it was clear to everybody around the studio that Stiller had an obsessive interest in the quiet, diffident young woman who played Elisabeth Dohna. He devoted hours to the scenes in which she appeared, taking them over and over again. He and the cameraman took endless trouble arranging the lighting and working out camera angles that would be most flattering to her. While the rest of the cast and the crew waited, Stiller coached her in every movement and piece of business. He often stopped the shooting to fuss over some detail of her make-up. Alternately patient and explosive, he kept the camera turning until Greta and the other members of the cast were ready to drop—and he had gotten what he wanted. "Making *Gösta Berling* was torture for her—she cried a great deal," a man closely associated with the production has said.

The attention Stiller lavished on his protégée created much interest and lively gossip around the studio. "None of us could understand why he was interested in this little nobody," Mrs. Stellan Claussen, a former actress who then held a managerial post at Svensk Filmindustri, once recalled. "To us she appeared to be just a shy, mediocre novice. However, the whole film world here stood in awe of Stiller. He was the cinema czar—and of course a great artist—who had his way in everything. We tried to make Greta one of our little family but we didn't get very far because Stiller scarcely permitted anyone else even to speak to her—he hardly let her out of his sight for a moment. As time went on, I remember, we nicknamed them 'Beauty and the Beast,' because she was really very attractive, especially her figure. That is what attracted people in Sweden, not her face. I can still see Stiller and that young girl—forever walking up and down, up and down, in the shade of that little grove just outside the studio. Stiller was always teaching and preaching, Greta solemnly listening and learning. I never saw anyone more earnest and eager to learn. With that hypnotic power he seemed to have over her he could make her do extraordinary things. But we had little idea then that he was making over her very soul."

Earnest and tractable though she generally was, Greta on at least one occasion blew up on the set as a result of Stiller's ceaseless pressure. Working over a difficult scene, Stiller, whose manner as a director has been described as that of "a torturing devil beyond compare," tried to make the frightened young actress perform by adopting his customary tormenting tactics. He continued to bully her until she finally shouted, "Damn you, Stiller, I hate you!" But he did not relent.

Such a show of temperament on Greta's part was exceedingly rare. She looked up to Stiller and tried to please him. During the filming of *Gösta Berling,* a journalist named Inga Gaate interviewed Greta and asked, among other things, if she found making movies difficult. "Terrible," Greta replied. "I have had a Gethsemane, but Stiller is the best human being I know. You never get angry or sad no matter how much he bawls you out. He creates people and shapes them according to his will. As for myself, I am a nice girl who gets very sad if people are unkind to her, although that may not be very feminine. Being feminine is a lovely quality which I may not have very much of." At the close of the interview Greta added, "You must not write up everything I say. I am one of those people who do not think, you see, who talk first and think afterwards." Stiller was annoyed when he read these remarks in the newspaper. He disliked reporters and encouraged Greta thereafter to shun them.

As the weeks passed, Stiller's sway over Greta's life began to extend beyond the studio. After work he sometimes drove her home in his roadster, an event that naturally brought many faces to the windows on Blekingegatan. On increasingly frequent occasions the two were seen together at the theatre or in fashionable restaurants like Bern's, where Stiller had a table permanently reserved. Often, when he was invited to a social function, he asked permission to bring his young friend. In this way he gradually introduced Greta to the society of actors, artists and writers in which he moved. He told her what to wear and what to say and did all he could to help her overcome her natural diffidence. One way to do this, he evidently felt, was to call upon her to entertain when they were out among his friends. Vilhelm Bryde has spoken of one such occasion when, during a party at his house, Stiller abruptly asked her to get up and sing. "She had a pleasant voice," Bryde has said, "and I remember she did some songs from the repertoire of Lili Zeidner, a popular revue artist. She sang until Stiller told her she could stop. She was very careful of the way she acted."

Unless Stiller pushed her into performing Greta was inclined to be pitifully silent and retiring on these excursions into the great world. The wife of a theatrical director who entertained Stiller and Greta at a large function during this period remembered that she said nothing during the evening beyond the civilities upon arriving and leaving. "She just sat in a corner and seemed to be lost," the hostess has remarked. The impression that Greta created on the rather sophisticated people to whom Stiller introduced her was not one of deep mystery but of plain simplicity. She seemed to them amiable and physically attractive —her incredibly long eyelashes were noticed by everyone—but almost totally lacking in personality. What her new acquaintances of this era did not know was that she had subjugated her natural childish charm and buoyancy in an effort to conform to Stiller's conception of what the character of "The Star" should be. Having shed the one and not yet taken on the other, she presented only a colorless façade.

Though Stiller's friends were puzzled by his attachment to what they considered a quite unpromising discovery, he was himself unswerving in his belief that he could make her accomplish great things. The dramatic critic Hjalmar Lenning, a friend of Stiller's, remarked to acquaintances after meeting Greta that he had found her "dull, uninteresting and very taciturn." Later on he asked Stiller if he really believed that she had a bright future as an actress. "You know," Stiller quietly replied, "she receives instruction excellently, follows directions closely. She is like wax in my hands. Greta will be all right. I believe in her."

By the time the filming of *Gösta Berling* had been completed, Stiller's dominion over his eager protégée was secure. She did nothing without his permission, saw only the people he wished her to see, and had assumed the name he wished her to bear. Having taken the necessary legal steps, she was now Greta Garbo. In name, at least, "The Star" had been born.

Chapter Seven

The first showing of *Gösta Berling's Saga* was held in Stockholm in March, 1924. Since the film was very long, running to almost four hours, it was shown in two parts, on separate evenings. Stiller accompanied Greta Garbo to the premieres, which were social events of some importance. The picture was not, however, an unqualified success.

While the popular reaction was generally favorable, the critical acclaim was restrained. One critic called the film "a beautifully staged failure." The others were less severe, though all complained of the liberties Stiller had taken in adapting the novel to the screen, particularly the addition of a happy ending. After seeing the cinema version of her work, Selma Lagerlöf said curtly, "Mr. Stiller has seen too many poor serials." The most thoughtful review of the film was contributed by Dr. Bengt Idestam-Almquist, writing under his nom de plume, "Robin Hood." He, like the majority of critics, took the position that while the film was "no masterpiece . . . it is, of course, in spite of its faults, one of the really great movies."

Neither "Robin Hood" nor any of the other critics devoted much space in their reviews to the newcomer Greta Garbo. Though her notices were small, they were on the whole good. The critics balanced criticism of her acting against enthusiasm for her appearance. "Robin Hood's" comment is typical. After the usual hedging statement that "it is too early to say much about Greta Garbo," he went on to observe: "She has several opportunities which she does not utilize. Spiritually she is too small for her part. But she is wonderfully beautiful in her Empire gowns and, in spite of her still-life acting, she is one of the bright spots in the movie."

To anyone viewing *Gösta Berling's Saga* today, nearly half a century later, Garbo is still one of the film's bright spots, though for different reasons. The interest of the modern viewer is, of course, to try to detect in the original Garbo evidence of those qualities that contributed to the Garbo of legend, the one whose image is enshrined in the minds of an admiring generation. Any resemblance between the two is almost purely coincidental.

In her first serious screen role the actress who was to become an international symbol of the cool, ethereal temptress looks as innocent and buxom as a cherub. Neither her appearance nor her performance reveals any incipient sign of that quality of metaphysical come-hither that was to make her name a synonym for the *femme fatale*. Piled on her head is a mop of long, dark hair that seems successfully to have resisted both brush and comb, her eyelids are weighted down with gobs of eye shadow, and her mouth is generously smeared with lipstick. Wearing a variety of low-cut gowns that permit the display of a rather ample bosom, she drifts woodenly through the picture, coming to life but once. This occurs in a rousing chase sequence, when she and the hero, escaping in a one-horse sleigh across a frozen lake, are pursued by a pack of "wolves"—actually a bunch of German police dogs, whose tails Stiller had had filled out with crepe hair and weighted with lead, the latter measure to prevent any inappropriate wagging. During the almost interminable pursuit across the ice, Garbo registers fright by furiously rolling her eyes, heaving her chest and crying *"Vargar! Vargar!"* as she flings her arm to indicate the approaching pack. The pursuers finally fall to scrapping among themselves, and hero and heroine gallop on to safety behind their trusty steed.

Ludicrous though all this may appear today, it was regarded as first-rate cinema fare in the early twenties. Stiller was widely praised not only for the sleigh-ride sequence but for many other similar episodes in the film, such as the great manor house fire, which were considered technically daring and unusually effective at that period in film history. Though the picture did not, to Stiller's disappointment, have the effect of transforming Garbo immediately into "The Star," he did not lose faith in his dream. The Swedish artist Einer Nerman, after seeing *Gösta Berling,* complimented Stiller and asked about the actress who played Elisabeth Dohna. "Her name is Greta Garbo," Stiller said. "She will be one of our greatest actresses."

At Stiller's insistence, Garbo had kept up her studies at the Academy during the filming of *Gösta Berling.* Whenever she was not required at the studio, she spent her days dutifully attending classes. Now that she was a fledgling movie actress and spending most of her leisure time in the company of the eminent director she was looked upon in a new light by her classmates. Their increased regard for her, together with a sense of relief at being away from Stiller's overwhelming presence, made the hours at the Academy pass quickly and enjoyably. As a second-year student she received a monthly salary of a hundred and fifty kronor; though this amounted to only a little more than thirty dollars, it was enough, combined with her film earnings, to make her independent. Furthermore, in addition to her classroom work, she was now having the useful and pleasurable experience of taking small parts in regular productions of the Royal Dramatic Theatre. Her first role on the so-called "Big Stage" was that of Mrs. von Brandt in the German comedy, *The Tortoise Comb,* which had a run of forty-three performances. After this she appeared as Fisher, a very pretty lady's maid, in J. M. Barrie's *The Admirable Crichton.*

While Garbo was pursuing her studies at the Academy, Stiller, following the Stockholm premiere of *Gösta Berling,* was engaged in editing a version of the film to be shown in Berlin. This was an important venture, since at that time a film that was a success in Berlin was almost certain to be a success all over Europe. After much shrewd bargaining, Stiller contracted to sell the German exhibition rights for 100,000 marks, a huge sum for that period. The buyer was the Trianon Film Company, a Berlin firm whose president was David Schratter. To close the deal, Schratter went to Stockholm, where Stiller informed him that a condition of the sale was that the Trianon Company pay all of his and Garbo's expenses to attend the Berlin premiere. She would need some new clothes to make the trip, Stiller said, and suggested that Trianon make an initial advance for that purpose of five thousand kronor. Schratter agreed to this and a few other of Stiller's last-minute conditions. At no time that he was conducting negotiations concerning Garbo, Schratter later said, did he ever lay eyes on her. It was Stiller who handled all her business affairs, including taking care of the advance for her clothes.

Early in September, 1924, Garbo, wearing the new finery that

Stiller had picked out for her, traveled with her mentor to the German capital. It was her first trip outside of Sweden, and she naturally found it exciting, especially since she was accompanied by a man of the world who knew how to travel in style. The Berlin premiere was held amid considerable fanfare. Photographs of Garbo appeared beforehand in the newspapers; outside the theatre were exhibited life-size cardboard figures of her and of the other stars of the film (most of whom Stiller had tactfully left in Stockholm in order to focus all attention on his protégée); and the German exhibitors had invited to the opening a large number of people prominent in both society and the arts. When Garbo and Stiller entered their box at the theatre, binoculars were trained on them from all directions, causing the young actress to push her chair back from the edge of the box. Stiller pulled it up again.

The film was a brilliant success in Berlin. The fashionable first-night audience applauded wildly when the picture was over and cried for Stiller to take a bow. He did and then, as the newspapers later reported, grasped the hand of his shy companion and propelled her to the edge of the box so that she might also acknowledge the applause. The German critics wrote rave reviews about *Gösta Berling,* describing it variously as "an unparalleled epic of the screen," "the height of filmic art," and "a masterwork of beauty and characterization." Garbo, too, fared better away from her native land. Like the Swedes, the Germans were much struck by her beauty—"a Nordic princess," "her bodily movements are like quicksilver"—but the Berliners also commented favorably on her acting, which appealed to them as "heartfelt," "soul-revealing" and "touched with *Weltschmerz.*" The picture settled down for a long run in Berlin. The exhibitors had figured on recovering their investment in four weeks. They got it back in one. From the Berlin showing alone Trianon cleared close to three quarters of a million marks.

The Trianon Company was so gratified with this bonanza that they got in touch with Stiller, who had returned with Garbo to Stockholm, and urged him to produce a picture for them. For bargaining purposes Stiller at first expressed only mild interest in the proposition; actually he was very keen about it. The next step he had in mind to advance Garbo's career was to produce a picture with her as the star. The Trianon offer looked promising for this purpose. At Stiller's suggestion, David Schratter traveled to Stockholm to discuss the deal.

While Stiller was busy making plans for her future, Garbo, now a minor celebrity, again resumed her studies at the Academy. During the next several weeks she appeared at the Royal Dramatic Theatre in *Violins of Autumn,* a Russian drama in which she had a small role as one of eighteen "Guests," and in an expressionistic Swedish work called *The Invisible,* in which she played "The Prostitute." Following these she was cast in the insignificant part of Mariette, a doctor's receptionist, in Jules Romains' famous farce *Knock, or The Triumph of Medicine.* As matters turned out, that was not only her final role at the Royal Dramatic but her last appearance on any legitimate stage.

In his prolonged negotiations with Stiller, David Schratter was impressed anew with the imperious director's talent for driving a hard bargain. As businessmen so often discover, the artist is apt to be a dreamer with a firm grasp of the mysteries of finance. After Stiller had worked out a contract for himself, guaranteeing him 150,000 marks for directing his first Trianon film, he took up a few other pertinent matters. "I have a contract with Greta Garbo," he told Schratter. "If you want me, you'll have to take her too." Schratter agreed. Garbo was given a five-year contract with an initial salary of five hundred marks a month. "Now, I also have a contract with the great young Swedish actor Einar Hanson," Stiller said, and Schratter, with a sigh, agreed to give Hanson a contract also.

The discussion then turned to the film Stiller was to make. The Trianon people were under the impression that he had agreed to produce a motion picture version of a sentimental German love story. The scenario for this had already been prepared. Stiller said he had a better idea. During the filming of *Gösta Berling,* he had read in a Stockholm newspaper a melodramatic serialized story written by a Russian refugee named Vladimir Semitjov. Impressed with the movie possibilities of the work, Stiller had bought the screen rights and with the help of the author and Ragnar Hyltén-Cavallius reworked it into a screen scenario. With great enthusiasm Stiller outlined the plot to Schratter.

The story concerned a young Russian girl of good family—the part to be played by Garbo—who, during the First World War, flees from Sevastopol on a Turkish barge with the intention of making her way across the Black Sea to Constantinople. There she plans to search for her fiancé, who has mysteriously disappeared into those parts. During the voyage, however, she is doped by some Turkish blackguards among the crew, and then taken to Asia Minor, where she is sold into a harem. The picture was to continue by showing her life as a concubine, her escape to Constantinople and her myriad adventures before being finally reunited with her lover. Stiller allowed that this would make a monumental picture.

Schratter was not so sure, but he eventually succumbed to Stiller's high-pressure salesmanship. Having gotten this much settled, Stiller broke the news that he planned to shoot most of the film in Constantinople. While Schratter held his head and muttered about expense, Stiller explained how, by producing the picture in Turkey, Trianon would not have to spend any money on sets. All the handsome backgrounds would be provided free. With Garbo and Hanson in the leading parts, the cast could be filled out with the addition of a few bit players, who, Stiller said, could be hired cheaply in Turkey. He also pointed out that he planned to use a great number of mob scenes and confidently predicted that the benighted Turks would turn out for these just for the fun of it. In the end Stiller had his way, as usual, in everything.

During all these involved negotiations, Stiller assumed that Garbo would acquiesce in the elaborate plans he was making for her. He was not wrong. When he told her that all arrangements had been made for their departure for Constantinople, she quietly informed the Academy and her family that she was leaving and packed her bags. Before or away from the camera she responded to Stiller's direction like an automaton. As she said of this period years later, "I had not anything to do with my own things at that time."

Chapter Eight

Toward the middle of December, 1924, the quartet of adventurous Swedes—Garbo, Stiller, Einar Hanson and Ragnar Hyltén-Cavallius—left Stockholm to try their luck in Turkey. After stopping over in Berlin to pick up a German camera crew, they continued on to Constantinople, arriving there shortly before Christmas. To their agreeable surprise, they were met at the railroad station by representatives of the Swedish and German legations. This attention pleased Stiller. He was in fine spirits. Perhaps because he was a Russian, he felt at home in that fabulous Byzantine setting. Also, he had plenty of money, and he was not small about spending it. With characteristic expansiveness he installed the camera crew in a fancy Russian pension while engaging splendid quarters for Garbo and himself and the other Swedes in the luxurious Pera Palace Hotel. On Christmas Eve he put on a big party for his cast and crew, to which he invited practically all the Swedish and German residents of the city. His Christmas gift to Garbo was a beautiful fur coat, the traditional token of affection of the older man for the younger woman.

Playing "The Grand Duke" to the hilt, Stiller promptly purchased two fine automobiles as well as two trucks. He turned one of the cars over to Hanson and Cavallius for their personal use. In the other he and Garbo drove around the city, taking in the polyglot atmosphere and looking for backgrounds. They were usually followed by one or both of the trucks carrying the camera crew and their equipment. From time to time the motorcade stopped while Stiller directed the photographing of a teeming street scene, a view of the breath-taking floating domes and minarets or some other picturesque sight he planned to use in the movie. He was in no hurry to get on with the work. He was enjoying himself and had time for everything.

Driving or on foot, Stiller spent day after day exploring with his wide-eyed protégée every nook and cranny of the ancient and incredible

En route to Turkey, 1924

city. They visited the mosques and tombs, feasted in the most elegant restaurants and whiled away the hours sitting in coffeehouses, where Stiller looked for characters that might be used in his film. On leisurely shopping expeditions they wandered through the hundreds of denlike stalls of the Grand Bazaar. Stiller loved to match wits in haggling with the native shopkeepers, and laid in a rather ample supply of Persian carpets. He also took great delight in buying Garbo elaborate oriental costumes. The most striking of these, according to Cavallius, was a beautiful Chinese gown of deep red silk lavishly embroidered with gold flowers. She appeared in this at a party given by the Swedish Legation and there gaily danced the Hambo, a boisterous Swedish folk dance, with Cavallius. Her spirits were as high as Stiller's.

While the joy continued unconfined, Stiller discovered that he had run out of money. He thought this a nuisance, especially since he hadn't yet got around to start actual shooting. He borrowed some funds from a Russian friend to take care of the emergency, and then wired the

Trianon Company, grandly requesting a million marks. Two days passed, and he received no answer. He wired again. Still no reply. Leaving his cast and crew with the admonition to be of good cheer, he took the train to Berlin. There he found that Trianon had gone hopelessly bankrupt. Any thought of continuing work on the Constantinople epic under Trianon's auspices was out of the question.

Stiller wired Hanson to bring Garbo and the other members of the company to Berlin. This assignment was easier ordered than executed, since none of the company had funds to make the trip. However, the Swedish Legation in Constantinople came to the rescue and bought railroad tickets for the three Swedes; the German Legation performed the same service for the camera crew. In spite of their bad situation, Hanson later told friends, Garbo seemed quite unconcerned. Dining with her the night before they were to entrain for Berlin, Hanson said something about their bad luck and expressed his concern about what they were in for next. Garbo was blandly reassuring. "Don't worry," she said. "Everything will be all right when we get to Berlin. Stiller will take care of everything."

A revealing glimpse of Garbo's utter dependence on Stiller and of her childlike and unquestioning faith in him came to light many years after the debacle in Constantinople. In 1937, David Schratter, the former president of Trianon who was then living in California, brought suit against Garbo to recover ten thousand dollars, which he claimed he had advanced to her during the period she worked for his firm. Though the suit never came to trial, Garbo's lawyers successfully contending that it should be barred because of the statute of limitations, Schratter's counsel was permitted, before the court dismissed the case, to question the actress about the matter. She acknowledged that it was Stiller who introduced her to Schratter but disavowed having borrowed any money from him. As the questioning continued, her artlessly phrased answers disclosed the extent of Stiller's domination of her existence:

QUESTION: Did you not eventually go to work for the Trianon Company, and weren't you given $1,250 a month?

ANSWER: I had nothing to do with those things. I don't know what conversations were going on. I was a little too young to determine those things, I think. I was under twenty-one.

QUESTION: Your arrangement with the Trianon Company terminated shortly after you returned from Turkey in 1925?

ANSWER: Well, all I know is that the whole thing busted, and naturally I did not understand anything about those things.

QUESTION: Didn't you once ask Mr. Schratter for an advance on your salary, and didn't he say that he could not advance you money, but that he would make you a personal loan instead?

ANSWER: No, I don't remember, because I did not have anything to do with any of those things.

QUESTION: Whom did you receive your money from during the period you worked for the Trianon Film Company?

ANSWER: I didn't receive any money, as far as I can recollect. There were fares to pay, for whom I don't know. We were merely taken along. I was merely a young actress working in it, and the people were merely put on the train and taken along. How they were paid I don't know.

QUESTION: Was Mr. Stiller acting as your representative as well as your director?

ANSWER: Yes.

QUESTION: He was, of course, interested in your personal welfare as far as advancement in pictures was concerned, I take it?

ANSWER: We did not discuss it.

What Garbo and Stiller did discuss, after she and Hanson had returned to Berlin, was whether they should go on to Stockholm, as they had expected to do. Stiller said he had made up his mind that they should all stay in Berlin. He had a number of irons in the fire, he explained, and assured them that something would turn up. The outlook was not promising. All the German film companies had been severely affected by the inflation. Stiller had been unable to find financial backing to resume production of his venture in Turkey. He had sought work as a director with the leading German motion picture firms, to no avail. The word had got around that he was a careless man with a mark.

Garbo in The Street of Sorrow

Though broke and in debt, he was keeping up appearances smartly. He had visited the moneylenders and was living in an expensive suite at the first-class Esplanade Hotel. He arranged for Garbo and Hanson to move in too. Stranded in a foreign country, they all did their best, as theatrical tradition requires, to put a good face on things.

They were rescued by a young German film director named G. W. Pabst, who was on his way to becoming one of the outstanding figures in the European cinema. Having recently turned from the theatre to motion pictures, he was then casting his second film. It was called *Die Freudlose Gasse,* exhibited later in America as *The Street of Sorrow.* The picture was to depict in starkly realistic fashion the devastating physical, moral and psychological effects of war as revealed through the lives of residents on a small, dark street in postwar Vienna. Pabst had assembled an excellent cast. It included such well-known players as Werner Krauss, Valeska Gert and the Danish actress Asta Nielsen, who was then the leading tragedienne of the European screen. He had, however, been unable to cast to his satisfaction the part of the elder daughter of an upper-class Viennese family impoverished by the war. It was the daughter's unhappy task to try to keep her family from starving without sullying her honor. Pabst had learned that Garbo, whom he had admired in *Gösta Berling,* was in Berlin, and set his secretary to calling the hotels to locate the Swedish actress. When reached by phone at the Esplanade, she told Pabst he would have to discuss the matter with Stiller and quickly turned the phone over to him.

Assuming his usual bargaining stance, Stiller said he didn't think Garbo would be interested in the part. However, on Pabst's urging, he agreed to take a look at the script. After studying it, he suggested a number of changes, especially in the part offered to Garbo, and let it be known that she might consider accepting the role if Pabst would meet her financial terms. For her work in the film Stiller demanded the exceedingly steep sum of four thousand dollars—to be paid, further-more, in United States currency. Pabst consented to this figure and method of payment. Then came Stiller's customary special conditions: Pabst's company would have to pay all Garbo's living expenses while the picture was being made; the film used in photographing the picture would have to be the most expensive kind on the market; Einar Hanson would have to be given work in the picture; and since, according to Stiller, Julius Jaenzon was the only person who could photograph Garbo properly, the Swedish cameraman would have to be hired for the picture. Pabst wearily agreed to all these demands, except the last. He explained that he had already engaged Guido Seeber, one of the best cameramen in Europe, and he could not be replaced. Stiller at length gave in on the matter of the cameraman, and contracts were signed.

On the first day of shooting Stiller accompanied Garbo to the studio. She was pale and visibly nervous. Meeting the other members of the cast, she was so uneasy that she was barely able to acknowledge the introductions. Stiller's first move was to seek out Guido Seeber, the cameraman, and treat him to a lengthy discourse on how to photograph Garbo. "He talked to me as if I'd never been behind a camera in my life,"

The Street of Sorrow

The Street of Sorrow, *with Jaro Furth*

Seeber said later. "He seemed even more wrought up than the frightened young woman he was so worried about."

Seeber and Pabst discovered, after they had shot the first hundred feet of film and looked at the results in the projection room, that Garbo did indeed present problems. Her nervousness was so plainly visible, in particular an apparently uncontrollable twitching in her cheek, that not a single foot of the film could be used. The scene, taken a second time, showed no improvement. Before trying again, Pabst suggested that Garbo take a rest; he talked with her and tried to relieve her anxiety. He had allowed neither her nor Stiller into the projection room; he wished to avoid upsetting her further and he was reluctant to acknowledge to Stiller that he and his cameraman were having trouble. Garbo nevertheless sensed that something was amiss, and when shooting was resumed her agitation had become even more noticeable. Seeber finally solved the problem. The next time the scene was filmed he operated the camera at a greatly increased speed; as a result, the nervous twitching in Garbo's face could no longer be detected on the film. Pabst then invited her into the projection room and complimented her warmly on her performance. Gaining confidence, she began acting with more assurance and conviction. Pabst continued to work with her patiently and carefully; he gradually expanded her part and invented additional opportunities for her to display her figure to advantage. Like Stiller, he photographed her primarily in long and medium shots, using close-ups only rarely.

Garbo proved to be a good workman. As a result of her training by Stiller, she followed Pabst's directions without a murmur of protest, and she was a model of industriousness. Pabst frequently kept the cast working for sixteen hours at a stretch; regardless of how late she worked, Garbo was usually the first person on the set every morning. She spent the entire day there, even if her presence was required for only a couple of hours. Pabst was also impressed by the fact that she always came to the studio well prepared. What he may not have known was that she had been rehearsed by Stiller until the late hours the night before.

By working at forced draft, Pabst completed *The Street of Sorrow* in thirty-four days. Though the picture has come to be regarded by film scholars as a major work, it was poorly received when first released. Critics complained that it was overly long, static and unconvincing. The picture failed as mass entertainment because it was too gloomy for popular taste, dealing as it did with hunger, greed, selfishness and lust. Furthermore, the film ran into censorship troubles in France, Austria and Russia and was heavily cut in several other European countries. A shortened version, exhibited in the United States in 1927, went almost completely unnoticed. One of the few critics who reviewed it expressed the consensus when he described it as "the least meritorious German picture of the year."

As for Garbo, she was lightly dismissed in America as "a simple and completely unsophisticated actress with a talent for expressing pathos and resignation." In Europe she was treated more generously. The well-known British director and critic, Paul Rotha, described her performance as "fascinating," and further observed: "By reason of the sympathetic understanding of Pabst, Greta Garbo brought a quality of loveliness into her playing as the professor's elder daughter. Her frail beauty, cold as an ice flower warmed by the sun, stood secure in the starving city of Vienna, untouched by the vice and lust that dwelt in the dark little street." All things considered, however, *The Street of Sorrow* did little to advance Garbo's career.

During the filming of the picture, relations between Garbo and Stiller became, for the first time since their association began, somewhat strained. Soon after shooting began Pabst made it clear that he preferred that Stiller stay away from the set when Garbo was working. Stiller submitted to the ban, but it angered him and aroused his jealousy, which could reach towering proportions. His nerves during these weeks were generally on edge. He was engaged in various business negotiations, but nothing had matured, and his disposition was generally snappish. It didn't help matters any that he was temporarily dependent for his living expenses on Garbo's salary. Furthermore, without consulting Stiller, she had been talking informally with Pabst, who had approached her, about the possibility of signing a long-term contract with his company. Pabst was very anxious to acquire her services, and pressed her to make a decision to stay on in Berlin.

When Stiller learned of Pabst's maneuvering, he flew into a violent rage. In one particularly stormy session in his suite at the Esplanade he accused his young friend in front of Einar Hanson of deceit, ingratitude and all manner of wrongdoing. Embarrassed and in tears, she promised to take no further steps without his approval. Changing from the outraged protector to the patient father, Stiller took her hands in his. "Stay with me, Greta," he said. "Moje knows what is best for you."

Chapter Nine

While Garbo was making *The Street of Sorrow,* Stiller had embarked on a business venture in keeping with his grandiose ideas. He had conceived a plan to form a gigantic combine of several European motion picture companies that would control some seven hundred movie theatres on the Continent. He had already enlisted the interest of UFA in Germany and Pathé in France. Also involved in the proposed deal was Ivar Kreuger, the fabulous Swedish financier known as "The Match King." Since Stiller was slated to be one of the top officials of the combine, he would, besides having a good thing for himself, be in a position to wield tremendous influence in promoting his protégée's film career. During the time that these intricate negotiations were in progress, however, there occurred another of those unforeseeable events that was to have a profound effect on his life and even more on Garbo's.

In the late spring of 1925, Louis B. Mayer, vice-president and production chief of Metro-Goldwyn-Mayer, was making a business and pleasure trip through Europe with his daughter Irene. While in Berlin, Mayer saw *Gösta Berling's Saga.* He was impressed by the scope of the picture, its resourceful photography and, most of all, what he considered its brilliant direction. A man who could turn out a picture like that, Mayer decided, belonged in Hollywood, and set out to capture him.

Mayer's action was in the spirit of the times. All the major Hollywood studios were then involved in conducting a wholesale raid on European cinema talent. Foreign films, especially those from Germany, had made a great impact on American producers and directors, and were also all the rage among the intelligentsia. Will Rogers remarked on this situation in his film *The Ropin' Fool,* made around this time. "If you think this picture's no good," Rogers said while twirling his lariat, "I'll put on a beard and say it was made in Germany, and then you'll call it art." Lured by fat contracts, foreign stars and directors were streaming into the California film factories in droves. Besides Victor Seastrom,

Stiller's confrere who had gone to Hollywood in 1923, other Europeans who followed the gold-dust trail included Ernst Lubitsch, Jacques Feyder, Fred Murnau, Emil Jannings, Conrad Veidt, Nils Asther, Greta Nissen, Ludwig Berger, Pola Negri and Erich Pommer, to name but a few.

Before meeting with Stiller, Mayer cabled Victor Seastrom to ask his opinion of his old colleague. Seastrom's reply was a glowing recommendation. Accordingly, when Mayer called on Stiller at the latter's suite in the Esplanade Hotel, he offered the Swedish director (Stiller became a Swedish citizen in 1921) a three-year contract at a starting salary of fifteen hundred dollars a week. For once Stiller, perhaps sensing that he had met his match, did not indulge in prolonged haggling over money matters. He did, however, put forth one provision: he would go to Hollywood, he said, only on the condition that M-G-M also put Greta Garbo under contract.

"And who is Greta Garbo?" Mayer asked, acting as if he hadn't noticed her in *Gösta Berling*. "First," Stiller began, "she is a great beauty, a type you get in front of a camera once in a hundred years. Second, she is a great actress, an actress who will be the greatest in the world." As Stiller was warming up to his subject, Mayer interrupted to suggest that it might be desirable for him to meet the young woman. Stiller called her into the room and introduced her to Mayer. His indifference was profound. As Garbo recalled some years later, "When we met with Mr. Mayer he hardly looked at me. I suspect he looked at me out of the corner of his eye, but I can't be sure he gave me even that much attention. The whole thing was arranged between Mr. Stiller and him." To make sure of signing Stiller, Mayer consented to give Garbo a three-year contract at a starting salary of three hundred and fifty dollars a week.

Back in Stockholm for a couple of weeks, Garbo told her family of her plan to go to America. She had gradually grown away from them since going out into the world with Stiller, but her mother, who still called her youngest child "Keta," wept on learning that she was leaving home for what perhaps would be forever. Her brother and sister, however, were excited by the news, much more so than Garbo herself. Then nineteen and very unsure of herself, she would have much preferred to continue her career in Germany or in Sweden. Going to America, even under Stiller's protection, filled her with concern. Her apprehension was increased by the fact that Stiller, for all his seeming self-assurance, had also gotten cold feet about the American adventure. At one point he had gone so far as to consult his lawyer about the possibility of breaking his M-G-M contract. Attracted by the financial and possible professional rewards that Hollywood offered him and the actress he was determined to make into a world-famous star, he had at the same time grave misgivings about the whole enterprise. In the end he told Garbo that they would go to New York, where he would decide whether they would go on to Hollywood. Stiller's friend Hjalmar Bergman, who talked with the director shortly before he left Stockholm, later wrote to Seastrom that Stiller was "so nervous it was almost frightening; if there are difficulties in New York, his nerves may not be able to take it."

Garbo and Stiller arrived in New York aboard the *Drottningholm* on July 6, 1925. The first difficulty they experienced was the heat. As their ship nosed into the Swedish-American Line pier at the foot of Fifty-seventh Street that sunny Monday morning, the temperature began to rise. By afternoon it had shot up to 86 degrees, and two local citizens, according to next day's newspapers, had died of heat prostration. It was the beginning of a prolonged heat wave, which Garbo and Stiller, accustomed to the cool Scandinavian climate, found almost unendurable.

To handle the welcoming of its latest importations, M-G-M selected one of its bright young public relations men named Hubert Voight, who subsequently became a ranking independent publicity expert in Hollywood. The chore to which he was assigned, Voight has since recalled, was more or less routine, though it did present certain difficulties. He was supposed to whip up New York newspaper editors' interest in a movie director who, though eminent in Europe, had scarcely been heard of in America, and in a young Swedish actress who was known to practically nobody in this country except Louis B. Mayer, and only dimly to him. Voight, without strenuously exerting himself, decided to adopt the familiar formula of identifying the unknown

Arriving in New York with Stiller

Swedish actress with a top-ranking American movie star. After glancing at some photographs of Garbo that had been forwarded from Stockholm, Voight decided to present her as "the Norma Shearer of Sweden." Working himself up into a small state of synthetic enthusiasm, he phoned the city editors to advise them of the Swedish Norma Shearer's arrival and suggest that they have reporters and photographers on hand to cover the momentous event.

As it turned out, only Voight, a Swedish-speaking Metro employee who acted as interpreter and a free-lance photographer named Jimmy Sileo (who had been paid twenty-five dollars in advance for the job) made up the welcoming party to greet the Norma Shearer of Sweden and her companion. They were both extremely co-operative in posing for pictures. Sileo took four, one of Garbo and Stiller leaning against the ship's rail and three of her alone. She gave every indication of being willing to pose for more, but Sileo, out on a hurry-up assignment, had brought only four plates for his camera. However, to please the eager young actress, he continued for the next twenty minutes to snap his empty camera at her as she sat on the rail, waved at the Statue of Liberty and assumed all the other shipboard attitudes that Sileo could think of. This business finished, Voight conducted the new arrivals to the Commodore Hotel, where Garbo promptly immersed herself in a tub of cold water. That was the way, Stiller later told friends, that she spent most of her time in New York.

Though Voight saw to it that prints of Sileo's photographs were delivered to all the New York papers, only two used them. The tabloid *Graphic* published the picture of Garbo and Stiller, and the *Herald Tribune* printed one of the actress alone. It showed her, dressed in a checkered suit with a long-waisted jacket, black pointed pumps, white blouse and white cloche, as she leaned against a bulkhead, waving and smiling. The picture was captioned: "A COMELY VISITOR. Greta Garbo, one of Sweden's most beautiful film stars, arrived here yesterday on board the Swedish-American liner *Drottningholm*. She has signed contracts to appear in several American motion pictures." It was true that Garbo had signed a contract, and since she was a minor, the document also bore her mother's signature, but Stiller was not satisfied with its terms; he had already decided to take up that matter as well as a few others with M-G-M.

While the staid New York *Times* didn't bother even to list the names of Garbo and Stiller among the prominent passengers on the *Drottningholm,* it did find space that day to report that Pola Negri, one of the reigning film stars, had been fined fifty-seven thousand dollars by the U. S. Government for failure to declare her jewelry on returning from Europe the previous May. The papers carried other news of somewhat more consequence. In the Middle West, a group of Republicans had begun to boom Calvin Coolidge for another term in the White House. England was calling on France to pay her scaled-down war debts, and the two countries were weighing a British suggestion that both break off relations with Russia. Down in Tennessee, the Scopes, or so-called "Monkey" trial, to test a state law forbidding the teaching of evolution, was about to open. The Teapot Dome scandal was being aired in Washington, and reputations were crashing almost audibly. The Prince of Wales, on a good-will tour, had taken time off to shoot a wildebeest in Southern Rhodesia. Gertrude Ederle was in England getting ready to attempt swimming the English Channel.

The New York that Garbo found, in the summer of 1925, glittered with prosperity. The stock market was doing fine, and anybody who didn't believe the country had reached a plateau of permanent prosperity was considered dull-witted if not un-American. There was a surplus in the U. S. Treasury, which Secretary Andrew W. Mellon planned to use to reduce the national debt. Prohibition was going full tilt, and the speakeasy had become a national institution. At Manhattan night clubs like the Mirador, Lido-Venice and Silver Slipper well-heeled patrons willingly paid a dollar for a ginger-ale chaser. On the night of Garbo's arrival in town the summer edition of the *Ziegfeld Follies* opened at the New Amsterdam with W. C. Fields, Ethel Shutta and Will Rogers. Elsewhere on Broadway Fred and Adele Astaire were dancing in *Lady, Be Good,* Willie Howard was carrying on in *Sky High,* and Lila Lee was starred in *The Bride Retires,* billed as "the world's greatest bridal-chamber comedy." Offered to the more serious-minded were such attractions as *What Price Glory, Desire Under the Elms,* with Walter

Huston, and *They Knew What They Wanted,* with Pauline Lord. At the top of the best-seller lists were Michael Arlen's *The Green Hat,* Edna Ferber's *So Big* and Sinclair Lewis' *Arrowsmith.*

Very few of these diversions were enjoyed by Garbo and Stiller, who found New York lonely and unattractive. Because of one vexing difficulty after another, they had to spend a little more than two months in the sweltering city. After a number of conversations with M-G-M officials, Stiller was persuaded to abandon the notion of trying to break his contract. This settled, the Metro executives were anxious for him to continue on to the Coast to begin work, but Stiller refused to budge until a revision had been made in Garbo's contract. He now brusquely demanded that her starting salary be doubled. M-G-M was vastly uninterested, even at half the price. Stiller worked for days trying to arrange an appointment to introduce her to M-G-M's president, Nicholas Schenck. He was always too busy. Instead, Stiller was turned over to a vice-president called Major Edward Bowes, who later acquired a considerable reputation as a judge of amateur talent.

Though Major Bowes shared the general Metro lack of enthusiasm for the Swedish Norma Shearer, he granted Stiller's insistent request that a screen test be made of her. With painstaking care Stiller spent a week supervising the making of the test. When it was shown to Metro officials, they all shook their heads. "She's too unusual," they muttered. Stiller tried to explain that this was precisely the quality that made her a great find, but nobody cared to listen.

When Stiller wasn't badgering M-G-M on Garbo's behalf, he roused her from her cold tub, and they went walking, if the heat wasn't insufferable, or to the movies. Though they both had only a most uneasy grasp of English, they had little trouble following the plots of the silent pictures. The cinema offerings on Broadway that summer included *The Lucky Devil* (Richard Dix and Esther Ralston), *The Lady Who Lied* (Nita Naldi and Lewis Stone), *The Freshman* (Harold Lloyd), *Don Q, Son of Zorro* (Douglas Fairbanks and Mary Astor), *The Gold Rush* (Charlie Chaplin) and *The Phantom of the Opera* (Lon Chaney). Studying American movies, Stiller felt, was beneficial to both himself and his companion, and they took in a great many of them.

Portrait by Arnold Genthe, 1925

Once in a while they called on one of Stiller's few acquaintances in New York. Among these was the well-known actress Martha Hedman, whom Stiller had known in Sweden. She invited the new arrivals to lunch and afterwards took them around to the studio of her friend Arnold Genthe, the famous photographer. "The newcomers were very much interested in the photographs they saw in my studio," Genthe recalled in his memoirs. "That kind of photography was something entirely new to them. 'I would love to have you make some pictures of me sometime,' Miss Garbo said. (We spoke in German, as she knew hardly a word of English at that time.) 'Why sometime?' I enquired. 'Why not now? You're here and I'm here, and I must make some real photographs of you to have visible proof that you are real.' She smiled, but protested earnestly. 'No, not now. Look at my dress, and I don't like my hair.' 'Never mind that,' I said. 'I am more interested in your eyes and in what is behind that extraordinary forehead.' And without any further preparation, Greta Garbo let me make a number of pictures of her. Her face had unusual mobility of expression and in the course of an hour my camera had captured a number of distinctive poses and expressions, all so different that it was hard to believe they were of the same girl." Masking out all but her classical facial features, Genthe revealed their mystical attraction—the heavy-lidded eyes, the perfect nose, the slightly parted lips.

Pleased with the results, Genthe showed the pictures to his friend Frank Crowninshield, editor of the sophisticated magazine *Vanity Fair*. "The pictures are very interesting," Crowninshield remarked, "but who is the girl?" "Greta Garbo," Genthe replied. "Never heard of her," Crowninshield said, "but perhaps I might use one of the pictures." "You can have it," Genthe said, "only if you give it a full page." Crowninshield agreed and scheduled one of the photographs for publication in *Vanity Fair*'s November issue. (It appeared under the caption, "A New Star from the North—Greta Garbo.") Genthe also sent a set of the pictures to Garbo, and one morning toward the middle of August she stopped in at his studio to thank him. She said that she had also come to bid him good-by. "They don't seem to want me," she explained. "They say I'm a type. I'm going back to Berlin." Genthe asked if she had

Arriving in Hollywood with Stiller

shown his photographs to the people at Metro. "No," she replied. "I want to keep those for myself. They have so many of me already." Genthe insisted that she bring the pictures to the attention of the M-G-M executives before taking any further steps to return to Europe, and she promised to do so.

Once the Metro officials had seen Genthe's arresting portraits, which Stiller laid before them, their chilliness toward Garbo suddenly vanished. The shy, frizzy-haired young hopeful they had seen in person now appeared in photographs as a handsome and oddly provocative-looking woman. If she could be photographed to look like that, Metro officials told each other, they could make something of her. Still, they were not inclined to boost her salary beyond three hundred and fifty dollars a week. Though Stiller doggedly insisted for a while longer on double that sum, he finally settled for four hundred dollars. He and Garbo then set out for California.

When they stepped off the train at the Los Angeles station, they were welcomed somewhat more imposingly than they had been in New York. Some twenty people turned out to greet them. Besides Metro publicity agents, an interpreter and other studio representatives, the group included Victor Seastrom, Karl Dane and a few other Scandinavian friends as well as two little girls in Swedish costume, each of whom presented Garbo with a bouquet. Holding the flowers and flanked by the moppets, she was photographed looking demure under her outrageously woolly hair-do. The reporters then put a few questions to the newcomers. Miss Garbo was asked where she planned to live in Hollywood. "I would like to find a room with a nice private family," she said.

Chapter Ten

Although any number of respectable Hollywood families would doubtless have been willing to take in Garbo as a boarder, she was advised that such living accommodations would be considered unbecoming to a movie star in America. At the suggestion of Victor Seastrom, Garbo and Stiller took up residence in Santa Monica, a placid suburban community near the ocean and fairly convenient to the M-G-M studios. Stiller rented a small house on the beach while Garbo moved into unpretentious quarters in the Miramar Hotel, located a short distance away. After their stifling and anxious stay in New York, they found the pleasant climate, ocean breezes and slower pace of life in California a relief. While getting settled and preparing to start work, Garbo spent most of her time at Stiller's house, indulging in her favorite pastime of swimming and sunbathing. A Swedish compatriot who visited Stiller at this time recalled having watched the young actress as she sat on the warm sands in front of the house. Wearing a rather commodious bathing suit, she was contentedly peeling potatoes. Nodding in her direction, Stiller said, "You will see that something will become of her."

Garbo was officially entered on the M-G-M payroll on September 10, 1925, but the studio showed no signs of being in a hurry to try to make something of her. Nor were Metro officials hasty about putting Stiller to work. For a while the newcomers were contented in their newfound leisure. They spent many days motoring about the countryside in the car that Stiller had bought, looking up friends among the Scandinavian colony and making a trip to San Francisco, where one of Stiller's brothers lived. "He and his wife invited Greta and me to dinner," Stiller later wrote to a friend in Sweden. "They were very kind and cried and carried on, but I could not feel anything."

As the days passed and the studio continued to display a marked lack of interest in himself and his protégée, Stiller became increasingly restive and broody. The whole thing was a mistake, he fretfully told his

Publicity shot of Garbo, 1925

Swedish friends; he and Greta should never have come to America. Affected by his moodiness, Garbo's spirits also sagged. "They were a melancholy pair," the wife of a Swedish actor then living in Hollywood has recalled. "It was partly because she made no success at all at the start. She was really quite unattractive then. Her hair was kinky, and her teeth were not good. Nobody paid any attention to her, and she was very unhappy. So was Stiller. They used to sit on the terrace, staring out at the ocean and looking gloomy. I remember we called them 'grandma and grandpa.'"

Once in a while the old-seeming couple stirred themselves and paid a visit to some of their Scandinavian friends, among whom were the Victor Seastroms, the Lars Hansons and an interior decorator named Erik Stocklossa. Many of the Swedes then resident in the film colony have recalled that when Stiller and Garbo called on them she showed more interest in spending her time with their children than with the grownups. "Whenever they were invited out," Erik Stocklossa once remarked, "she would ask, 'Have they any children?' If the answer was yes, she would always come and devote all her time to the kids." She was especially fond of the Seastroms' children, and often brought little presents to them.

After a month of enforced idleness, Stiller began a campaign of polite but steady harassment of M-G-M to secure a part for Garbo and a directorial assignment for himself. His dealings at the studio were mainly with Irving Thalberg, the brilliant and hard-driving "boy genius" of the film industry, who, at twenty-six, had zoomed from an office boy at Universal to production manager at M-G-M. From the beginning he and Stiller didn't get along well. Stiller was not pleased to take orders from a man sixteen years his junior, whose film experience, Stiller felt, was a drop in the bucket compared to his. Thalberg, on his part, considered Stiller loud, overbearing and unreasonably demanding. Furthermore, Thalberg had not developed unlimited enthusiasm for Garbo from his one perfunctory meeting with her and from looking at the screen test made in New York. In an effort to whet his interest Stiller supervised the making of another series of tests. When these were viewed by Thalberg and Mayer, they were quite favorably impressed, though they complained about her hair and teeth. Mayer suggested that she have the necessary dental work done immediately and that she also visit the studio's chief make-up man, who would create a more attractive coiffure. Stiller saw to it that both steps were taken. Then, ten weeks after her arrival in Hollywood, Garbo was given her first part.

She started her American career close to the top, having been cast as the female lead opposite Ricardo Cortez in a moderately ambitious picture called *The Torrent*. The studio assigned Monta Bell to direct it. This was a disappointment as stunning and profound to Garbo as it was to Stiller, for both had confidently assumed that he would be selected as the director of her first American film. Had they known this would not be the case it is doubtful if either would have come to Hollywood. She was so frightened at the prospect of working with a strange director, in a huge studio where she felt lost and among people whose language she did not understand, that she told Stiller she preferred to give up the part and go home. He rejected this notion instantly; she undertook the role.

Though Monta Bell directed the picture, Stiller was responsible in large measure for Garbo's performance. Except for the first day, Stiller did not appear on the set, but every evening he rehearsed Garbo in the next day's scenes, coaching her in every movement and every expression. This regimen, though taxing, was necessary because she was not prepared to cope with the Hollywood method of directing. "The American director," she said in an interview at this time, "tells his players to act the scene as they feel it—and then he makes suggestions. In Sweden we are instructed exactly how the scene must be played before the camera is turned." As a result of careful preparation, Garbo unfailingly reported on the set ready to act the scene as she, and Stiller, felt it. Though staying away from the set, Stiller delivered Garbo to the studio every morning and called for her every night, continuing to keep her securely under his wing.

He had time to perform this daily chore, since, despite his persistent proddings, M-G-M had still not assigned him to a picture. Dispirited and suffering from recurrent attacks of what he thought was lumbago, he nevertheless put a good face on things, except in letters to friends in

The Torrent (*above*) *with Ricardo Cortez* (*below, left*) *with Lucy Beaumont*

Sweden. Late in November, 1925, he wrote to his friend Axel Nilsson in Stockholm: "I would like to make my millions now and get away from here, but I guess I will have to wait at least 3 years. . . . The Americans are very nice and very uninteresting. There is nothing here of Europe's culture. All of America seems to be some sort of society which now and then breaks the law. . . . Greta is starting work for a well-known director, and I think she has got an excellent part. If she only has the energy she will make millions. . . ."

As shooting of *The Torrent* progressed, Metro officials began to show keen interest in the young actress they had so reluctantly acquired. Several of them, including Irving Thalberg, made a practice of dropping in to look at the "rushes" (each day's shooting run off in a projection room at the studio), and their comments were uniformly enthusiastic. Slowly and dimly they began to sense that they had stumbled upon something quite out of the ordinary.

In itself Garbo's first American film was something less than monumental. It was based on a rather stringhalted story by Blasco-Ibáñez, the prolific Spanish novelist who enjoyed a great vogue in the twenties. Several of his works had already been filmed with phenomenal success, in particular *The Four Horsemen of the Apocalypse,* which had the result, among others, of raising Rudolph Valentino from obscurity to stardom. *The Torrent* was drawn on a much smaller scale.

Garbo portrayed in this film the role of Leonora, a Spanish peasant girl with a first-class singing voice who falls in love with Don Rafael, the son of the rich local landlord. His domineering mother forbids their marrying. To show that she means business she forecloses on the house where Leonora lives with her parents, though permitting the girl's mother to remain as a scrubwoman. Don Rafael, a spineless type, accedes to all this, but it hurts him inside. Leonora, however, is more spirited and goes to Paris, where she becomes famous as an operatic star known as La Brunna. Her bell-like tones and other gifts are so highly esteemed that she attracts a throng of admirers, including a few grand dukes and the king of Spain. They outdo each other in showering her with diamond bracelets, ermine capes and other trinkets. Still, she can't get the shallow but handsome Don Rafael out of her mind. Wearing her most luxurious furs, she returns to her native village, matrimony being her intention. A flood breaks loose at this point and while the waters rage about them Leonora and Don Rafael damply protest their love to each other. Owing to renewed maternal objections, they are thwarted again and for good. At the end Don Rafael has married a woman of his mother's choice, fathered two children and become a paunchy, prematurely old man who is very unhappy at the turn of events. Leonora, while going on to greater heights as a diva, beautiful, loved and envied, is equally unhappy and sings while her heart is breaking.

Garbo made a good impression on the other members of the cast and on the crew that worked on the picture. She arrived at the studio at seven and left at six. She was earnest, agreeable, hard-working and, unlike some other European importations, given to no displays of temperament. Her inability to speak English prevented her, even if she had wished, from mixing easily with the other people on the set. In spare moments at the studio she was being tutored in English by an interpreter who had been assigned to translate for her. She also practiced her English with the chief cameraman, William Daniels, with whom she struck up a pleasant and lasting acquaintance. "I didn't teach Garbo to speak English," Daniels has remarked, "but we used to talk a lot, and I would correct her on certain things. We understood each other, and talked about things we both knew—movie talk. The first time I heard her speak English was when we were making *The Torrent.* Garbo was sitting in a sleigh on the back lot. She suddenly said, 'I'm important.' 'Why, you're the most important person around,' someone replied. Then she said, 'Important Garbo—important sardines—just the same.' The word she was trying to use, of course, was 'imported,' but she thought she had made a fine sentence."

The Torrent was completed two days before Christmas, in 1925. Among the interested spectators at the preview, held soon after the first of the year, were Garbo, Stiller, the Victor Seastroms, the Lars Hansons and other members of the Scandinavian colony. "We all thought the picture was a flop and that Garbo was terrible," Lars Hanson later remarked. "In our opinion it didn't amount to anything. Stiller was raving mad, he thought it was so poor."

The picture did perhaps contain a few imperfections, such as Garbo's costumes. These were a sight, as Joseph Alsop, the thoughtful syndicated columnist, observed in 1935, after having seen the film again. "Miss Garbo was clothed in a series of the most improbably hideous garments conceivable by the human mind," Alsop remarked. "The effect of one touching scene wherein Miss Garbo, sated with operatic triumphs, revisits her childhood farmstead is quite destroyed by her appearance in a dress that must have been designed for Maggie in 'Bringing Up Father.'" Another touching scene occurs when the flood, richly described in a subtitle as "a torrent as furious and relentless as the passion in the hearts of the lovers," is at its height. While trees, houses and human beings are being swept away in the angry waters, Don Rafael risks his life making his way to Leonora's house with the intention of rescuing her. He is somewhat surprised, considering the circumstances, at her composure, for she is lying down reading a book. Scarcely losing her place, she bids her drenched caller step into the next room and put on some dry clothes. He returns wearing one of her ermine and moleskin coats. With Don Rafael looking like a displaced Eskimo and Leonora in a modified Mother Hubbard, the star-crossed lovers roll their eyes and heave their chests to indicate their mutual affection.

Even in 1926, scenes like that struck some perceptive filmgoers, including most of Garbo's Swedish friends in Hollywood, as implausible. In addition, her countrymen were inclined to be critical of her acting. "We thought her very clumsy, the way she walked and handled herself," a well-known Swedish actress who was then in Hollywood with her husband has said. "But the Americans found her movements attractive. 'Ah,' they said, 'she walks like an animal.'"

That is indeed very nearly what they did say. "She is lithe, quick and graceful," Mordaunt Hall wrote in his review of *The Torrent* in the New York *Times*. "Miss Garbo is dark, with good eyes and fine features," he added in speaking of her "undeniable prepossessing appearance," and went on to remark: "She is never at a loss for an expression or gesture, and in most of the scenes she appears to be at ease before the camera. Miss Garbo takes full advantage of the numerous opportunities to display her ability as a film actress and she easily cap-

With Ricardo Cortez in The Torrent

tures the honors by her performance." *Variety* agreed. Said the trade paper: "This girl has everything, with looks, acting ability and personality. She makes *Torrent* worthwhile. Louis Mayer can hand himself a few pats on the back for having brought this girl over from the other side."

Richard Watts, Jr., the discerning critic of the New York *Herald Tribune,* also gave Greta Garbo's initial American performance a favorable, though somewhat more restrained, notice. "In the leading role," Watts wrote, "Greta Garbo, Swedish screen star, makes her American debut. She seems an excellent and attractive actress, with a surprising propensity for looking like Carol Dempster, Norma Talmadge, Zasu Pitts and Gloria Swanson in turn. That does not mean that she lacks a manner of her own, however."

What was to become known as the Garbo manner was but faintly discernible in *The Torrent,* but there were intimations. "She was beautiful then," Joseph Alsop wrote in 1935 of Garbo in her first American film, "but not as she is now, when she seems the embodiment of Francis Bacon's wise remark that 'There is no excellent beauty that hath not some strangeness in the proportion.' Her hair was darker, her face more fully rounded, her eyes less wholly unreal. She had an air of youth about her, and more than a trace of immaturity. In her acting, she sketched in what she is now, but only sketched it. . . . Once or twice she wore that cloak of tender irony which she can put on at will today. But she was still distinctly embryonic."

Chapter Eleven

Pleased with the critical and box office success of *The Torrent*, M-G-M decided, in the familiar Hollywood fashion, to repeat the formula. With one exception, the ingredients of Garbo's next film were the same as before: another improbable Blasco-Ibáñez story, this one laid in South America and called *The Temptress;* another popular sexy Latin lover as the hero, this time Antonio Moreno; and another exotic and implausible role for Greta Garbo, this one being the part of Elena, a beautiful, worldly and heartless woman whose slavish admirers range from bankers to bandits. There was to be one difference in this confection, however. Stiller was assigned to direct it.

Now that he had been given a chance to direct his protégée, his dark mood disappeared. He was full of excitement and enthusiasm. "At last," he told Lars Hanson, "they'll see what Greta can do." Anxious to make something special of *The Temptress,* Stiller labored over the script and developed a number of unusual ideas he thought would be effective. He planned, for one thing, to open the picture with a lively circus scene complete with tumblers, acrobats, clowns and dancing bears, which, as the camera moved away, would be revealed as an entertainment at a lavish private party. Telling Hanson of his plans, Stiller confidently predicted, "We'll show them a thing or two."

Trouble started brewing the minute Stiller stepped on the set. "When I got there ready to start," he later told his friend Ernest Mattson, "I saw fifty people standing around. 'Who are all these people? What are they doing here?' I asked. I was told that one was an assistant director, another was an assistant producer, somebody called a script girl and so on. 'Take them away,' I said. 'I don't need them. All I need is a camera and actors.' But they all stayed."

In practically no time Stiller succeeded in antagonizing Antonio Moreno. Since Stiller felt that the hero of *The Temptress* should be clean-shaven, he ordered Moreno to get rid of his mustache. This ruffled

The Temptress

the sensibility of the swarthy Prince Charming, and an angry scene ensued. Later, to achieve an arty effect, Stiller got ready to make a shot of Moreno's feet under a table next to Garbo's; for the purpose of heightening the contrast, Stiller said Moreno would have to wear shoes several sizes too large for him. Moreno, who was proud of his small feet, refused and retired in very bad humor to his dressing room. He stayed there pouting until Stiller gave in on the matter of the footwear. Relations between the two remained sour. Whenever a scene between the hero and Garbo failed to please Stiller, he laid the blame on Moreno. A star, and accustomed to being handled like one, Moreno bitterly resented this treatment.

Playing his usual role of a tyrant with a megaphone, shouting, gesticulating and running about, Stiller alternately irritated and amused the other members of the cast. An interpreter had been placed at his disposal, but Stiller seldom bothered to use him, preferring to try to make himself understood with his meager, faulty English and by gestures and pantomime. This means of communication caused endless difficulties. Frustrated by his inability to explain his ideas, Stiller was often sent into a rage. Then he would circle around the actors and shout at them in a mixture of Swedish, English and German. To the other people on the set, except for Garbo, his instructions were comically confusing. When he wanted the cameraman to start shooting, he said, "Stop," and when he wanted him to stop, he said, "Go." In one scene he wanted a group of extras to applaud. "Now," he shouted, "all explode." Word got around the studio that all was not going well on *The Temptress* set.

On the afternoon of the fourth day of shooting, a cablegram was delivered to Garbo, informing her of the death of her sister Alva in Stockholm. Alva, who is remembered by many people as having been prettier than her sister, had herself begun a motion picture career in Sweden. She had appeared in a small role in a romantic film called *Two Kings* and seemed to have a rather promising future in the cinema when she was stricken and died of tuberculosis. As soon as Garbo informed Stiller of the tragic news, he dismissed the entire cast and took her home. His action did not make a hit with the budget-conscious front office.

Metro officials were further perplexed and exasperated by Stiller's working methods, which seemed to them utterly chaotic. "Stiller tried to work in Hollywood the same way he had worked in Sweden, where the head office often didn't know any more about what he was doing than the title of the picture," Lars Hanson has said. "He had his own particular way of making a picture. He shot scenes as he wished, not necessarily in sequence and not necessarily the ones he intended to use. He liked to shoot everything, and then make the film what he wanted it to be by cutting. He could never stick to a schedule. He would plan to shoot a scene calling for a mob of extras and then leave them standing around idle all day while he worked on something else, often something very trivial. Mayer and Thalberg were very upset. They went to see the rushes, and they couldn't recognize what he was doing. They had no idea of even what he was trying to do. And Stiller, because he could speak hardly any English, wasn't able to explain what he was doing and satisfy them. I remember Thalberg saying to me, 'Is the man mad? Has he ever been behind a camera before?' Thalberg talked to Stiller and tried to get him to work in a more orderly way, but it did no good."

Stiller was infuriated by the interference from the front office. "They brought me here to direct because they liked my methods," he told Hanson. "They say they are something special. Then they won't let me use my methods. Instead they try to teach me how to direct."

One night, after Stiller had been working on *The Temptress* for ten days, he was summoned to Thalberg's office. His quarters, on the second floor of the M-G-M administration building, had a large window that overlooked an alley, from which, when it was dark, anyone passing by could observe what was going on inside. One passer-by that night was Albert Lewin, a Metro producer who was then Thalberg's assistant. "I came walking down the alley," Lewin has said, "and it was dark—we all worked late in those days—and I looked up into Irving's office. He and Stiller were talking. Irving was walking back and forth—he always walked around when he talked—and he was tossing that familiar twenty-dollar gold piece up in the air, catching it and tossing it up again. I couldn't hear what was being said, of course, but it was plain that a very lively discussion was in progress. It was a curious sight, a

The Temptress (*above*) *with Antonio Moreno*

kind of dumb show. As I stood there I saw Garbo walking up and down the asphalt street alongside the old wardrobe building. She would look up into the office where Irving and Stiller were talking, watch the characters inside for a moment and then walk away again. I watched her for quite a time as she continued that pacing up and down, up and down. She was obviously very agitated. I hadn't met her then, and I didn't speak to her. She was still pacing when I finally walked away. She knew that a great decision was being made that night, and she was waiting for the word."

Stiller came out of Thalberg's office with news as distressing to him as it was to Garbo. He had been summarily removed as director of *The Temptress*. The picture was to be turned over to another director. No other assignment had been offered to Stiller.

His dismissal, understandably, plunged him and Garbo into a state of profound melancholy and resentment. An indication of her despair is revealed in this letter, which she wrote at that time to Axel Nilsson, a mutual friend of Stiller's and hers in Stockholm:

Dear Nisse:

Thanks for your nice letter. I meant to write to you so often, but I am like Moje—I don't get beyond the planning.

Perhaps you know what things are like? Well, Nisse—it has been difficult here, you might even say terrible!—I don't want to tell you how I have felt.—When this thing happened to Moje, I thought the sun would never rise again.—Can you understand, Nisse, why Moje should always have such difficulties?—always so much to fight against! Moje, who is one of the best persons in the world. However, I still hope that everything will turn out all right. . . . You should have seen Moje, as sweet and submissive as he could be. He got so tired and depressed that he said he could not continue. I felt terribly sorry for Moje. . . .

God bless you,
Greta

There was ample reason why she might also have felt sorry for herself. She had not recovered from news of her sister's death when

The Temptress

she was stunned by the embarrassing failure of the man whose life was so closely intertwined with her own. After *The Temptress* fiasco, Stiller was laid low with despondency, and he was also ailing physically. As he sat on his terrace brooding, Garbo went about propping him up with pillows and doing what she could to cheer him up. The person whom she most admired and who had been for so long a mountain of strength had begun to crumble.

Instead of being protected, she was now forced into becoming the protector, a role for which she was poorly prepared. "She had developed no ideas or opinions of her own at that time," Lars Hanson has said. "Whatever thoughts she had were thoughts she borrowed from Stiller. She was still just a little girl from the South Side, young and inexperienced. For her, life was like walking on a marsh." At the same time she was supposed to be a glamorous and sophisticated movie star, another role that she found confusing and burdensome. The gulf between what she was and what the studio was grooming her to be was immense. With Stiller in eclipse, she was alone and adrift and out of her depth. Her feelings of insecurity and bewilderment, combined with her long, taxing hours at the studio, made this a period of intense strain. Night after night, she confided to a Swedish actress, she walked the floor until daybreak and sometimes in desperation knocked her head against the wall. She was in limbo.

The pervasive gloom lifted a bit when Stiller rallied sufficiently from his depression to seek work. Though he was still under contract and being paid by M-G-M, it was evident that he would never be given another chance to work there. However, Paramount had recently brought over from Germany a brilliant producer named Erich Pommer, who was an admirer of Stiller's work. Over the vociferous objections of Paramount executives, Pommer borrowed Stiller from Metro to direct *Hotel Imperial,* a spy thriller set in Austria during the First World War. Heading the cast were Pola Negri and James Hall. Pommer, whose reputation rested on his skillful collaboration with directors, wisely allowed Stiller to work in his own manner, and Stiller plunged into his task with frenzy. He wrote the scenario for the film in nine days. "I saw Stiller when he was getting ready to start shooting *Hotel Imperial,*"

Lars Hanson has recalled. "He was bursting with energy. He showed me the script of some scenes he was preparing to do—mass scenes of people in a square. According to the script, that was to take three weeks of shooting. Stiller did it in three days. He was so very anxious to succeed that he worked until he was green in the face."

Meanwhile, Garbo had finished *The Temptress,* which had been completed under the direction of Fred Niblo. Again, the Swedes in the film colony turned out in a body for the preview, and again they shook their heads collectively in disapproval. Stiller was so violently exercised that he sought out Thalberg in the lobby after the performance and berated him in German for having ruined Garbo as well as an excellent script. Thalberg did not speak German, so he simply nodded his head and said, *"Ja . . . ja . . . ja,"* about the only German word he knew. Finishing with Thalberg, Stiller rejoined his friends. "When I was at Metro," he said, "that fellow pretended not to know any German. Now I find he speaks it fluently."

Stiller and the other critical Swedes again badly misjudged American filmgoers. The New York *Times* considered *The Temptress* "a distinguished piece of work," and commended the producers for, among other things, not "pandering to popular appeal by portraying a happy ending." The ending was indeed lugubrious. After her sizzling rompings on the Pampas, Garbo, as Elena, winds up in Paris bereft of the only man she ever loved (the identical fate that had befallen her in *The Torrent*), though she had previously had more than a nodding acquaintance with a packet of other gentlemen. "Those men did not love me," she cogently explains in a subtitle to her one true love. "They loved my body; it was never for my happiness, but for theirs."

Despite its florid subtitles and spurious plot, *The Temptress* was another distinct triumph for Garbo. "I want to go on record as saying that Greta Garbo in *The Temptress* knocked me for a loop," wrote Robert E. Sherwood in the old *Life.* "I had seen Miss Garbo once before, in *The Torrent,* and had been mildly impressed by her visual effectiveness. In *The Temptress,* however, this effectiveness proves positively devastating. She may not be the best actress on the screen—I am powerless to formulate an opinion on her dramatic technique—but there is no room for argument as to the efficacy of her allure. . . . *The Temptress* is a lavish, luxurious picture, with all known forms of audience appeal. It would, however, be pretty dreadful were it not for the individual and unassisted efforts of Greta Garbo, who qualifies herewith as the official Dream Princess of the Silent Drama Department of *Life.*"

The newly crowned princess was showered with much other critical acclaim: "a magnetic woman" . . . "a finished actress" . . . "remarkably well suited to the role" . . . "such a profile, such grace, such poise" . . . "makes every scene in which she appears a telling one." Realizing what Stiller and his friends and she herself thought of her performance, Garbo read these notices with a sense of increasing wonderment.

Chapter Twelve

Movie stars, as everybody knows, are America's untitled aristocracy. Because of their station in life, they wield a wide influence on fashions and morals. They are adored by some and envied by many. To be in their presence is deemed a privilege, to be presented to them an honor. Such is the fascination of the make-believe aristocracy that thousands upon thousands of words are daily communicated about them in newspapers and magazines, on radio and television. Unlike many privileged classes of a more ancient order, the movie aristocracy is not considered a burden by the masses. On the contrary, the common people gladly support the West Coast nobility in a style to which few of them have been accustomed by making voluntary contributions at box offices scattered throughout the land.

While willingly granting special privileges to the aristocracy, the common people also sternly insist that their betters fulfill special obligations. Chief among these is the unwritten law that members of the aristocracy must never lose the common touch. There are many accepted ways by which they may show respect for this rule, such as signing autographs and making public appearances. Most important, members of the nobility are expected to make themselves accessible at all times to journalists and readily answer any question pertaining to their personal and professional lives; give their views on love and marriage, on war and peace, and on the relative merits of various kinds of nightwear; smilingly pose for photographs; and in other ways make a steady effort to prove that, for all their fine feathers, they are really just folks.

When Garbo was elevated to the cinematic aristocracy, she was faced with the problem of trying to conform to its paradoxical code of behavior. She did her best to adjust to it. For example, whenever M-G-M asked her to pose for publicity photographs, she acceded without protest. The extent of her co-operation is indicated by the nature of some of the publicity shots made at that time. On one occasion she con-

Early Hollywood publicity shots (above and opposite)

sented to pose sitting in a chair next to a full-grown lion at Gay's Lion Farm, the threadbare publicity angle relating to the fact that Leo is part of the M-G-M trade mark. Another time she donned a track suit and spent the better part of an afternoon being photographed with the University of Southern California track team. One of the pictures, remarkable in retrospect, shows her with the team's coach, Dean Cromwell. Holding a starter's revolver in his hand, Cromwell is standing alongside the young actress, who, wearing light running pants, black jersey, stockings rolled below her knees and regulation track shoes, is crouched on a starting line like a sprinter. Her blond hair is falling over her right eye as she looks up at the camera and smiles winningly. Other early publicity shots show her playing a ukulele, standing in front of her hotel and waving amiably at the camera, holding a baby monkey, modeling her "new fur-trimmed leather coat," and greeting a visiting maharajah and his aides. For good reason she was known, in the beginning, as "the pet of the publicity department."

Publicity shot, 1926

After her success in *The Torrent,* curiosity about the new star began to develop. A few alert journalists requested interviews, which she granted. These meetings were arranged through the studio, which supplied an interpreter as well as a representative of the publicity department whose function was to assist the new star to say the proper things. To judge from the results of these interviews, she had very little to say. Her comments were largely confined to rather obvious observations, such as how much larger everything seemed in Hollywood—the studios, number of technicians and so on—compared to the motion picture industry in Sweden and on how film directors there work harder than those in America. In one interview she was quoted as having paid tribute to "the efficiency of the Metro-Goldwyn-Mayer organization," a politic remark but hardly a sparkling one. She apparently said nothing whatever about herself. If her interviewers made any inquiries of a personal nature, their questions went unanswered. They departed knowing little more about her than when they had arrived.

That she failed to provide interesting copy was not owing to a disinclination to do so. She tried. But she was severely handicapped. For one thing, she was heavily burdened with inhibitions, as most Swedes are. To generalize on national characteristics is always rash, but the Swedes themselves readily acknowledge that as a people they suffer from an ingrained reserve that complicates their personal relationships. Unlike their Scandinavian neighbors, the hearty Norwegians and spirited Danes, the Swedes are cautious and tentative and inclined to be suspicious of the motives of others. Being incapable of spontaneous cordiality, they are often mistakenly judged to be haughty and antisocial. Actually, the Swedes' desire to be sociable is as strong as that of any other people, but the temperamental barriers standing in the way of their doing so are formidable.

As a purely Swedish product, unleavened by any alien strain of vivacity or impulsiveness, Garbo was almost stiflingly inhibited in her meetings with Hollywood newspapermen. Genuinely shy and timid, she was exceedingly ill at ease in their presence. Furthermore, she was constitutionally incapable of talking about herself, as her classmates at the Dramatic Academy and many other people had already discovered. In addition, she was conscious, as she had also shown at the Academy, of her lack of extensive formal schooling. For all these reasons, being interviewed was an ordeal for her. There was still another reason. Stiller, who disliked newspapermen, had advised her to be wary in talking with them, a piece of advice that added to her difficulties. All things considered, it is understandable that Garbo made a vapid impression on American reporters and magazine writers in her first encounters with them.

American journalists, however, are enterprising, perhaps none more so than contributors to movie fan magazines. By using their ingenuity and unbridled imaginative powers, fan magazine writers are able to endow each Hollywood star with a distinct public personality. It matters little whether the public personality bears much relation to the private one. The important consideration, in the cinematic scheme of things, is that every star have a label. For example, when Garbo arrived on the Hollywood scene, Mary Pickford had been tagged as "America's Sweetheart," and Clara Bow was in her glory as "The It Girl." Garbo, a reclusive foreigner, plain-seeming, inarticulate, and with no apparent marked attributes of a positive nature to exploit, presented a somewhat more difficult problem. But the personality manufacturers were equal to the challenge.

While *The Temptress* was being filmed, Garbo was interviewed by a representative of *Motion Picture Magazine* named Rilla Page Palmborg. Her husband, who spoke Swedish, was also present at the interview and acted as interpreter, though as the author pointed out in her article, "It was amazing to hear her speak such good English, for she knew scarcely a word of it when she arrived." It was also noted that Miss Garbo's accent was "charming" and that her voice was "deep and low." She was described as being "tall, awkward and self-conscious. She wore a plain little suit, badly in need of pressing. Her eyes were shaded with a green visor drawn over her forehead. . . . She said that the bright California sun hurt her eyes."

Nothing of a sensational nature developed during the rest of the interview. Miss Garbo remarked that she was "frantic" when Stiller was dismissed as director of *The Temptress,* but made no further comment on that subject. She observed that "everything over here is strange and different," that the M-G-M studio "is so large it confuses me. I would get lost if someone did not take me to the many stages where we work," and that she had been too busy to become homesick. Of America she said, "You all hurry so much. Everyone goes on the run. We do not rush so in Sweden. . . . In America you are all so happy. Why are you so happy all the time? I am not always happy. Sometimes yes, sometimes no. When I am angry, I am very bad. I shut my door and do not speak." As to her career, she said only that sometime she would like to play the part of a "good girl."

On the basis of these rather scanty and by no means obscure or ambiguous remarks the author wound up her article, which was published nine months after Garbo arrived in Hollywood, with the prophecy: "Greta Garbo will fascinate people, but I wager she will always remain more or less a mystery." To add emphasis to this point, she attached to the article a factitious but provocative title—"The Mysterious Stranger."

And so, in such a way as this, the legend began.

Chapter Thirteen

Once the legend was born, events conspired to make it grow. Directly after completing *The Temptress,* Garbo was cast opposite John Gilbert, "the screen's perfect lover," in *Flesh and the Devil.* No sooner had shooting started than reports of a heady romance between Gilbert and his new leading lady began to circulate. Nobody at the studio did anything to discourage these rumors. The director of the picture, Clarence Brown, let it be known that he considered the love scenes he had made of the two principals the best he had ever filmed. He explained the reason. "I am working with raw material," Brown said rather breathlessly. "They are in that blissful state of love that is so like a rosy cloud that they imagine themselves hidden behind it, as well as lost in it."

Before Garbo's affair with John Gilbert was over, it had become a matter of international interest and taken on legendary dimensions. "In the full flower of their romance," the Hollywood chronicler Adela Rogers St. Johns once wrote, "Gilbert and Garbo were added by movie fans to the list of immortal lovers, Romeo and Juliet, Dante and Beatrice, Anthony and Cleopatra. They portrayed love between man and woman as Shakespeare wrote it into his sonnets to the Dark Lady."

Though Gilbert may not have been a collective modern counterpart of Dante, Romeo and Anthony, he was nevertheless a notable figure of the twenties. Extremely handsome, with coal-black hair, dark, burning eyes and flashing white teeth, he was without dispute the most popular male star of the silent screen. In 1926, when he met Garbo, M-G-M was paying him ten thousand dollars a week. Under Erich von Stroheim's direction, he had made a tremendous hit the year before as Prince Danilo in *The Merry Widow,* which cleared around four million dollars and contained love scenes never before approached, according to one critic, "for frank sensuality and passion." Following this success, he had scored an even greater triumph as the doughboy Jim Apperson in *The Big Parade,* which turned out to be the biggest box office sensation since

With John Gilbert in Flesh and the Devil

The Covered Wagon. "That was worth doing," Gilbert once said of his role in *The Big Parade.* "All the rest was balderdash."

Essentially a bitter and unhappy man, Gilbert had never wanted to be an actor. His parents were members of a third-rate traveling stock company; they were divorced when he was a baby, and his childhood, he recalled in a short autobiography, was a miserable period when he was at times "hungry enough to eat out of garbage cans." His schooling was meager and sporadic and ended, like Garbo's, when he was fourteen. After a succession of menial jobs, he entered motion pictures as a fifteen-dollar-a-week actor, though his overwhelming ambition from the start was to be a director. To secure his services as an actor, he was subsequently often promised a chance to direct, but he was never given an opportunity to work behind the camera, being demonstrably too valuable in front of it. This disappointment nettled him all his life.

To his friends in the film colony Gilbert was known as a very gay blade, reckless, temperamental, slightly mad, a rollicking companion and a generous and convivial host. He was also a man who, as one of his friends has said, "had a tendency to overcapitalize romance both on the screen and off." Before encountering Garbo, Gilbert had been twice married and twice divorced, first to a movie extra and then to the well-known stage and screen actress Leatrice Joy. Neither marriage had lasted long. Though Gilbert's public personality, as depicted in the fan magazines, was that of the dashing, wholesome outdoor type, fond of tennis, swimming and yachting, it was his drinking that Miss Joy complained of in seeking a divorce.

A man who made enemies almost as easily as friends, Gilbert developed a large following of film people in and out of the studios who considered him monumentally conceited and as uncivil, rebellious and irritating as a spoiled child. Perhaps his most outspoken critic was the late Jim Tully, the big, burly, so-called "hobo writer" who had a disenchanted view of the motion picture colony in general. Writing about Gilbert in *Vanity Fair,* Tully led off by remarking, "His emotion is on the surface. His nature is not deep. His enthusiasms are as transient as newspaper headlines." And went on from there to observe, among other things, that the idol of moviedom was "not a gifted actor." On one occasion Gilbert and Tully came to blows. "It looked to me as if he'd fan himself to death," Tully said afterward in speaking of the outcome. "So I put him to sleep for his own protection."

Gilbert was twenty-nine and Garbo was twenty-one when Clarence Brown introduced them on the set of *Flesh and the Devil.* "It was love at first sight," Brown once said, "and it lasted through many years." There is no doubt that Gilbert fell headlong in love with the young actress. Her beauty, shy manner, intriguing accent, long lashes, cool charm—all this was new to him and exciting. And the handsome, smiling Gilbert was something new to Garbo, who had led a secluded life with a brooding and demanding older man as her only male companion. Her response to Gilbert's gaily insistent attention was quick, though it was not in her nature that it should have been precipitous. She was a young woman, inexperienced at riding in the lists of love.

Because of their work, Garbo and Gilbert spent all of their days together, and Gilbert took advantage of every opportunity to press his

Flesh and the Devil, *with John Gilbert*

cause. The opportunities were many and suitable. In the picture they were making they portrayed a man and woman hopelessly and violently in love. However dated and droll most of *Flesh and the Devil* seems when seen today, the passionate love scenes between Gilbert as Leo and Garbo as Felicitas, who in the film was married to Lars Hanson, project a quality of conviction beyond the most accomplished play-acting. "Never before has John Gilbert been so intense in his portrayal of a man in love," wrote the critic of the New York *Herald Tribune* in reviewing the film. "Never before has a woman so alluring, with a seductive grace that is far more potent than mere beauty, appeared on the screen. Greta Garbo·is the epitome of pulchritude, the personification of passion. . . . Frankly, never in our screen career have we seen seduction so perfectly done."

Off the set, Gilbert and Garbo were also getting better acquainted. They often dined together, and the young actress became a rather frequent visitor at Gilbert's Tower Road mansion, set high on a hill overlooking Beverly Hills. Sometimes on Sundays they took off in one of Gilbert's sleek, high-powered roadsters for a day's drive and a picnic in the mountains. They were calling each other now by pet names. Gilbert's favorite for Garbo was "Fleka," irregularly derived from the Swedish *svensk flicka,* meaning "Swedish girl." Another was "Gee-bo"; at other times he referred to her as "The Swede" or "Swede." Her nickname for him was "Jacky," which, because of the Swedes' difficulty in pronouncing the letter *j,* she pronounced "Yacky."

Nobody at this time—and but once later—ever heard Garbo talk in public about "Yacky," but he couldn't keep quiet about his new Swedish friend. "Garbo is marvelous," he said by way of beginning one paean. "The most alluring creature you have ever seen. Capricious as the devil, whimsical, temperamental and fascinating. Some days she refuses to come to the studio. When she doesn't feel like working, she will *not* work. Garbo never acts unless she feels she can do herself justice. But what magnetism when she gets in front of the camera! What appeal! What a woman! One day she is childlike, naïve, ingenuous, a girl of ten. The next day she is a mysterious woman a thousand years old, knowing everything, baffling, deep. Garbo has more sides to her personality than anyone I have ever met."

When *Flesh and the Devil* was finished, Gilbert asked Garbo to marry him—a proposal that he was to make more than once again. Put off by his Fleka, Gilbert abruptly entrained for a vacation in New York. There he was asked about the romance in which the country was beginning to take considerable interest. "Garbo is a wonderful girl," Gilbert told reporters. "We are merely good pals." The romance had temporarily cooled, but it was far from over.

Whatever thoughts Stiller may have had about his protégée's straying from his dominion he kept to himself. As far as his Swedish friends recall, he never referred to the subject directly, though he expressed his displeasure at the role she was given to play in *Flesh and the Devil.* "Those fools at Metro will ruin her," he said. Actually, Stiller was so immersed in his own affairs that he paid attention to little else. He was fighting to rescue his own professional life. With *Hotel Imperial,* which he was directing, he hoped to salvage his Hollywood career. Never before had his friends seen him work with such frenzy. He slept hardly at all and ate practically nothing. He was often racked with rheumatic pains. He had the notion that he could rid himself of them and harden his body by vigorous exercise and swimming in the ocean. Frequently he went swimming when the water was much too chilly for comfort, and more than once showed up at the Lars Hansons' house after such a Spartan dip shivering with cold.

At the preview of *Hotel Imperial,* which was attended not only by Garbo in company with the other Swedes in Hollywood but also by Irving Thalberg and many other film executives, Stiller was so nervous and exhausted that his face was chalk white. "He hadn't slept a wink the night before," Lars Hanson has said. "He was so eager that the picture would be a success. I remember that he was so worn out and wrought up when we talked with him in the lobby before the picture that he began to cry and ran into the lounge to compose himself." The preview audience gave the picture a very warm reception. Thalberg later told Lars Hanson that Metro had made a mistake in not holding onto Stiller.

Preceded by a sizable advertising and promotion campaign, *Hotel Imperial* was a success when it opened at the Paramount Theatre in New York, both with the critics and at the box office. During its first week in Manhattan, the picture took in the very satisfactory sum of eighty-seven thousand dollars. After Stiller had thus demonstrated his talent in terms of dollars and cents, Paramount offered him a contract at twenty-five hundred dollars a week. He accepted. "Now that I have such a good contract," Stiller remarked to Lars Hanson, "I'm going ahead and make one more picture. It will be genuine garbage, but I'll do that one and go home with the money." The Lars Hansons were also planning to return to Sweden. So was Garbo. "I'm not staying much longer," she told the Hansons when they talked about leaving Hollywood. "Moje and I will go home soon."

Chapter Fourteen

Owing in no small part to its well-publicized love scenes, *Flesh and the Devil* was a smashing box office hit. The critics divided the acting honors equally between "the screen's perfect lover" and Garbo. She was now established as a star. After but three American films, she had joined the company of Gloria Swanson, Pola Negri and Norma Shearer, who, as film scholar Lewis Jacobs has remarked, were "the prototypes of the ultra-civilized, sleek and slender, knowing and disillusioned, restless, oversexed and neurotic woman who 'leads her own life.'" That was not, however, the kind of woman that Garbo, or Stiller, thought it was in the best interests of her career to continue to portray. When M-G-M selected as her fourth picture an inane work titled *Women Love Diamonds,* in which she was again cast in a role she described as that of a "stupid seductress," she balked, for the first time. She refused to report to the studio to be fitted for costumes, explaining to the Metro officials by phone that she didn't want to play "any more bad womens."

Back of her refusal to show up for work was another consideration of more importance. Taking Stiller's advice, she had decided she would make no more pictures unless Metro gave her a substantial increase in salary. She was then in the second year of her three-year contract, and by its terms was being paid six hundred dollars a week. Since John Gilbert, with whom she had been co-starred, was taking home ten thousand dollars a week, both she and Stiller—especially Stiller—felt that an upward revision in her salary was in order.

When her discontent over the matter of legal tender was communicated to M-G-M, Louis B. Mayer invited her, late in November of 1926, to come to his office for a chat. After the usual pleasantries, he got down to the reason for her visit and asked what figure she had in mind for her weekly pay check. Five thousand dollars, she replied. It may have been a coincidence, someone has remarked, that a slight earthquake was recorded in the Hollywood area about the time Garbo announced that figure. Mayer offered an increase to twenty-five hundred dollars a week, but his new star, having been coached by Stiller, a master negotiator, said she was not interested in any compromise. To think of giving her, a newcomer who had been on the payroll for little more than a year, five thousand dollars a week, Mayer explained, was completely out of the question. In that case, Garbo said, she thought she would go home, and she did.

She stayed away from the studio for the next seven months, despite all threats and entreaties by the Metro high command. Because of her recalcitrance, she was put on suspension by M-G-M, which meant that she received no pay and was forbidden to work for any other motion picture company. In further countering her stay-at-home tactics the studio hinted that, since she was suspended and therefore in effect an unemployed alien, she might have trouble renewing her passport when it expired unless she came to terms. Outwardly Garbo showed no signs of alarm; privately she was deeply worried and confused, as she revealed in a letter written at the time to her friend Lars Saxon, a Swedish publisher and author, whom she addressed by his nickname, Lasse.

You cannot imagine how many things have happened since you heard from me last. Twice I have turned my back on the studio and gone home. Threats—nothing has helped. I have not returned until I calmed down. I was given a part right after finishing my second film. I was tired and nervous. Besides, it was a "vamp part." I asked to be spared it, but they said no. I stayed home for more than a week, but then I went back and played it. Believe me, that was a big scandal. They think I am mad! Then there was still another ugly part with one of the worst directors there is. And Garbo went home the second time. This is something nobody does here. But I get so nervous over these idiotic things that I lose my head. People say that they are going to send me back home. I don't know what will happen. Haven't shown up at Metro for over a month. Oh, oh.

My second film [The Torrent] *has now been shown here. Lasse, I apologize to everybody for it. Terrible, the story, Garbo, everything is so rotten. It is no exaggeration—I was below criticism. I can't blame anyone, either. I was depressed, tired, couldn't sleep, everything wrong, but the basic matter is probably that I am no actress. I am so worried about what will happen with me. But when you take the devil aboard ——*[Swedish saying: When you take the devil aboard, you must row him ashore.]

I suppose you have read in the papers about me and a certain actor, but I am not, as they say here, "going to get married." But they are crazy about news. That is why they have picked on me. I get violently home-sick at times, and now that Christmas is approaching I feel like crying. Just imagine being home then, with the snow, the wonderful atmosphere in the town, seeing people eager and loaded down with parcels. This is the third Christmas that I am away from Sweden, and I feel so unhappy and treated in such a stepmotherly way. Can you understand it? It is so childish to be that way when one can't go home anyway and ought to be grateful for a position that millions would thank God for. Well, that's the way it is.

Stiller has now completed his film with Pola Negri [Hotel Imperial]. *It is excellent. European and consequently full of atmosphere. The ending is American but so tasteful that you forgive it. But every-body has to adjust to conditions here and to what the public is believed to want. I hope that Stiller, who did not get much kindness at home, will become one of the best, if not the best here. He is now with Paramount. I have to stay at Metro, where no one cares about me, sad to say.*

Metro's unhappy and intractable star knew, of course, that Stiller and several other of her countrymen were making plans to return to Sweden, and she was attracted, in her dejected frame of mind, by the prospect of going with them. So she remained quite silent in the face of Metro's arguments and warnings, repeating only when necessary that all she wanted was "more mon-ee," which, as Jim Tully once observed, "are the saddest words ever heard by spiritual men engaged in the craft of the cinema." The men at Metro, both spiritual and secular, were baffled. They were up against what they had never encountered in a star: genuine, complete indifference. This quality, as they were to learn, would always be Garbo's chief weapon in getting her way.

Throughout her extended war of nerves with M-G-M, Garbo had the moral support of John Gilbert. Her defiance of the Metro bigwigs, with whom he had had many lively and often bitter skirmishes, appealed to his rakish nature, and he encouraged her to stand pat in her demands. He had another and more personal interest in continuation of the strike. After announcing in New York that he and Garbo were just pals, he had hurried home to resume the pursuit with increased ardor; his lady's idleness created favorable conditions for romance. With time on her hands and Stiller again deep in the direction of a picture, Garbo whiled away hours on end at Gilbert's house on the hill.

Gilbert's close friend Carey Wilson, a Metro producer who was then unmarried, was living in Gilbert's house during this period and accordingly saw a great deal of Garbo, with whom he struck up a warm friendship. "She was in love with Jack, and he with her. There is no doubt about that," Wilson once remarked. "We used to sit around the pool and talk by the hour. She never talked about herself, but she used to ask lots of questions about Jack. She wanted to understand him. 'Why does Jack do this?' she would ask, or 'Why does Jack do that?' I knew that Jack wanted to marry her, but that subject never entered the conversation. It would have meant talking about her personal affairs, and that she refused to do."

Gilbert taught Garbo how to play tennis, and though her form was unconventional—she grasped the racket around the middle of the handle instead of at the end—she developed into quite a good player. She worked seriously at improving her game. Wilson recalls one period when, Gilbert being busy at the studio, he and Garbo played a singles match every day for sixteen days in a row. On the sixteenth day, she was the winner, for the first time. "Now I never play you singles again," she told Wilson. "She didn't say why," Wilson said. "Evidently she had reached some goal."

When together with Gilbert and Wilson, she was almost always in gay spirits and seemed to fancy herself as a kind of third musketeer. Gilbert and Wilson each wore a loose-fitting, wrap-around polo coat with a belt that tied like a sash. One day Garbo appeared wearing a coat exactly like theirs. "Now I'm one of the boys," she announced. Wearing their identical coats, the trio often went out together to the movies, excursions that Garbo seemed to enjoy. "Here we go, three fellows out for a good time," she would say as they roared off in one of Gilbert's sporty cars. She was interested in perfecting her English, and when either Gilbert or Wilson used a word or expression she didn't understand, she usually said, "Come on, I'm one of the boys. Tell me what it means." Sometimes, when the three friends were sitting around after dinner, she would get up and say, "I take a walk." It was understood that she liked to walk by herself, and she would disappear alone into the hills above Gilbert's house. She had been warned that there were snakes in the hills. "So?" she replied. Often she stayed away until long after dark, and more than once Gilbert and Wilson set out to look for her. When she returned from her solitary walks, she would be greatly amused if the boys showed signs of having been worried about her.

With the boys or with Gilbert alone Garbo was talkative, natural and seemingly content. When Gilbert invited other guests to his house, however, she was stricken speechless and displayed an uncontrollable urge to flee into the hills or back to her hotel. Gilbert, who enjoyed having a great many people around him, undertook the task of trying to make her feel at ease with his friends. His principal training ground for bringing her out socially were his Sunday buffets, which had become a kind of local institution and were usually attended by some two dozen actors, actresses, producers, directors and other film people. Among the more or less regular guests were Lilyan Tashman, Edmund Lowe, Arthur Hornblow, Jr., Edwin Knopf, Diana and George Fitzmaurice, Alice and Barney Glazer, and Sarah and Herman Mankiewicz. Congregating late in the morning, Gilbert's guests played tennis, swam, talked shop and wound up the day with a buffet supper.

Gilbert hoped that in the casual and relaxed atmosphere of these gatherings Garbo would lose some of her shyness and learn to enjoy his way of living. Encouraging her with smiles and playful sotto voce comments, he escorted her among his guests, talking with this one and that, and tried to instill in her a confident social manner. "Jack wanted her to be the semi-official chatelaine of the house on the hill," Carey Wilson has said. "She was one of the sweetest and finest persons I ever knew, and she tried to play that role as Jack wished, but it was hard for her. Sometimes, when the buffet had been prepared, Greta would

Publicity portraits, 1927 (above and opposite)

become very nervous and uneasy if the guests were slow in beginning to eat. She would go around to Jack and whisper anxiously that the food was ready but nobody was eating. 'Well, just go and tell the people it's time to eat,' Jack would say. But things like that she couldn't do. What was second nature for him was agony for her."

Regardless of her tentative social attitude, she held total fascination for Gilbert. "I would rather spend an hour with Fleka than a lifetime with any other woman," he told a friend. But he wanted to spend a lifetime with her—at least, he wanted to make her his bride. "Gilbert pleaded and begged that they should marry, but Garbo just did not want to," the director Clarence Brown once said. "I have heard her say, while she looked at him and shook her head, 'John, you're such a child.'" Child or man, Gilbert was a single-minded suitor who, taking these gentle rebuffs in stride, refused to abandon the case. He was so confident at one point that his quest was about to succeed that he announced publicly that he and Greta Garbo were planning to marry. Such a union, one of the newspapers enthusiastically remarked, would "place the ultimate diadem on his brow." But Gilbert, in a rather touching statement, later modified his announcement by saying, "I am engaged to Miss Garbo, but I don't know whether she considers herself engaged to me."

On at least two occasions Gilbert seemed close to winning the ultimate diadem. Once, according to Carey Wilson, Gilbert was in a state of great elation and excitement because he was sure he had convinced his Swedish friend that they should marry, quit everything and go away on a year's yachting trip through the South Seas. So certain was he that this dreamy plan would be realized that he spent over $100,000 in buying and refitting a handsome two-masted schooner, which he christened, in Garbo's honor, *The Temptress*. As matters turned out, Gilbert had miscalculated the extent of his inamorata's interest in matrimony; the intended bridal craft never put to sea bearing the newlyweds.

On the other occasion Gilbert persuaded Garbo to elope. To minimize the chances of a change of heart, he hurried her into his fastest car and drove at high speed to Santa Ana. When they reached the marriage license bureau, however, she bolted and ran to a hotel, where with maidenly dexterity she hid in the ladies' room until after Gilbert had disconsolately given up. Then she took a train back to Los Angeles alone.

For weeks following this fiasco Garbo and Gilbert didn't speak to each other. When they resumed amicable relations, Gilbert's ardor had not perceptibly dampened. On Garbo's part the hectic, romantic period of her association with Gilbert was at an end, to be replaced, she hoped, by friendship. "Many things have been written and said about our friendship," she remarked in the one interview in which she ever publicly referred to Gilbert. "It is a friendship. I will never marry. . . . But you may say that I think John Gilbert is one of the finest men I have ever known, American or otherwise. He is a real gentleman. He has temperament. That is, he gets excited—has much to say sometimes —but that is good. I am very happy when Metro-Goldwyn-Mayer say I am to do a picture with Mr. Gilbert. He is so fine an artist he lifts me up and carries me along with him. It is not just a scene I am doing —I am living."

Metro-Goldwyn-Mayer would also have been very happy to have Garbo make another picture with Gilbert, but she remained adamant on the matter of money. It was indirectly through Gilbert that this seeming impasse was broken. He introduced her to his business manager and agent, an extremely able Hollywood figure named Harry Edington, who had negotiated Gilbert's so-called "million-dollar contract." She and Edington got along well. "He became convinced that I was not as terrible as the papers made me appear," she once told a Swedish friend. "He sympathized with me and understood that what I wanted was not to make a fuss. I hate fuss. I wanted only the opportunity to make good pictures."

Bearing in mind that she also wanted to make a decent income, Edington went into a huddle with the Metro executives. As a result of his skillful negotiating and his client's cool indifference, he eventually produced a contract that she found quite satisfactory. The new contract, which she signed on June 1, 1927, stipulated that she work for Metro for the next five years and be paid a starting salary of five thousand dollars a week. This sum was to be gradually increased over the years until in the fifth the weekly pay check would reach six thousand dollars. One of the unusual and attractive features of the contract was its provision that she be paid every week in the year. This was different from the standard contract of Hollywood players, which calls for their being paid only forty weeks in a year; if they work more than this, they are paid for the extra time, but the studio is not contractually obligated to keep them on the payroll for more than nine months in any year. Garbo and Edington took the position that since she was available to work the year around there was no reason the studio shouldn't get up the money every week. It was a quaint notion, worth well over an extra quarter of a million dollars to the actress during the life of the contract.

Another of its novel features was that it did not obligate Garbo to pay Edington the usual agency commission of ten per cent of her salary. In fact, she had to pay him nothing at all. Edington considered her a "prestige item" on his roster of clients, and was willing to represent her gratis. She did not object to this arrangement. Edington, however, did not go unrewarded. With Garbo's knowledge and approval, M-G-M demonstrated its appreciation to Edington for having been instrumental in boosting the Swedish star's pay check and thus helping to relieve the firm of a good piece of money by putting him on the Metro payroll at a sizable salary, at the same time permitting him to continue his regular agency business. Such financial hocus-pocus made the Hollywood wheels go round.

Though Garbo was now receiving the respectable income, even by Hollywood standards, of $260,000 a year, she showed no signs of extravagance, aside from buying a secondhand black Packard limousine and hiring a Negro chauffeur to drive it. She continued to live in her small suite at the Miramar Hotel, and began to shop around for a reliable savings bank.

Chapter Fifteen

The success of Garbo's protracted strike against M-G-M added one more bright thread to the fabric of her legend. A virtual newcomer to Hollywood, she had quietly but firmly defied its mores by disputing the wisdom of Louis B. Mayer, one of the film community's most powerful chieftains. She had taken issue with him on the highly sensitive subject of money, and she had made her will prevail. The fact that the maneuver had been initiated by Stiller and carried through by Edington did not detract from the distinction that the coup conferred on Miss Garbo. She was given credit for outsmarting one of the smartest men in the business. Her legendary character was now endowed with another element: sagacity.

As her business manager, Edington took steps to see that this newly acquired reputation for astuteness was perpetuated. From reading the stories that had been published about his new client he realized that her remarks in print did not always sound like conversational pearls. Acting on the proposition that silence never betrays, he advised her to stop giving interviews, except any that he might approve. This advice she accepted with alacrity and relief. In addition, Edington used his influence at M-G-M to put an end to the practice of using his client in circus-type publicity photographs. No longer did she have to pose with lions and monkeys, nor, for that matter was she thereafter required to take part in any other publicity stunts.

By design and by happenstance Greta Garbo was gradually being fashioned into the legendary figure who was to become known as "the Swedish Sphinx," mysterious and wise. She needed to be invested with one other quality, Edington felt, and that was dignity. He considered the ban on interviews and conventional publicity as steps in the right direction but insufficient to elevate her in the public mind from a movie star to a great actress. After pondering how to effect this transformation, Edington was struck with an inspired notion. He decided that she should

With John Gilbert in Love

no longer be spoken of as Greta Garbo; instead she was to be called, with simple dignity, just Garbo, as if she were a latter-day Bernhardt or Duse. Edington's idea was happily accepted by the M-G-M publicity department, and it wasn't long before the word "Garbo" could mean only one thing—in English or nearly any other language—the woman of legend.

On her return to the studio, Garbo behaved in the manner she thought appropriate to a star who has been raised to the upper ranks. All the other leading actresses, like Lillian Gish (whom Garbo much admired) and Marion Davies, employed colored maids to attend them in their dressing rooms. After her strike, Miss Garbo arrived at M-G-M with two colored maids. To Edington and some of the other people around the studio, the presence of the dual attendants seemed almost excessively dignified. One of the maids accordingly departed.

In keeping with her rise in stature, Garbo was next cast in the title role of an adaptation of Tolstoy's classic, *Anna Karenina*. The title of the film, which was a modern-dress version of the novel, was thoughtfully changed to *Love,* possibly because John Gilbert was again co-starred with Garbo and, reports of their romance being in wide circulation, Metro could see no serious disadvantage in being able to advertise the picture with the potent and timely caption, "John Gilbert and Greta Garbo in *Love.*"

Shooting the picture was something of a trial, owing to displays of temperament by the two principals. The director originally assigned to the film, Dmitri Buchowetsky, had to be relieved because he was unable to get along with its stars. He was replaced by the more diplomatic Edmund Goulding, who also ran into heavy weather. "Gilbert was feeling his oats," a man who was on the set has recalled. "He wanted to show Garbo how clever he was. Every scene meant his interference with Goulding. He insisted on trying to direct the picture. Garbo insisted that she could not act if anyone watched her. She even asked if the set couldn't be fenced in so the electricians would have to stay outside. This was tried, but it proved impractical." Garbo also frequently complained of being "so tired I must go asleep," and made a practice of retiring between every scene to her dressing room to rest and drink hot coffee, a pot of which was kept brewing on a hot plate by her maid.

The director's work was made no easier by the inconstancy of the personal relationship between Gilbert and Garbo. On some days they seemed the warmest of friends; on others, they were barely on speaking terms. Whatever the state of their private relations, Miss Garbo habitually deferred to Gilbert on all professional matters. Whenever a question arose, her customary comment was "I ask Jack."

Despite the troubles of production, *Love,* when exhibited, brought forth a shower of praise from the critics and a rain of cash at the box office. "Greta Garbo is more beautiful than ever before" . . . "outshines any other performance she has given to the screen" . . . "an exceedingly impressive picture" . . . "beautifully done and the twin stars leave nothing to be desired"—such were the rave notices when the picture opened in New York. At the premiere the management saw fit to emphasize the nature of the film by projecting an enormous,

Love, *with John Gilbert*

With Lars Hanson in The Divine Woman

blood-red heart on the stage curtains during the playing of the overture.

Even without benefit of such tasteful showmanship, *Love* fared exceedingly well in Sweden. Garbo's earlier pictures had not swept the cinema critics in her homeland off their feet. For the most part they had taken the position that she was a capable actress with important possibilities but, on the basis of what they had seen, lacking maturity. Their generally aloof attitude was largely dispelled by her performance in *Love*. "Greta Garbo has never been better," wrote Sweden's best-known film critic, the pseudonymous Robin Hood. "In her first American pictures she was something different from this: a sensual body, thin and wriggling like an exotic liana, plus a couple of heavy eyelids that hinted at all kinds of picturesque lusts. But gradually Miss Garbo has worked her way towards becoming a real artist, an actress with depth and sincerity. What she gets out of the part of Anna Karenina, which is far from easy, is always engrossing, often touching, sometimes even human and great."

The time had now come, M-G-M decided, to feature Garbo as a star in her own right. Since she was to carry her next picture unsupported by an actor with demonstrated box office appeal, Metro's best minds were set to the task of choosing the proper vehicle. There was much deliberation, and out of it came what the studio considered a plum: Garbo would portray Bernhardt. The script was to be adapted (as it turned out, very loosely) from Gladys Unger's play about Sarah Bernhardt called *Starlight,* in which Doris Keane had appeared a couple of years before. Metro executives thought the title of the play too tame for a cinematic work, so they changed it to something with a more seductive sound—*The Divine Woman.* They cast Lars Hanson opposite the star and engaged a group of experienced supporting players, including Lowell Sherman, Polly Moran and John Mack Brown.

Here was a film situation that captured the wholehearted interest of Mauritz Stiller. His protégée playing the great Sarah—a chance to show the world that his discovery was a truly great actress, as he had always proclaimed; his good friend and fine actor Lars Hanson as the male lead; a sensible and interesting script; a congenial European locale; a good supporting cast—altogether, Stiller felt, a picture made to order for him to direct. Excited by the prospect, he pulled what strings he could to land the director's assignment. He failed. Instead of Stiller, M-G-M handed the directing job to his old colleague, Victor Seastrom. For Stiller, much as he loved Seastrom, that was the final humiliation.

Stiller had now come to the end of the road in Hollywood. After the success of *Hotel Imperial,* he had directed not one more picture, as he had planned, but two: *The Woman on Trial,* with Pola Negri and Einar Hanson, and *The Street of Sin,* with Emil Jannings and Fay Wray. Both were failures. He had gotten into a squabble with Paramount during production of the Jannings film, and had left the studio with bad feelings on both sides. Blacklisted by both Paramount and Metro and ailing in health, Stiller packed his belongings and headed for home. There was no delegation to see him off at the Los Angeles railroad station—only Seastrom and Garbo. Both she and Stiller wept when he kissed her good-by. "I will see you soon, Moje," she called as Stiller waved farewell from the departing train. That was the last time she saw her mentor.

When Stiller returned to Sweden, he was suffering from a lung ailment and also, though he did not then know it, from an incurable circulatory disease. He refused to consult a doctor, relying instead on massage and vigorous exercise, both measures aggravating rather than helping his condition. He never complained, however, and appeared to his friends to be in good spirits. Wanting to be in the thick of things, he sold his house outside of Stockholm and moved into an apartment in the city. In April, 1928, he signed a contract to produce and direct the musical play *Broadway.* He plunged into this task with his customary enthusiasm and nervous excitement. After the opening-night perform- ance, he walked the streets until dawn with his friend Olof Andersson, who has recalled that Stiller was alternately elated and severely de- pressed. When he bought the morning papers and learned that the musical had received very good notices, he broke down and wept.

This success, after so many failures, revived Stiller's ebbing confi- dence. Again he was full of great plans. He began negotiations looking toward the production of a film in England. He even considered tackling

Hollywood again. His friend Ester Juhlin showed him a script that he thought had the makings of an extraordinary film, and they discussed taking it together to America, traveling by way of Madeira, where Stiller planned to sojourn in the hope that the island's beneficent climate would improve his health. Stiller's attorney, Hugo Lindberg, once recalled that his client and good friend talked of this venture at a party they both attended in the fall of 1928. The two men left the party together. "When we were out in the night air, Stiller began coughing very badly," Lindberg has said. " 'You can't go on like this,' I told him. 'Something must be done.' But he just passed it off. He said he'd be all right and started talking about something else. Three days later he collapsed and was taken to the Red Cross Hospital."

It was there that Victor Seastrom, who returned to Stockholm with his family in November, found his old friend. "The moment I entered his room I saw a man marked by death," Seastrom has said. "What a reunion. He had left Hollywood a year ago, so happy to go home. He knew that I was coming and had been expecting me impatiently. He cried like a child when he saw me." Quickly composing himself, Stiller was soon talking at a great rate. Ever a man of the world, he had arranged with his doctor to allow him to mark Seastrom's return in style; a nurse brought in a bottle of champagne, and the two old friends drank a bit of it out of sherry glasses. "If I live, it will be thanks to you," Stiller said as Seastrom prepared to leave.

Every day thereafter Seastrom visited Stiller, who was eager to hear all the news, especially about Garbo. She had written a few letters, but Stiller had dozens of questions. Seastrom was able to talk glowingly of her work with him in *The Divine Woman,* which on the whole had been well received. Following that, she had played a glamorous Russian spy in *The Mysterious Lady,* directed by Fred Niblo, the man who had replaced Stiller as director of *The Temptress*. When Seastrom remarked that *The Mysterious Lady,* aside from Garbo's performance, had made a generally indifferent impression, Stiller said with a touch of bitterness that he wasn't surprised. Her popularity was steadily rising, Seastrom went on, and she had also completed *A Woman of Affairs* (the screen version of Michael Arlen's fabulously successful novel *The Green Hat*), yet to be released. She was then in the middle of making her eighth American film, *Wild Orchids,* in which she was being supported by their countryman Nils Asther. Metro had been working her hard, Seastrom said, perhaps too hard for the good of her health. When she finished her current film, though, she was going to have a few weeks off, and she was coming home for Christmas. Stiller, excited by this piece of news, cheerfully predicted that he would be out of the hospital by the time she returned.

But his condition worsened after an operation for the removal of several ribs. "One day when I came home after having been with him for several hours," Seastrom has said, "the nurse at the hospital called me on the phone and said that Stiller wanted me to come back as soon as possible because he had something very important to tell me. I hurried back to the hospital again and was with him for more than an hour waiting eagerly for what he wanted to tell me. But he talked only about indifferent things. The nurse finally came in and said she could not allow me to stay longer. Then Stiller suddenly got desperate. He grabbed my arm in despair and would not let me go. 'No, no,' he cried. 'I haven't told him what I must tell him!' The nurse separated us and pushed me toward the door. I tried to quiet and comfort him, saying that he could tell it to me tomorrow. But he got more and more desperate. His face was wet with tears. And he said, 'I want to tell you a story for a film. It will be a great film. It is about real human beings, and you are the only one who can do it.' I was so moved I didn't know what to say. 'Yes, yes, Moje,' was all I could stammer. 'I will be with you the first thing in the morning and then you can tell me.' I left him crying in the arms of the nurse. There was no morning."

Stiller died on November 8, 1928, at the age of forty-five. Seastrom cabled the message of Stiller's death to Garbo. The wire was delivered to her on the set of *Wild Orchids,* where she was playing a love scene with Nils Asther. "She turned deathly pale," one of the men who was on the set has said. "I thought she was going to faint. She walked slowly away from all of us, as if she were in a trance. When she got to the other side of the building, she stood there leaning against the wall with her hands pressed against her eyes for several minutes. Then she pulled

The Divine Woman (*above*) *with Lowell Sherman*

herself together, came back and continued the scene. She didn't say a word to anyone about what was in the wire."

Stiller left no will and, contrary to published reports, bequeathed no material goods to his protégée. Through the courtesy of his executors, however, she later acquired an exceptionally good portrait of her mentor. Stiller's cash estate amounted to 626,000 kronor, or a little over a quarter of a million dollars, nearly all of which he had left on deposit in three separate banks in Santa Monica. His intention, his attorney Hugo Lindberg believed, was to leave the money to his two brothers in the United States. It developed, however, that Stiller's creditors, chiefly Svensk Filmindustri, claimed the entire amount; even that was not sufficient to pay off all his debts. That Stiller died bankrupt and at a comparatively early age did not come as a total surprise to his friends. As they were well aware, he had always lived beyond his means, financially as well as emotionally.

Whether Stiller was in love with Garbo and she with him is a matter on which his closest friends have never agreed. Lars Hanson, who spent untold hours with them in Sweden and in Hollywood, was of the opinion that there existed between them a bond of mutual affection, respect and dependency but never the normal ties of love. Victor Seastrom and Axel Nilsson, also intimate friends of both Stiller and Garbo, have expressed a somewhat different view. According to Nilsson, Garbo once told him, "If I were ever to love anyone, it would be Mauritz Stiller." And Seastrom has remarked, "At one time, Moje was without any doubt in love with Garbo, and she with him."

All such speculation is idle and unnecessary. For by her actions through the years Garbo has revealed more clearly than any words what Stiller meant to her. From the day of his death she has been engaged in a never-ending search to find someone to take his place.

Chapter Sixteen

"After Moje died," Greta Garbo once told a Swedish friend, "I could not sleep or eat or work. For me it was a time that was very black. I wanted to drop everything and go back to Sweden, but the studio said no. They shook their heads and said, 'You must be faithful to us and to your work.' I said to them, 'You will have something dead on the screen. It will have no life.' But they wouldn't let me go."

An impairment in Garbo's acting, caused by her grief and sense of loneliness, was discerned dimly by the critics. When *Wild Orchids*, the picture she was making at the time of Stiller's death, was released, Richard Watts, Jr., writing in the New York *Herald Tribune*, paid tribute, as was his custom, to Miss Garbo as "an alluring personage," "a beautiful woman" and "expert actress." At the same time, however, he felt compelled to add that "her role is hardly as striking as the part of her husband, which Lewis Stone, that splendid actor, handles with his customary expertness." Other critics were also inclined to reserve their major praise for Lewis Stone and Nils Asther, while choosing temperate expressions, such as "effective," "well-timed" and "not without subtlety" to describe Garbo's performance. She had not been wholly wrong in her foreboding.

Her sorrow was alleviated to some extent by her preparations for returning to Stockholm for Christmas. It was to be her first trip home since becoming a film star, and she planned to go in style. She enlisted the assistance of Lilyan Tashman, who was known as one of Hollywood's best-dressed actresses and whom Garbo had met through John Gilbert, to help her select a new wardrobe. "She has bought some really divine things," Miss Tashman reported at the time to a friend. "Several smart tweed traveling suits, two lovely velvet dresses, a gorgeous gray fur coat, heavenly evening gowns in which Garbo will look—well, as only Garbo can look. She also bought some beautiful things with lace on them. I was surprised—she can't tell real lace from machine-made. She would always

The Mysterious Lady (*below*) *with Conrad Nagel and Gustav von Seyffertitz*

turn to me and ask, 'But, Tashman, how do you *know* it is handmade?'"

Wearing her new fur coat, Garbo boarded the *Kungsholm* on December 8, 1928. She was pursued by a throng of reporters and photographers. In contrast to the almost aggressively willing spirit she had displayed toward the press on her arrival in New York less than four years before, she now refused to utter a word or pose for a single picture before being escorted to her stateroom by officials of the steamship line. Her behavior naturally increased the fervor of the newspapermen, who scrambled all over the ship and devised various stratagems in an unavailing effort to get a word from her. One witness to this hectic pursuit was Captain Ragnar Ring, the commercial film producer who had given Garbo her first chance before a motion picture camera and who was also returning home on the *Kungsholm* after a business trip to America. Ring was puzzled by the antics of his former employee. "Why can't she say a couple of friendly words to the reporters and show her enticing smile for a few seconds to the photographers?" he remarked when later relating the incident to a friend in Sweden. "Then they wouldn't bother her. As a clever woman she should know that." Ring was not the first person to ponder this matter, nor the last.

He had reason to be discouraged about the possibility of Garbo's adopting a friendly attitude toward the press or even toward old acquaintances by an incident that happened the second day at sea. Ring sent his card by a steward to Garbo's cabin together with a note saying that if there was anything she wanted he would be delighted to be of assistance. The steward returned with the reply: "Miss Garbo wants only to sleep."

On the third day out Garbo emerged from her cabin for the first time. She was not sporting any of her smart new clothes. She was wearing instead a woolen skirt, plain pullover sweater, gray wool stockings, low-heeled shoes, black cloth coat and black beret. As she walked on the promenade deck, Captain Ring, indefatigable in his effort to be friendly, approached her, bowed and kissed her hand. "Good morning, Captain Ring," she said. "We have met before." "Yes," Ring said. "I helped you take your first steps in front of the camera." "I remember," Garbo said, but gave no indication of wishing to reminisce. Ring

The Mysterious Lady, *with Gustav von Seyffertitz*

changed the subject, and together they strolled into the salon, where they sat and passed the time of day chatting about the advent of talking pictures, recent Swedish films and other impersonal matters. As time for lunch approached, Ring invited Garbo to accompany him to the dining room.

Arriving there, they were ushered to the captain's table, where they were introduced to a group of distinguished fellow passengers who had visited the United States to attend the wedding of Count Folke Bernadotte, cousin of the Crown Prince of Sweden, and his American bride, the former Estelle Manville. Among the returning members of the wedding party were Count and Countess Carl Bondi, Count and Countess Wachtmeister (the Count, a royal equerry, owned one of the oldest and largest estates in Sweden), and twenty-one-year-old Prince Sigvard, second son of the Crown Prince. It was hard to tell, Captain Ring has remarked, who was the more impressed—the actress from Stockholm's South Side or the assorted nobility. Whichever was the case, the luncheon went very well. Everyone at the table, in particular Countess Wachtmeister and Prince Sigvard, was very friendly and attentive to Garbo. She in turn was animated and gay. When she left her luncheon companions, they expressed the hope of seeing her again at dinner. She disappointed them by eating alone that night in her cabin. However, during the remainder of the voyage, she graced the captain's table with her presence on several occasions. By the time the ship reached Gothenburg, Garbo had struck up a warm friendship with Countess Wachtmeister, and the actress had also strolled and danced with Prince Sigvard, who was plainly smitten.

At Gothenburg, Garbo was met by her mother and brother, her friend Mimi Pollack and her husband and what looked like a sizable share of the city's population, who had turned out in a milling mass to glimpse and cheer the returning heroine. Also on hand was a large group of reporters and photographers. Being then, as later, somewhat more kindly disposed toward Swedish rather than American newspapermen, Garbo granted a brief shipboard interview. "Yes, I am glad to be back," she said, "but not, as you might think, because I hate Hollywood. People talk a lot of nonsense about Hollywood. Let me tell you there are just as many temptations in Gothenburg or Stockholm as there are over there. In Hollywood you think mostly about working. I have had to work harder than most, and I am very tired now. I have come home to rest. Will you please let me rest? I shall *sleep* in Stockholm."

Escorted by a bodyguard of police, Garbo was conducted from the ship through the crushing mob to a taxi; two of its windows were broken by surging admirers before the machine was able to move on to the railroad station, where Garbo and her friends and relatives boarded a train for Stockholm. Most of the newspapermen who had greeted her went along on the same train, and continued their journalistic efforts en route. The photographers queued up outside her compartment and took turns snapping pictures of her. When one of them showed up for his third turn, Garbo rose and waved him away. "Man, think of my feelings!" she said. This remark, when printed in the newspapers, was taken up and repeated as a choice Garbo mot.

Any thoughts she may have had of getting much sleep in Stockholm were dispelled soon after her arrival there. The welcoming crowd in her native city was even bigger than the one in Gothenburg. Again a phalanx of policemen had to protect the terrified actress from her cheering, enthusiastic countrymen as she made her way from the train to the automobile that was at length able to bore its way through the crowd and take her to the small apartment that her brother had rented for her in the center of the city. The press followed her car in taxis. She had to flee into her apartment and lock the door to avoid further encounters with the persevering photographers. Beneath headlines of imposing dimensions the story of her arrival was splashed over the front page of every newspaper in Stockholm.

It was a triumphant homecoming. To Garbo's disgust, however, the Swedes' curiosity about her turned out to be no less insatiable than the Americans'. She was besieged with requests for interviews, deluged with social invitations from old friends and total strangers, pestered by stage-struck boys and girls asking her help and hounded by promoters with business propositions of every description. Her phone rang almost incessantly, until she had it disconnected. When she went for a walk, people followed her. When she went shopping, crowds collected and

A Woman of Affairs (*below*) *with John Gilbert*

stared at her. Compared to this existence, life in Hollywood was serene.

One morning she quietly left her apartment and taxied to the office of Hugo Lindberg, the attorney who was acting as executor of Stiller's estate. Garbo asked Lindberg for permission to look at Stiller's possessions, which were in storage, awaiting auction, at Frey's Express. "I went with her," Lindberg recalled, "and I remember vividly how she walked about the room, touching this item and that. She seemed very moved and talked about Moje in a hushed voice, almost a whisper. 'This was the suitcase he took to America,' she said, picking up the bag. 'And these rugs—I remember when he bought them in Turkey.' We stayed for quite a time while she walked around among the furniture and paintings and all the other things and made sad little comments. Then we started back to my office. As soon as we were on the street people recognized her and began to follow us. Greta walked faster and faster as the crowd grew bigger and bigger. Finally it got to be enormous and we were practically running. When we were back in my office at last, Greta was very upset and nervous and seemed almost on the verge of tears. She sat down in a chair, took off her hat and threw it on the floor. 'People are mad!' she exclaimed."

Before leaving, Garbo asked Lindberg for directions to find Stiller's grave. He told her in what part of the Jewish section of the North Cemetery, on the outskirts of Stockholm, Stiller had been buried, and offered to accompany her there. "Thank you," she said. "I will go alone." Lindberg escorted her to the street, where a knot of the curious still remained, and helped her into a taxi.

Despite the pandemonium that her appearances in public created, Garbo managed in one way or another to wrest some enjoyment from her Swedish sojourn. She spent a quiet, homely Christmas with her mother and brother, who had moved from the old flat on Blekingegatan to a larger apartment on the South Side, the section of the city that Mrs. Gustafsson could not be persuaded to leave. On New Year's Eve, Garbo was the guest of Mimi Pollack and her husband at a party they gave at the Strand Hotel. She drank champagne, danced and sang and joined wholeheartedly in the merrymaking. Sometime after midnight she was joined by Prince Sigvard, who had finished the celebration

Wild Orchids (*above*) *with Lewis Stone* (*below*) *with Nils Asther*

with his family. The Prince brought with him his very good friend, Wilhelm Sorensen, who was later to spend much time in Garbo's company both in Sweden and in Hollywood. Tall, slender, good-looking, carefree and ingenuous, Sorensen was the son of a wealthy Swedish industrialist. Then in his early twenties, Sorensen was one of Garbo's most devoted admirers. He has never forgotten their first meeting. When Prince Sigvard made the introduction, Garbo peered at Sorensen with a quizzical smile for a couple of seconds, then plucked the white handkerchief from his breast pocket, flicked it across his cheek and said gaily, "Well, what kind of a sailor are you?"

Sorensen, alone or with his royal chum, began spending as much time with Garbo as she would allow. She allowed a good deal, since she often needed a male escort. Sorensen had a car, was always available to squire her about the city when she had errands to do, and he was unattached. "Garbo has always liked to have around her men without consequences," Sorensen once said. She accepted invitations to dine with him on a couple of occasions at his family's mansion, where they were joined by Prince Sigvard, who was no less dazzled than Sorensen and found this way of meeting Garbo in private very convenient. At times, however, she became bored with the effusive attentions of the two infatuated young men. When they called at her apartment during this period, she sometimes sent them away as abruptly as if they had been strangers. Her capricious behavior served only to heighten their yen. Inevitably, the newspapers began to hint at a budding romance between the actress and the Prince. These reports irritated Garbo, but she said nothing about them in public until after she had returned to America, where a reporter asked about rumors of her royal romance. "I don't play around with kids," she replied.

She preferred to spend her social hours in Sweden with adults, like the Count and Countess Wachtmeister, at whose country estate she was a guest for several days. She also accepted invitations to a few small functions at which, she had been assured in advance, only people she knew well would be present. Harald Molander, a Swedish film executive, has recalled one such occasion, a dinner party attended by Garbo and a number of other people from the stage and screen. "She was not

With Lewis Stone in Wild Orchids

then so shy and mysterious," Molander has said. "In fact, that evening she was as gay as anyone there. After dinner all the guests were supposed to put on a little individual performance. I remember Garbo sang an American cowboy song. She did it very cleverly."

As Garbo's women friends knew, however, gaiety was by no means her customary mood. Alone with them she was generally taut, anxious and morose. She smoked without letup, and she suffered constantly from insomnia. She had a deep dread of being alone, especially at night; whenever she went out in the evening, she elicited a promise from one of her women friends to see her to her apartment and sit up with her until she fell asleep, no matter what the hour. Wooing slumber, she often took hot baths in the middle of the night and plied herself with nightcaps of hot chocolate made with rich cream. "After this," one of her friends has remarked, "Greta would throw herself on the couch, weeping and bemoaning her tired state. With her head cushioned at last on the other woman's lap she would gradually calm down and finally go to sleep. It was a nightly ordeal."

Though Garbo's friends were aware that she planned to start back to Hollywood early in March, she kept the exact date of her departure a tightly held secret and was thus able to slip out of Stockholm without having a brush with reporters and photographers. With an actress friend she was driven by Sorensen to Gothenburg. As soon as the party arrived there Garbo was recognized, and the customary crowds took up the chase. Several hundred people jammed the pier as she and her two friends boarded the *Kungsholm*. When Garbo kissed Sorensen good-by just before he started back down the gangplank, there was a roar of delight from the onlookers. Whatever they may have conjectured, the kiss, as far as Garbo was concerned, was the equivalent of a friendly handshake.

When, a couple of weeks later, the studio received word from its New York office that Garbo had entrained for Hollywood, M-G-M made plans for a suitable reception. Metro executives, newspapermen and a mob of fans were on hand to meet her train at the Los Angeles station. She wasn't on it. She had gotten off instead at San Bernardino, where she was met by John Gilbert, ebullient as ever. He had sent her a flood of cables while she was in Sweden and had tried in vain to reach her by phone. In the three months she had been gone he had talked of her incessantly to his friends. They knew that he regretted the bitter quarrels he and Garbo had had before she left and that he had high hopes of reviving his tempestuous romance with "The Swede." He still thought that things would turn out as they do in the movies, with the screen's two great lovers united in holy matrimony.

For Garbo, being back with Gilbert was, to be sure, more fun than playing around with kids, but absence, in her case, had not had the advertised effect of making the heart grow fonder. Before she and Gilbert had reached Hollywood, they were quarreling again. According to Gilbert, Garbo told him, "You are a very foolish boy, Yacky. You quarrel with me for nothing. I must go my way. But we need not part." That was not the speech Gilbert had hoped to hear from his leading lady. He came to the conclusion at last that his affair with his obstinate Fleka had no chance of a happy ending.

Chapter Seventeen

Quite alone now, Garbo set out to build a new, independent existence. Packing her belongings, which were few, for she has always believed in traveling light, she moved out of the Miramar Hotel, a residence that evoked many memories of Stiller. She took a small suite in the large and fashionable Beverly Hills Hotel. Probably its most unobtrusive guest, she was never seen about the premises, except when she walked quickly through the lobby, her face shielded by the brim of her hat, to and from the elevator. Not once did she go near the hotel's swimming pool or dining room. The meals she took at the hotel were served in her suite, and she ate in solitude. Nearly all her Swedish friends—the Lars Hansons, the Victor Seastroms and most of the others—had gone home to stay. Since she was no longer seeing Gilbert, about all she had to keep herself occupied was her work.

That came far from satisfying her. She had tired of playing the siren whose charm led men to ruin. On her way back from Sweden she had been interviewed in New York by a reporter from the *Times,* who asked her what role she would most like to undertake. "Joan of Arc," she replied. "But it probably wouldn't go well. I would like to do something unusual, something that has not been done. I would like to get away from the usual. I don't see anything in silly love-making. I would like to do something all the other people are not doing."

Instead of Joan of Arc, however, Garbo was cast as Arden Stuart in *The Single Standard,* a work adapted from the novel by Adela Rogers St. Johns. In the role of Arden Stuart, Garbo portrayed a "free soul," a young woman quite as troubled and restless as the Maid of Orleans, though for somewhat different reasons. Arden, being in revolt against the code that allows young men to have dalliances with chorus girls but obliges young ladies to restrain their amorous enthusiasms, shows how modern she is by first falling in love with her chauffeur. This attachment winds up poorly. To avoid a scandal, the chauffeur, who,

The Single Standard (*below*) *with Nils Asther*

inexplicably, is an English lord in disguise, does the decent thing by committing suicide. After a short spell of brooding, Arden chances to meet at an art exhibit one Packy Cannon (Nils Asther), an ex-sailor and ex-pugilist turned painter. Next day she and Packy board his yacht, the *All Alone,* and set sail for an extended holiday together in the South Seas. Because Packy has ideals about love, this affair also winds up dolorously; he brings Arden back to port and sails away alone to the Orient. With one exception, Arden's friends are outraged by her free-wheeling behavior. The exception is Tommy Hewlett (John Mack Brown), a long-suffering old admirer who takes Arden to the altar. When, three years later, Packy returns from the Orient, Arden has become a mother. Such is Packy's charm, however, that she comes very close to booking passage with him again on the *All Alone.* At the end motherhood triumphs. Arden watches Packy's yacht depart as she nestles in the solid comfort of her husband's arms. *The Single Standard* was advertised as the picture giving Garbo her first "100 per cent American role." It also gave her more opportunities for silly love-making, but little else.

While on location at Catalina Island during production of *The Single Standard,* Garbo learned of John Gilbert's sudden marriage to the well-known actress Ina Claire, an event that came as a considerable surprise to the entire movie colony. Gilbert had met his most recent bride one week after Garbo had returned from Sweden. After a three-week courtship he and Miss Claire flew to Las Vegas and married. Garbo received the news from an eager reporter who chartered a plane and flew to Catalina with the first edition of a newspaper carrying the story under a banner headline reading "John Gilbert Weds Actress." (His bride, a star of the legitimate stage and not accustomed to second billing, complained that the story should have been headlined, "Ina Claire Weds Movie Star.") Encountering Garbo on the set between scenes, the reporter handed her the newspaper spread open to reveal the glaring headline. She glanced at it, scanned the story and returned the paper. "Thank you," she said. The reporter began pressing her with questions about her reaction to the news. "I hope Mr. Gilbert will be very happy," she said, and walked away.

The fact that Garbo declined ever to say anything further in public about Gilbert's marriage did not prevent the Hollywood columnists and fan magazines from speculating at great length on how she felt about it. Some said that Gilbert had jilted Garbo and that she was so heartbroken she planned to give up her career and retire to her native land. With an equally omniscient tone other journalistic seers reported that Gilbert had threatened to kill Garbo or himself or both unless she consented to marry him, that she had said she never wanted to see him again and that he had married Ina Claire on the rebound.

Aside from her great annoyance at the continuing and ever more fanciful stories about the affair, Garbo was not, according to people who were close to her at the time, much affected by the denouement of her friendship with Gilbert. "Greta was in love with Jack Gilbert for fourteen days, then she was through," an actress who saw Garbo often during the Gilbert period has said. "That's an overstatement, of course, but not very over. She'd had enough of his craziness, and she was glad to be through with him. But Gilbert was still in love with her." The latter observation was confirmed some years later by Gilbert, speaking in his customary rich and beautiful prose to a woman friend. "Lots of people live and die without ever knowing that one great love," he said. "Thank whatever gods there be, I didn't. There's never been a day since Fleka and I parted that I haven't been lonely for her. And I think she has always been lonely for me."

A few months after Gilbert and Garbo had parted she was driving down Sunset Boulevard with a young Swedish admirer who was visiting her. Gilbert passed them in his convertible. "*Gott,* I wonder what I ever saw in him," she said. "Oh well," she added, "I guess he *was* pretty."

When the commotion stirred by Gilbert's marriage was at its height, Garbo made up her mind to remove herself as far as possible from the madding crowd. That she was living at the Beverly Hills Hotel was now common knowledge. To get a fleeting glimpse of her, members of that curious and incomprehensible species known as fans took to hanging around the hotel lobby, to the irritation of the management and the extreme disgust of Miss Garbo. She pretended not to see them as she marched through the lobby and acted as if she were deaf in refusing their persistent entreaties for autographs.

One morning around seven o'clock a well-dressed young woman walked into the hotel lobby and took a chair facing the elevator. She sat there hour after hour scanning the guests as they emerged. Shortly after noon, Garbo walked out of the elevator and through the lobby to the porte-cochere, where her chauffeur-driven car awaited her. The determined fan who had been waiting for her scampered after the actress. Instead of approaching her, however, the fan dashed down the drive and disappeared into the shrubbery a few yards ahead of Garbo's car. As the star's secondhand limousine started down the drive the devoted fan jumped from the shrubbery and threw herself across the road. Garbo's chauffeur slammed on the brakes and screeched to a stop a few inches before the prostrate form. The girl jumped up and ran to the back window of Garbo's car. "Please, Miss Garbo," she said, thrusting a pad of paper and a pen into the startled actress' face, "may I have your autograph?" "*Gott!*" Garbo exclaimed. "Are you all right?" The fan, with a triumphant look on her face, said she felt fine. "Drive on," Garbo told her chauffeur, as the fan was hustled off the premises by the doorman.

Soon after this disturbing incident Garbo left the Beverly Hills Hotel and took up a new residence. Where she was living not even the studio nor her few friends knew. She kept the address of her new abode a secret for several weeks. For all practical purposes she had dropped off the face of the earth. The only person who knew where she had gone was Harry Edington, her business manager, who at Garbo's request had found her a private house that suited her fancy and enabled her, for a while at least, to escape the eyes of prying strangers.

The house Edington had rented was situated at 1027 Chevy Chase Drive, a quiet residential street in Beverly Hills. A conventional, two-story structure of California-Spanish architecture, it had eight rooms and three baths, including two bedrooms and a bath on the second floor; since Garbo almost never entertained, this part of the house was kept closed off. She occupied the master bedroom on the ground floor, on which there were also a living room, dining room and library as well as a servant's bedroom and bath. Behind the house was a garden planted with lemon trees and at the rear of the garden was a swimming pool. A high, rose-covered cement wall separated Garbo's property from the one adjoining hers at the far end of the garden. She asked Edington to try to persuade the owner of the house she had rented to erect similar walls on the two other sides of the property; this effort to provide more or less complete privacy was unavailing.

Having acquired the house, Garbo requested Edington to make arrangements for help; she wanted a Swedish couple, the woman to cook and the man to serve as butler and chauffeur. Edington lined up a number of prospects through an employment agency. The first couple Garbo interviewed were a young pair named Gustaf and Sigrid Norin. Though they didn't let on, they were not experienced domestics. Gustaf had come from Sweden with the hope of breaking into the movies but had had no luck; his wife, though a good cook, had never held a job before. They were low on cash and thought it would be a living as well as a lark to work for Garbo. She talked to them briefly in Swedish, and said they could have the job.

Gustaf and Sigrid helped their mistress move into her new home. The task was not arduous. She had rented the house furnished, and brought her own belongings, which consisted of one trunk, three suitcases and a few assorted boxes, to her new residence in a taxi.

After she had lived in the house for several weeks, she asked Adrian, the costume designer at M-G-M, to come out and rearrange the furniture in the living room. He did the best he could, considering the rather commonplace objects he had to work with, and afterwards suggested that some new drapes, slipcovers and other refurbishing would do much for the rooms. In these suggestions Garbo showed no interest. She seemed to care nothing about trying to make the place her own. "I don't remember that she bought one thing for the house, even a vase," the butler Gustaf later recalled. Satisfied to take the house as she found it, Garbo lived in it as if it were a hotel, even though it was the first house she had lived in during the twenty-four years of her life.

Chapter Eighteen

While Garbo was living her reclusive existence on Chevy Chase Drive, her legend was growing apace. The fact that she now vanished after working hours like a phantom into the dusk and kept herself almost completely inaccessible added another fillip to the gathering mystery. The journalists responsible for keeping the world informed on the thoughts and deeds of America's aristocracy were consistently thwarted in their efforts to discover why she had taken up these strange, hermitlike ways and how she spent her hours. Nobody seemed to know. This did not keep the more talented journalists from writing about Miss Garbo, however. Some capitalized on their lack of information by explaining in a few thousand words what they had not been able to discover about the actress whom they variously described as "Hollywood's Number One Mystery," "The Woman Who Lives Behind a Wall," "The Scandinavian Sphinx," and so on. More interesting perhaps, and certainly more valuable in the developing legend, were the articles that made no pretense of presenting mundane factual information but dwelt instead on the loftier plane of character analysis. Of the efforts in this latter category probably none was more richly rewarding, in its way, than one published in *Pictorial Review,* written by Palma Wayne and titled with clinical neatness "A Woman of Scandinavia."

"She is a woman about whom it is easier to feel than to speak," the article began, a trifle discouragingly. "When with her one is aware of being with some one trembling with a terrible nostalgia which cannot be seen. Of a turbulent storm of inner discontent, but there is no phrasing of it on that calm and untouched face. Here is a personality so unusual, so hard to define when its atmosphere is touched, one marvels what brings it so much force when it casts its shadow on the screen."

Making a stab at defining the unusual personality, the author went on: "There is no mystery here, unless it is that mysterious and unbear-

"The Swedish Sphinx"

able ache that lies at the mainspring of humanity. Many generations of fine, rugged, slow-thinking people of the soil have gone to create this timber. Then suddenly through some unexplained transition, from out of this stern, simple background, comes a mechanism so finely adjusted, so sensitively attuned to some inner high strain, some unreached transports she can not herself sustain it, and in the whole world for her there is no rest. . . . She was born with that same thing Chopin came into the world with, and which his Slavonic mother called *'zoll'* and the Germans *'velt-schmerz.'* A world-pain, life-hurt.''

At length, after probing other corners of Miss Garbo's soul, the author concluded: ''There you have her. This tall, white, Scandinavian woman, who marches to some unstruck music, inscrutable, authentic, and sure.''

As a matter of fact, when this tribute was published, Garbo was listening, if not exactly marching, to the music of Sophie Tucker, many of whose records together with a phonograph were among the furnishings of the house on Chevy Chase Drive. The songs of ''The Last of the Red-Hot Mamas'' evidently helped to soothe Garbo's life-hurt, since she played them oftener than any others. Her taste in literature, as her Swedish couple observed, was also down to earth. Though she occasionally read novels (some in Swedish and German as well as in English), her favorite reading matter consisted of movie fan magazines. Gustaf the butler had instructions to keep his employer supplied with the latest issues of all the screen magazines; Garbo pored over them by the hour, marking the articles about herself. Every few weeks she had Gustaf wrap up a bundle of these and ship them to her mother. Mrs. Gustafsson, in turn, frequently dispatched a parcel of European magazines and newspapers containing articles about her illustrious daughter. If, in his magazine shopping, Gustaf made a mistake and bought two copies of the same issue, Garbo sent him back to the stationery store with the duplicate to get a refund. Once in a while he was also given the chore of returning magazines in which Garbo had found no article about herself and negotiating a refund for them too.

Garbo displayed a highly developed sense of economy in other directions. Perhaps the fact that she had never before been in charge of running a house made her more than normally cautious about avoiding extravagance and seeing to it that her help had little opportunity to cheat her. The day Gustaf went to work Garbo informed him that he was to be in charge of doing all the buying for the house and that the monthly budget for all household expenses, including food, was not to exceed a hundred dollars. By using considerable ingenuity and shopping at cash-and-carry markets, Gustaf managed to hold the first month's expenditures down to eighty-five dollars. However, after Garbo had examined the bills at the end of the month, she called Gustaf in and complained that he had been too loose with the money. He promised to try to do bettter, but was unable to shave the expenses any finer, and there were more complaints. "We found we couldn't please her, no matter how we schemed," Gustaf said later. "She scolded on general principles. It was a comedy at the end of every month."

Gustaf was entrusted with other financial responsibilities. "A few days after we took charge of her house," he has recalled, "Garbo handed me fifty dollars in cash and a little black book. She said the money was to make purchases for her from time to time. I was to get a receipt for everything I bought. Then I was to enter every purchase, with the date it was bought, in the little black book. Each receipt was to be pinned on the page of its entry. At the end of the month Garbo went over this book, drawing a line through each item and receipt as she checked them off. Believe me, I saw to it that they balanced to a cent."

Gustaf was not authorized to spend any of the petty cash fund for newspapers. Using his own money, however, he customarily bought a morning paper on the way home from driving Garbo to the studio. At her request he left the paper in her bedroom after he had finished with it. This sensible practice enabled Garbo to avoid a minor but regular daily expense. She availed herself of another economy by having Sigrid, the cook, put up her lunch, which Garbo carried to the studio in a brown paper bag.

Sigrid was also in charge of taking care of Garbo's wardrobe, which was not extensive. Her preference in clothes ran to plainly tailored tweed and jersey suits. With these she wore men's shirts and ties, of which she had a large assortment. She seldom wore anything except men's oxfords. "I used to buy most of her shoes," Gustaf said. "I bet she had a dozen pairs of these tan shoes sitting in her closet. Often when I brought home a new pair she had ordered, she would say, 'Just the thing for us bachelors, eh, Gustaf?' "

For company around the house Garbo kept several pets—a chow dog, a pair of black alley cats and a parrot. She thought the parrot very amusing, and spent hours teaching it to say, "Hello, Greta," to make a noise like a Bronx cheer and to imitate the throaty way she laughed. While she was away at the studio during the day, the parrot spent a good share of its time calling out, "Come here, Gustaf! Come here, Gustaf!"—a command the bird evidently heard often enough to be able to pick up without any special coaching.

Most of Garbo's recreations were solitary ones—swimming in her pool, lying in the sun, walking and horseback riding. She liked especially to walk in the rain, partly because it provided a kind of natural screen that isolated her from people. Wearing a man's slicker, she would leave the house when the first drops began to fall and be gone for hours. As she strode along the sides of the roads winding up into the canyon she was often hailed by considerate motorists who stopped to offer her a lift. Fearful of being recognized, she refused such offers by simply shaking her head and keeping on the move. Despite the dark glasses and floppy hat, she was occasionally recognized on her walks during fair weather. Once a group of five children tried to stop her and persuade her to give them her autograph. Garbo ignored them, and began walking faster, soon breaking into a brisk trot. The youngsters, keeping up their pleas, chased her all the way to her house, where Gustaf dispersed them. Returning from another walk, she was accosted a few blocks from her house by two middle-aged women who fell into step on either side of her and started to babble that they were admirers and neighbors and wished to invite her to join their community garden and bridge club. Garbo responded to this invitation by keeping silent and quickening her pace. Undaunted, the ladies stepped up theirs and continued prattling until Garbo finally took off at high speed and after sprinting a block or so handily outdistanced the winded clubwomen.

In rain or shine horseback riding was Garbo's favorite sport. When not working, she usually spent part of three or four afternoons a week on the bridle path in Bel Air, a fashionable community adjacent to Beverly Hills. She customarily started out around four o'clock, when few people were on the trail. Though she sometimes walked to the stable, a distance of some three miles, she was usually driven there by Gustaf, who had instructions to park the car as close as possible to the entrance of the barn. To avoid any casual contact with the other riders Garbo always mounted and dismounted inside the barn instead of in the courtyard. She opened an account at the stable, and when her first month's bill came due, the manager asked for her address so he could mail her statement. Unwilling to reveal where she lived, Garbo told him simply to hand her the monthly bill and she would send a check.

On Sunday afternoons she generally went to the movies, sometimes in Beverly Hills but more often in Pasadena, Long Beach or some other nearby town, where she felt the chances of not being recognized were fairly good. She always had Gustaf drop her off a couple of blocks from the theatre; approaching the box office, she pulled her head inside her coat collar, jerked down the brim of her hat and scampered inside. She was very much impressed by Gary Cooper's acting and seldom missed one of his pictures. She also made a point of seeing every film directed by Ernst Lubitsch and Erich von Stroheim—in her opinion two of the most gifted directors in Hollywood. She usually saw her own pictures two or three times, on different occasions.

Garbo's temperament, like that of most Swedes, was markedly affected by the weather. Accustomed to a cool, damp climate, she had difficulty getting used to the long, dry spells common in southern California. During these periods she often became restive. "I can't stand this dry weather any longer," she would say. "I must have some rain or I'll go crazy." Her solution to this problem was childishly simple and direct. "She would go out into the garden," Gustaf said, "turn on the sprinklers and walk through the spray until she was drenched to the skin. Sometimes she would put on her bathing suit. Often she was fully dressed. She did this time and again. She would play around in the spray so long that the garden was flooded."

However soothing these watery romps may have been to Garbo's spirit, they sometimes had the effect of bringing on a cold, an ailment to which she has always been susceptible. Like Stiller, she relied for the most part on natural measures to ward off or cure any impairment of her health. In addition to her long walks, swimming and sun-bathing, she also worked out in the garden with a pair of dumbbells and further toughened herself by throwing around a medicine ball, which she frequently heaved by mistake into the flower beds. When she afterwards complained to Gustaf about the sorry condition of the beds, he got into the habit of indicating in his reply that it was hard to raise flowers in a gymnasium, a remark Garbo did not regard with amusement. To prevent catching a cold she also sprayed her nose and throat several times a day. Despite all these measures she was frequently stricken. "The minute she felt a cold coming on," Gustaf said, "she would make an appointment for treatment in a Hollywood Turkish bath, where the water came hot from a natural mineral spring. No one ever seemed to recognize her down there, and she went often. She often took the massages and baths when she didn't have a cold, especially if she was tired or nervous, as she usually was when making a picture."

Garbo spent much more time fretting about her health than about her appearance. That seemed to concern her very little. All she had on her dressing table was a box of face powder and a silver toilet set— no creams or other facial preparations. Once in a while she rubbed a piece of ice over her face "to freshen up a bit," as she put it. Her perfume collection consisted of one bottle of gardenia, which she almost never used. She stayed away from beauty shops, preferring to take care of her hair herself. After shampooing it under the shower, she rinsed it in camomile tea, which Sigrid brewed for her from camomile seeds.

Since Garbo's figure seemed to be unaffected by the food she ate, she was able to relish the hearty, substantial Swedish fare that Sigrid prepared. Even on the help's day out Garbo usually took her meals at home, eating alone either in the garden or at the kitchen table. Her talent for cooking was extremely limited, so Sigrid usually left a cold roast and a vegetable salad in the refrigerator and some potatoes ready for frying on the stove. Having observed her mistress around the kitchen,

Sigrid felt it useful to leave on the potatoes a note reading, "Stir often when over fire." As far as food was concerned, Garbo at that time had few eccentricities, though she occasionally treated herself to a cluster of raw garlic, being of the opinion that it was good for her health and also perhaps for her *zoll*.

Chapter Nineteen

After a long spell of being in virtual hiding behind the walls of her house on Chevy Chase Drive, Garbo gradually emerged. She moved out of her seclusion with the alert, cautious timidity of some woodland creature leaving the safety of its bower, and she ventured but a short distance. On the way she made a few hesitant acquaintances that developed into friendships. From then on she had a social life of her own, peculiar in some ways, narrowly restricted and for the most part subterranean.

Without exception, Garbo's small circle of friends were Europeans. The one she had known longest was Nils Asther, the Swedish actor with whom she had worked in *The Single Standard*. Renewing her friendship, she occasionally invited Asther to lunch or dinner, and they made a few trips to Lake Arrowhead, a mountain resort, together. She also picked up her friendship with John Loder, an English actor, and his wife, both of whom Garbo found attractive. She had first met the Loders at a party at Pickfair, the estate of Mary Pickford and Douglas Fairbanks, which Garbo had attended with John Gilbert in the period when he was trying to transform his reluctant Fleka into a social butterfly. Through Stiller she had earlier become acquainted with Emil Jannings and his family, and through them, in turn, she met another couple who became her close friends. They were Jacques Feyder, a Belgian who had made a reputation as a brilliant film director in France before being brought to Hollywood by M-G-M, and his handsome French wife, a well-known actress on the Continent. With Asther, the Loders and Feyders—all Europeans, all able to speak German (the language Garbo preferred next to Swedish), all professional people—Garbo felt at ease, being under no obligation to play the part of the mysterious actress. In the company of these good friends she made little jokes and sometimes acted as silly as a schoolgirl.

Garbo's friendship with Jacques Feyder and his wife ripened after he had been selected, owing partly to Garbo's urging, to direct her in a picture called *The Kiss*. In this work she played the young wife of a rich and jealous older husband, whom she finds it necessary to liquidate and of whose murder she is acquitted by the adroit courtroom tactics of the young attorney (Conrad Nagel) who is the object of her affection. However threadbare its plot, *The Kiss* has always been of interest to serious filmgoers for two reasons; it was Garbo's last silent film, and it was directed with consummate artistry. Garbo enjoyed working with Feyder, whom she admired professionally as well as personally, and she also took pleasure from the fact that Mrs. Feyder was on the set nearly every day. After work the three often went to the Feyders' house for dinner, and even once in a while to Garbo's.

Her little group of friends was increased by the unexpected appearance in California of Wilhelm Sorensen, Prince Sigvard's young friend with whom Garbo had become acquainted in Stockholm. Garbo was informed by wire of his arrival on a freighter docking at San Pedro, and drove there to meet him. Sorensen dined that evening with Garbo at her home and was a guest overnight, that being the only occasion, in the memory of the help, that the guest room was occupied. The following morning Sorensen took up quarters at a hotel in Hollywood, but he visited Garbo's house nearly every day during the remainder of his visit, which turned out to be an extended one.

Sorensen, unable to settle down to entering his father's manufacturing business, had come to Hollywood with the vague notion of finding congenial work in the movies. There was nothing vague, though, in his desire to see Garbo again. He was understandably surprised to find that her life in Hollywood was not as glamorous as he had imagined it would be. After working all day at the studio, she came home with little interest in doing anything except having a swim, eating dinner and sitting around in the garden or taking a walk before retiring at ten o'clock. Once Sorensen had become accustomed to the nature of Garbo's hemmed-in existence, he enjoyed being a part of it. She invited him to use her pool whenever he wished, a privilege she had extended to nobody else, and after he had bought a car, frequently allowed him to drive her to and from the studio. In time Sorensen took to accompanying

Garbo to the movies and to small social gatherings. "You must be around me," she once told Sorensen. "But if I ever got sentimental," he remembered, "she would always say, 'Don't drink so much,' and push me away."

As a present for his hostess Sorensen brought a small, sculptured bust of himself, which Garbo placed on the piano in her living room. This was one of the few personal touches visible anywhere in the house. The others included two framed photographs, one of her brother and one of Stiller. In a mothproof bag in her clothes closet she kept another memento of Stiller—the plaid suit she had worn when she traveled with him to Turkey. She sometimes showed this to sympathetic visitors and not infrequently spoke of Stiller in an indirect way, always referring to her late mentor as "He." In certain situations she would remark, as though to herself, "He says I must do this," or "He doesn't want me to do that." To some visitors it almost seemed at times as if there were a specter in the house.

Though moody on occasion, Garbo was generally good company

With Conrad Nagel in The Kiss

when with her new friends. To their pleasant surprise she invited all of them to have dinner and spend Christmas Eve at her house—the first time she had given a party. In preparation she bought a large Christmas tree and splurged on decorating the house with holly and poinsettias. With Sorensen she went shopping at a five-and-ten-cent store, where she bought decorations for the tree and some comical little presents for her guests, who included the Loders, Jacques Feyder (his wife had returned to Europe), Asther and Sorensen. After dinner Garbo played Santa Claus and distributed the gifts, which included such things as a boy's necktie for Feyder, a set of dominoes for Asther and a pair of lady's garters for Sorensen. Everyone had a jolly time laughing at Garbo's funny, inexpensive presents.

During this period, when Garbo was being pictured as leading the life of a confirmed hermit, she was actually getting about a good deal, in a quiet way. With Sorensen as her escort she once went so far as to attend a dinner party given in her honor by Pola Negri, whom Garbo had met through Stiller and whose talent she had always admired. This function, Garbo felt, demanded that she look her best; she accordingly decided that for once she would have her hair done at a beauty parlor. Being afraid to go alone, she had Sorensen accompany her to the beauty shop in the Ambassador Hotel. While her hair was being fixed, he sat outside the booth and conversed with her over the partition in Swedish. When the battery of beauticians, following her suggestions, had finished, Garbo presented a rather unusual sight. She had had her hair waved and arranged in a novel style resembling a half-opened parasol. Her gown for the occasion was equally sensational, being a green silk creation that had been to the cleaner's and shrunk so that the hem was at her knees. "She looked like Clara Bow," Sorensen has recalled. One of the guests at the party had the gallantry to compliment Garbo on her new coiffure. "You know," she replied, "one often makes mistakes in life," a remark which the other guests thought so humorous that it was taken up as a running joke among them.

Besides attending a limited number of private social functions, Garbo also occasionally went out in public. She and Sorensen once in a while dined at a restaurant called the Russian Eagle, which Garbo

The Kiss, *with Lew Ayres*

liked because it was a dimly lighted establishment she could visit without much chance of being recognized. Accompanied by Feyder, Sorensen and the Loders, she also enjoyed on occasion dropping in at the Apex Club, a noisy cabaret located in the colored section of Los Angeles. This honky-tonk place appealed to her not only because she liked the jazz music and floor show but also because its combination of little light and much cigarette smoke made it as hard to pick her out as if she had been in a thick fog. Perhaps her most daring excursion into public was her attendance, with Feyder and Sorensen, at a recital given by the Spanish dancer La Argentina at a theatre in Los Angeles. This adventure did not work out well, since the audience seemed to divide its attention about evenly between the dancer on the stage and the actress and her escorts in their box. To avoid embarrassment to herself and to the performer, Garbo and her party left the theatre at the first intermission.

In the darkness of a movie house Garbo felt more comfortable, especially when she had Sorensen as her willing escort. They attended the movies often. One Sunday afternoon they went to a theatre in Beverly Hills to see *The Love Parade,* starring Maurice Chevalier and directed by Ernst Lubitsch. When they came out of the movie house, Garbo walked over to the curb and sat down on it. Placing her chin between her hands, she stared into space for what seemed to Sorensen to be several minutes. He finally asked what was bothering her. After a pause, she said, "I must sit and think. I am so happy to know that pictures like that can be made." Rising at last, she asked Sorensen to drive her to a florist's shop, where she bought five red roses, after which they drove to Lubitsch's home. When Lubitsch, summoned by the butler, came to the door, Garbo tossed him the roses, threw her arms around his neck and said, "Ernst, I love you, I love you for this picture." Pleased enough, Lubitsch insisted that she and Sorensen come in and join the guests he was entertaining at dinner. To Sorensen's surprise, Garbo accepted; she and Lubitsch then sat down together and discussed the picture at length, completely oblivious of the other guests and of the food that was set before them.

Content with her little circle of friends, Garbo resolutely refused to have anything to do with the conventional social life of the film colony. When Mary Pickford invited her to a dinner in honor of Lady Mountbatten, a visitor to Hollywood and a guest at Pickfair, Miss Garbo declined with thanks. Miss Pickford then wrote Miss Garbo a long letter, in which she transmitted Lady Mountbatten's overwhelming desire to meet Miss Garbo. This pleading missive brought no results. "It would be the same old thing," Garbo said to one of her friends. "Strangers staring at me and talking about me. I would be expected to dance, and I despise dancing. I can't do it." Marion Davies also entertained Lady Mountbatten at dinner; Miss Garbo, again invited, again declined. Lady Mountbatten was persevering, however. Making a visit to the M-G-M studio, she sent word through a high studio official to the set where Garbo was working to explain that she was on the lot and would love to stop in for a minute to meet her. Miss Garbo sent back word that she was too tired. She gave the same brush-off to another distinguished visitor, Alistair MacDonald, a son of England's then Prime Minister, who was being given a conducted high-level Hollywood tour and had indicated strongly that he hoped not to leave town without meeting the Swedish star. When all other measures for effecting a meeting had failed, including the intervention of John Loder, Clive Brook and that of nearly every other member of the British colony, a very special invitation was tendered to Garbo to attend a farewell banquet given by the studio in the young Britisher's honor. "I am sorry," she replied. "But I am sick. I cannot come."

Though Garbo was naturally less arbitrary in dealing with her close friends, even they at times found her social manner somewhat capricious. Always unpredictable about keeping engagements, she preferred to drop in to see her friends without warning and at her convenience, sit around for a while and then depart as abruptly as she had arrived. John Loder once remarked that he could not "remember that she ever made one definite appointment, even a dinner engagement, a day in advance. 'Perhaps I will drop in to see you tomorrow night,' is the nearest intimation of her intentions that my wife and I ever got. Many a night Mrs. Loder and I stayed at home on one of Garbo's half promises that she would call. Sometimes she would appear. Often she wouldn't. She never took the trouble to as much as telephone when she didn't come. If anyone happened to drop in before Garbo's arrival, she would steal quietly away without even ringing the doorbell. She positively refused to meet any of our friends."

There were also times when Garbo positively refused to see anyone, including her own friends. When this mood was on her, she would tell her butler, "Gustaf, I am not at home to anyone. Remember, not anyone." Then, regardless of who called or phoned—her friends, the studio, her business manager—she remained positively incommunicado. On more than one occasion the Loders or Jacques Feyder stopped by her house when they were certain that she was in, only to be informed by Gustaf that she was not at home and that he had no notion when she would be. "After they had left," Gustaf said, "she would call me to her and say, 'Who was that, Gustaf? What did he say? Do you think he believed that I was not here?' If I said I thought he suspected she was there, she would roll over on her side and laugh, as though she thought it was a good joke."

During these spells of self-imposed seclusion, which lasted from a few days to a week or more, Garbo lounged around the house and garden, sleeping, reading and lying in the sun. Sometimes she would scarcely stir out of bed for two or three days at a stretch, except for a swim and a sun bath. When she did get up, she ambled around the house as a rule in her bathing suit and an old bathrobe. She made no effort ever to explain the reason for her periodic retreats. Because of her curious social behavior and simple tastes, Garbo's friends fell into the habit of referring to her among themselves as "the Peasant of Chevy Chase."

To the world, however, Garbo was something quite different, as she realized. This other self, the fabled creature of mystery, she regarded alternately with distaste and quiet amusement. One day as she was driving on Sunset Boulevard with Sorensen in his secondhand Buick convertible, a number of screen stars, including Joan Crawford, whizzed by in their chauffeur-driven limousines. "Imagine," Garbo said to her companion, "I read last night that I was queen of the movies, and look at me now, riding around in this old car. *Gott,* what a funny joke."

Chapter Twenty

As queen of the movies, Garbo found herself at the close of the 1920s in the uneasy situation that is the lot of all who wear a crown. Hollywood was in the throes of a revolution set off by the advent of talking pictures. The arrival of sound suddenly and radically changed every aspect of movie-making. In the hectic transformation from silent to talking pictures the established cinematic aristocracy was uprooted. Old favorites whose voices failed to satisfy the demands of the new medium were banished. To survive in the new order was hard enough for stars whose native tongue was English. For non-English-speaking players, like Pola Negri, Emil Jannings and a great many other Europeans, the challenge posed by American talkies proved impossible to meet. Foreign talent departed from Hollywood in large numbers.

In these circumstances it was natural that the future of Greta Garbo, the Swede who had reigned supreme in the silents, should have been a matter of greater public interest than that of any other star. Moviegoers had seen many high-ranking members of the nobility vanish into obscurity after confronting the microphone. What fate, they anxiously wondered, lay in store for the queen of the movies when she, too, was required to speak?

Neither Garbo nor M-G-M showed any inclination toward haste in providing an answer to this question. In fact, Garbo's last silent picture, *The Kiss,* went into production almost two years after *The Jazz Singer,* the first feature-length talking picture, was released. Public enthusiasm for the talkies had become so marked by the end of 1929, however, that Metro decided Miss Garbo's speaking debut could not wisely be longer delayed. With her approval the studio selected as the vehicle for her first talking picture Eugene O'Neill's grimly sentimental play *Anna Christie.* This work, originally a Broadway success starring Pauline Lord, had been made into a film in 1923 with Blanche Sweet in the title role. Though its morality had become somewhat outdated by the end of the Roaring Twenties, the play offered one distinct advantage to Garbo: as Anna, she played a young woman who had been brought to America from Sweden as a child. Garbo's accent could thus be turned into an asset.

In her first talking picture she was up against a supporting cast made up of players with long stage experience. George Marion, who created the role in the original Broadway production, played Anna's father. Charles Bickford was cast as Matt Burke, the Irish sailor who falls in love with Anna but is repelled upon learning of her scarlet past, which she describes as the time she "worked in a house in Sain' Paul." The part of Marthy Owen, the boozy wharf rat, was entrusted (and, as it turned out, with great wisdom) to sixty-year-old Marie Dressler, who made her first stage appearance at the age of five. In advertising *Anna Christie,* M-G-M put the emphasis where it unquestionably belonged; the picture was billed under the bold, galvanic slogan, GARBO TALKS.

Anna Christie opened at the Capitol Theater in New York on March 14, 1930. The dedicated Garbo admirers who packed the theatre waited with breathless anxiety for her first words. To prolong the suspense, Clarence Brown, who directed the film, shrewdly delayed Garbo's appearance until the picture was well into the second reel. Finally, the door of the "ladies' entrance" of a waterfront saloon opens and there stands Garbo. She is wearing nondescript clothes, she looks wan, and she carries a battered suitcase. For nearly a full minute she doesn't speak. Putting down the suitcase, she slouches over to a table and wearily sits down. A waiter approaches. At last, Garbo utters her first words: "Gimme a visky. Ginger ale on the side." As the waiter goes to fetch her drink, she turns her head to call after him, "And don' be stingy, ba-bee."

Garbo's first speaking performance, described by one critic as "the most eagerly and fearfully awaited cinema event since the talking pictures got into their stride," was a triumphant success. "Her voice," wrote Richard Watts, Jr., "is revealed as a deep, husky, throaty contralto that possesses every bit of that fabulous, poetic glamour that has made this distant Swedish lady the outstanding actress of the motion picture world." Garbo's voice captivated other critics, who described it as "alluringly deep-toned," "sensationally effective," and as a "haunting, husky growl."

Anna Christie

With Marie Dressler in Anna Christie

Anna Christie, *with George F. Marion and Charles Bickford*

Her acting was also greeted with plaudits. Of all the tributes showered on Garbo for her interpretation of Anna, probably none was less unrestrained than that of Robert E. Sherwood, the noted playwright and biographer. He began his review of *Anna Christie* by observing that the M-G-M publicity department was advertising Garbo as "the greatest living actress." "While it is always a pleasure to any critic to dispute the extravagant claims of the press agents," wrote Sherwood, "I find myself unable, on this occasion, to utter a word of protest. . . . An actor or actress to deserve that most misapplied of all epithets, 'great,' must possess intelligence, grace and power in high degree. Miss Garbo is liberally endowed with the three essential qualities. Her intelligence and grace were revealed in all her silent films, from *The Torrent* to *The Kiss*. Her intense power bursts forth for the first time in *Anna Christie*."

Garbo did not agree. She was not pleased with *Anna Christie*. Because of her practice of never looking at the daily rushes, she did not see the picture until after it was completed. She attended a showing of it with Jacques Feyder and Wilhelm Sorensen at a theatre in Beverly Hills. "Isn't it terrible?" she whispered to them time and again as the picture unfolded. "Who ever saw Swedes act like that?" Her displeasure and agitation increased as the film progressed. With her friends she walked out long before it was over. Though disappointed in her own performance, she was greatly impressed with Marie Dressler's. The morning after she had seen *Anna Christie,* Garbo drove to Miss Dressler's home and presented the veteran comedienne with a large bouquet of chrysanthemums.

With a completely different cast, except for Garbo, M-G-M also made a German-speaking version of *Anna Christie* for distribution abroad. Garbo plunged into this enterprise with enthusiasm. She felt more at ease in the company of Europeans, and she was especially pleased that Jacques Feyder had been selected to direct the German version. She worked with him on the script, making changes in several scenes and altering the translation made by the studio. It was clear to Garbo's few friends that she enjoyed making *Anna Christie* in German and that she was pleased with the result. "Garbo thinks this is one

Anna Christie

of the best pictures she has ever made," Sorensen, who managed with Garbo's help to land a role in the foreign version, told a friend at the time. "And she gives most of the credit to Jacques Feyder."

The reception of *Anna Christie* proved that Garbo talking was an even more magical figure than Garbo mute. M-G-M was vastly relieved. Garbo's contract had two more years to run. During that time, Metro attempted to make capital out of its most valuable property by keeping her almost constantly at work. In twenty-four months she completed six pictures in rapid succession: *Romance, Inspiration, Susan Lenox: Her Fall and Rise, Mata Hari, Grand Hotel* and *As You Desire Me*. None added much to her reputation. Only "the greatest living actress" could have survived the banality of most.

In the majority of these films Garbo played her now familiar role —"the unhappy heroine of many amours, who finds that true, and rather infantile, love has entered her life and thereupon proceeds to suffer and suffer." Nobody, it was acknowledged, could suffer more beautifully than Garbo. Still, some filmgoers who were not confirmed Garbo addicts began to feel that enough was as good as a feast. Only in *As You Desire Me* (the screen version of Pirandello's mystical play) and in *Grand Hotel* (which also starred John Barrymore, Joan Crawford, Wallace Beery, Lionel Barrymore and Jean Hersholt) did Garbo have a vehicle of any consequence. Of *Grand Hotel* John Mosher wrote in *The New Yorker:* "In spite of the brevity of her appearances, against what many a star would call ground odds, Garbo dominates the picture entirely, making the other players merely competent performers, in my opinion; giving the tricky, clever film a lift, a spring, such as pictures without her, without that intense, nervous vitality she's got, cannot possess. By her walk alone, her gait, Garbo is exciting, and it doesn't need the folderol of grand dukes and pearls that this story gives her, the so conventionalized role of the beautiful première danseuse, to lend her that exasperating enchantment vaguely described as 'glamour.' " The rest of the half dozen pictures added up to a series of personal triumphs over material that ranged from commonplace to ludicrous. The films, as the critics described them, were either "sadly unconvincing," "uninspired," "so unworthy" or "nothing exceptional." Miss Garbo's performances, however, were always either "compelling," "brilliant," "perfect" or "impeccable." It was a tribute to her "exasperating enchantment" that she came through this spate of mediocre pictures bearing the title, conferred upon her by the New York film reviewers, of "The Magnificent One."

More uncompromising critics were of quite another mind about the Garbo films of this period. Granting that her vehicles were for the most part shoddy, the discerning critics, of whom perhaps Mary Cass Canfield, author and playwright, was the most perceptive, also found Miss Garbo's acting not always up to the mark. In a trenchant article titled "Letter to Garbo" and published in *Theatre Arts Monthly,* Miss Canfield, after saluting Garbo for her beauty, grace, glamour and refusal to be exploited in the conventional Hollywood manner, observed:

"Yet, your fascination and your finesse, in short your glamour, although it exercised an almost hypnotic influence on your public, could not quite hide the fact that, for some years, your acting was curiously uneven. And that in such films as *Anna Christie, Mata Hari* and *Grand Hotel,* your playing was, more often than not, a highly finished piece of somnambulism. You were clever and sophisticated; but emotionally, Miss Garbo, you were walking in your sleep. Your Anna Christie was a wind-blown dryad, quite adequate in make-up and attitude; and never once touched the core of the character. . . . Your performance was picturesque, of course, but there was no wisdom in it and there were no tears.

"*Mata Hari,* intended as a high-pressure thriller, yet more than foggy in its scenario, was a concoction which would scarcely have given any actress much of a chance to write a human document. But you merely walked through it, like some superior and unperturbed mannequin."

Continuing her stern appraisal, Miss Canfield added: "Although *Grand Hotel* is plainly melodrama, smartened up with a cosmopolitan veneer, and is neither a great play nor presents anything more than snapshots of character, Miss Leontovich, who created your role in the New York stage production, rewrote the script in terms of her own Slavic temperament; and managed to make us feel the heroine as a woman in pain, a disillusioned being, reconciled to life by a brief passion and once more hopelessly at odds with life when the fire was extinguished. But you, gracefully going through the motions of acting this picture, let reality slide, inspired us with no agony on your behalf, lived little your-

Romance (*below*) *with Lewis Stone*

self. Your reflection of the heroine's tempestuous changes of mood was a surface artifice, overacted and without inner flame. And your gaiety was stillborn, unconvincing.

"This remoteness was, at that period, your drawback—a drawback so serious that it barred you from being, in any sense, a great actress, although you had the outer graces and the pliable mind which are of use to the great actress. You appealed to our aesthetic instinct; you could not touch us. For you were unaware; and all your suavity could not conceal the paralysis of your imagination. . . ."

However unsparing this criticism, it would have been acknowledged by Garbo herself, without a murmur of protest, as legitimate. She was her own harshest critic. As one of her closest friends said at the time, "She is supercritical of her work to the degree of being almost self-destructive." Throughout this artistically lean era Garbo was quite constantly unhappy not only over the roles she was given but over her interpretation of them. She had long since sickened of playing what she had earlier called "bad womens." In her anxiety to be cast in a different, challenging role she had argued with Louis B. Mayer and wrangled with Harry Edington, her business manager and agent—eloquent indications of her deep concern, for she has always abhorred being party to a quarrel. But Metro seemed to take the position that people went to see a Greta Garbo movie to see Greta Garbo, and the corporate mind could not be changed. It was the old story, always accentuated in Hollywood, of the artist and the money-changers.

The somnambulistic quality of Garbo's acting during this period did not arise alone from repugnance over her stereotyped roles and an unconscious desire to escape from them. The sense of remoteness that she revealed on the screen had its origins also in her private life. To the few people who knew her, she seemed to have become even more remote, moody and troubled. Her professional acquaintances saw this side of her character only on rare occasions, as, for instance, the time that a director approached her on the set where she had been working for many hours. "You look tired, Miss Garbo," he said. "You'd better go home. You must be dead." There was a long pause before she replied. "Dead?" she finally sighed. "Dead? I have been dead many years."

Chapter Twenty-one

"Genius, for all who manifest it," says André Maurois, "is an exigent and dangerous companion; for a woman more than for most." The truth of this tenet had been made blindingly clear to Garbo by the early 1930s. Her dangerous companion had, on the surface, served her well. Garbo now had all the haberdashery of success. She was famous and wealthy. Her artistry had won her the respect of her colleagues, the adoration of untold millions and the profound appreciation of international intellectuals who ordinarily thought movie stars were trash. She was acclaimed the most beautiful woman in the world. And she was still young, in her middle twenties. The natural, psychological question was: why, with all this, was she a weary and tormented soul, confused in mind and heart? She had in abundance everything the human condition requires—except, perhaps, love.

Since Stiller, Garbo had encountered no men who were giants. Reaching out for mastery, as her disposition dictated, she found the would-be masters cast up by Hollywood to be only life-size and therefore unacceptable. She seemed to be, as Maurois has said of George Sand when she was at about the same ago as Garbo, "a woman thirsting for love and worthy to beloved, yet incapable of that humility without which no love is possible." Of men generally Garbo became disenchanted. Among other reasons, she felt she had been betrayed by a couple of former male companions who had talked in public, albeit with exquisite discretion, of their friendship with her. "That's men again," Garbo had said bitterly in *Anna Christie*. "Oh, how I hate 'em, every mother's son of 'em." Those words, it began to appear, expressed Garbo's own inner feelings.

Her desire to escape from the eyes of the world became obsessional. She was no longer content with her house on Chevy Chase Road; word had reached the public that she lived there. Fans began writing her at home, and a few boldly came to the door and asked for her. Further-

With Robert Montgomery in Inspiration

more, the houses on either side were two-story structures, from the upper floors of which it was possible to see into parts of Garbo's garden and pool. The feeling that she was being spied upon made her uneasy. She had a Nordic version of a persecution complex in an un-violent but definite form. To avoid being looked at she sometimes got up at five in the morning to have a swim and waited until after dark to take an evening dip. Tiring of having to resort to such stratagems, she packed up and moved into another house in Beverly Hills that Harry Edington had found for her. The new residence, on Camden Drive, had

Inspiration

With Clark Gable in Susan Lenox: Her Fall and Rise

the advantage of comparative isolation, but the noise of streetcars operating on a trolley line a block and a half away kept Garbo awake at night. Though she had taken a year's lease on the house, at six hundred dollars a month, she soon decided that it wouldn't do.

Moving again, she settled her few belongings into another rented property, this one on San Vincente Boulevard in the Brentwood section of Santa Monica. The Brentwood house, surrounded by enormous cypress trees that hid it completely from the street and from neighbors on all sides, satisfied her desire for seclusion. "This is where I will live as long as I stay in Hollywood," she told Edington the day she moved in. Gustaf and Sigrid, the young Swedish couple who had handled Garbo's household affairs, had left her employ; they had never been able to please her and had wearied of her constant scolding. She now had a Negro chauffeur to drive her old limousine. To do her cooking and housekeeping she hired an elderly, closemouthed Alsatian woman who wore pince-nez and hairnets. Though a good cook, Garbo's housekeeper was somewhat inept at serving; she had a habit of dropping dishes, but never a word about her mistress.

Having shut herself off from the world, Garbo became almost frantically jealous of what she called her "private life." In the past she had read all the flimflam the fan magazines published about her, including their ever recurring and nonsensical speculations on her affairs of the heart, with rather good-natured amusement. Articles of this nature now infuriated her. She instructed Edington and M-G-M to see that nothing whatever was printed about her life away from the studio. She refused to speak to former close personal **and professional** associates whom she suspected of having talked **about** her to anyone. She became violently upset at the mere possibility that a single word about her might be breathed by one of her friends. As one of them told a reporter at this time, "She is slightly mad in this particular—quite unreasonable —but I admire and love her sufficiently to respect her wishes fully."

Garbo's circle of friends, small to begin with, had drastically narrowed. The Jacques Feyders had returned to Europe; so had many members of the German colony, among whom Garbo had numbered several acquaintances. Wilhelm Sorensen, her young Swedish admirer and escort, had also gone home. Garbo was not, however, without close friends. Probably the most devoted were two talented women, Salka Viertel and Mercedes de Acosta.

Intellectual, sophisticated, witty, good-looking and the mother of three sons, Salka Viertel had come to Hollywood in the late twenties with her husband, Berthold, whose work in the German cinema, particularly his direction of the film *Adventures of a Ten-Mark Note,* had attracted the attention of American producers. After putting in a stint on the West Coast, Berthold Viertel (who is supposedly the central character in Christopher Isherwood's novel *Prater Violet*) left to resume film-making in Europe, returning periodically to visit his family, who remained in Hollywood. Like her husband, Mrs. Viertel had had a brilliant and colorful existence before coming to America. Born in Poland, she had gone to Germany, where she joined Max Reinhardt's famous theatre. Her career as an actress on the German stage had been distinguished, and she had also at one time organized and managed her own repertory company. In Hollywood she soon became one of the brightest members of the German colony.

Not long after her arrival in California, Mrs. Viertel was introduced to Garbo at a dinner party given by one of their mutual German friends. The two women—both European, both lonely in America, both actresses—quickly discovered that they had much to talk about. Conversation with Mrs. Viertel, Garbo found, was not only easy but interesting, lively, warm and rewarding. Like a child finding a grownup who understands, Garbo responded with a wide-eyed eagerness bordering on disbelief. Throughout the evening, according to one of the male guests present, Garbo seldom wandered from Mrs. Viertel's side, and when, at a late hour, Mrs. Viertel left to go home Garbo bade her good-by with apparent reluctance. At noon the following day, Mrs. Viertel answered her doorbell. Opening the door, she found Garbo, who had walked from her house, a distance of some three miles, to continue the conversation. It lasted throughout the afternoon.

Subsequently, Garbo met her valued new acquaintance quite frequently in the homes of their German friends. On those occasions, Mrs. Viertel has remarked, "we often poured out our lonely hearts to each other, and by and by Greta and I became friendly." Their friendship ripened during the course of their work together in the German-speaking version of *Anna Christie,* in which Mrs. Viertel played Marthy Owen, the role originally created on the screen by Marie Dressler. Though Garbo, handicapped by her social claustrophobia and the simple egotism of an undeniable artist, had been far from outgiving with other friends at this period, Mrs. Viertel found her "truly wonderfully kind and thoughtful." The unfathomable, magical quality in Garbo's make-up that has always bewitched intellectuals seemed to cast its spell with great force on Mrs. Viertel. In later years she may have revised somewhat her estimate of Garbo's character, but in the days when the friendship was burgeoning Mrs. Viertel was given to describing Garbo without abashment as "an individual apart from all others, a beautiful and ennobled soul."

The singularity of Garbo's character appealed also to her other close friend, Mercedes de Acosta. Five years older than Garbo, a woman of courtly manners, impeccable decorative taste and great personal elegance, Miss de Acosta was born into a socially prominent New York family of distinguished Spanish lineage. She was the youngest of four sisters known as "the beautiful de Acosta girls," the eldest of whom became Mrs. Philip Lydig, one of the fabulous figures of her generation. Like her sister, Miss de Acosta early revealed "a passionate and intense devotion to the art of living," and she was endowed as well with a high spirit, energy, eclectic curiosity and a varied interest in the arts. Not long after her debut she published her first volume of poetry, *Moods.* She was then nineteen. In 1921 she was married to Abram Poole, the fashionable American painter who was then beginning to make his reputation; they were divorced in 1935.

Soon after their marriage Poole did an imposing, full-length portrait of his wife. She is wearing a straight black gown, a cockade hat—she has always had a taste for historical headgear and footwear—and buckled shoes of a model known in France as Duc de Guise. The shoes, like everything else she wore, were made to order. The face is in profile and shows a small head dominated by a proud nose; it is a strong, intense profile with (her friends thought) something of the hauteur of a falcon. The portrait also shows remarkable, long, slender hands. The hands and face stand out against the dark background like marble, adding to the cold, imperious air of the picture. Short of stature, always dressed picturesquely if eccentrically, perfectly tailored and groomed, Miss de Acosta became a famous and noticeable first-night personality at New York and Paris theatres. Her streetwear, particularly her severe hats and whimsical coats, came to be much remarked during her walks on Park Avenue. Tallulah Bankhead, with her reckless gift for caricature, once described Miss de Acosta as looking like "a mouse in a topcoat."

During the twenties, Miss de Acosta, who was inadequately described in a contemporary newspaper interview as "a very charming young woman of society who absolutely refuses to butterfly her way through life," vigorously pursued her literary career, publishing two more volumes of verse and two novels. In addition, she composed two works for the theatre; one, *Sandro Botticelli,* was produced by the Players Company at the Provincetown Playhouse in New York and ran for three weeks; the other, *Jehanne d'Arc,* was produced by Norman Bel Geddes in Paris and had a somewhat longer run. Both plays starred Miss de Acosta's friend, the eminent actress Eva Le Gallienne.

Migrating to Hollywood, where she worked as a scenario writer, Miss de Acosta took up residence in a modest, handsomely furnished house in Brentwood, not far from Garbo's. Before long the actress and Miss de Acosta met and became good friends. There was much about her neighbor, considered even in her New York and European circles as a vivid, stimulating and unique personality, to fascinate the less experienced Garbo. Having traveled widely, Miss de Acosta was a cosmopolite with a cosmopolitan outlook on life. Having associated by choice with creative people, she had an aristocratic appreciation of, and familiarity with, the arts generally, whether modern and *à la mode* like Picasso's pictures, or the music of her friend Igor Stravinsky, or the paintings of Giotto. She had, in addition, an esoteric interest in religious philosophies, and over periods had devoted herself to St. Francis of Assisi and Thomas Aquinas, of whose works she was an avid reader. Later she threw her impassioned interest into Buddhist beliefs and poetry, and finally traveled to India to pursue her inquiry into Far Eastern religious thought.

As part of her worldly education, Miss de Acosta had become a connoisseur of food. At her table she served only vegetarian dishes, remarkably ingenious and toothsome. She refused to eat animal flesh, as she also refused to wear furs, owing to her tender respect for animals, a respect inspired by St. Francis and the Yoga philosophy. This love for creatures and for the poetry of nature itself may well have been an original bond between her and Garbo. In all their manifestations, Miss de Acosta's tastes were refined, exotic, luxurious and elegant.

Generously, she undertook the task of teaching Garbo something of literature, music, poetry, painting and the essences of taste and elegance. She supplied her interested and appreciative but somewhat phlegmatic pupil with books and escorted her to concerts and galleries. They were often seen together, Garbo usually hiding behind the customary dark glasses and floppy hat, her companion wearing the distinctive, eye-catching costumes that she affected. Miss de Acosta tried to help Garbo overcome her desperate fear of crowds by a process of inducing a calming mental attitude. The system was not lastingly successful. Often lonely in her own house, Garbo became a frequent visitor at Miss de Acosta's.

Despite the admiration and affection of her friends, Garbo was given to periodic spells of moodiness. It was reported in Hollywood that she would actually sit on the top step of her basement stairs and peer for hours into the dark cellar. Gossip also said that, though she was given a complete set of Ibsen, she preferred *Peter Rabbit,* which she kept on her night table. This choice of reading matter would not necessarily be regarded as extraordinary by literary people, for *Peter Rabbit* is considered by many English critics to be stylistically and in the realm of fantasy second to *Alice in Wonderland.*

Sometimes, too, when the mood was on her, Garbo would revert to her old habit of shutting herself off from everyone with no word of explanation. One day shortly before Christmas in 1931, a close friend called at Garbo's house, keeping an appointment made the day before. "Miss Garbo has gone out," the housekeeper said. The caller asked when

Miss Garbo was expected to return. "I really couldn't say," the housekeeper replied. "She has gone out to New York."

Without informing anybody outside of her household, Garbo had packed a bag and gone East to spend the holidays by herself. She slipped into New York unobtrusively and registered at the Hotel St. Moritz as "Gussie Berger." Her presence in Manhattan was not discovered for several days. During this time she went to the theatre frequently, usually buying two seats on the aisle so that she would have nobody sitting immediately next to her on either side. To avoid being recognized she customarily entered the theatre just after the curtain had gone up and bolted the second the final curtain came down.

On at least one occasion, Garbo's devious theatregoing tactics defeated her purpose. This occurred when she attended a performance of *The Barretts of Wimpole Street* starring Katharine Cornell. The ensuing contretemps is a striking illustration of the fabulous effect that Garbo's mere physical presence was capable of creating. "There was no indication of any kind that she was in New York," Miss Cornell has recalled in her autobiography, "and one Wednesday matinee a woman with her coat collar pulled up, hat pulled down, hands held across her face, walked up to the box office and bought a ticket. Her mysterious behavior attracted the attention of the doorman, and he sent an usher down to see if she was quite well. The usher went up to her, looked, gasped and came rushing back gibbering. 'It's Greta Garbo!' In a minute the word was all over the theatre—backstage and frontstage. We couldn't get the curtain up because the actors were so busy peeking through holes in the curtain."

Miss Cornell, however, was not certain that the mysterious spectator was actually Greta Garbo, nor were some other members of the cast. A great many young women at the time were doing all they could to look and act like Garbo, and besides there were rumors that on the set she used doubles or stand-ins who enjoyed impersonating her in public. In an effort to settle the lively argument going on backstage, Miss Cornell summoned her husband, the director Guthrie McClintic, who was at home and who had once been introduced to Garbo in Hollywood, to rush to the theatre. Peering from the wings, McClintic identified the customer in question as the genuine article. His identification was not, however, accepted as positive by several other persons backstage. Matters were still up in the air when, some twenty minutes after the curtain had gone down, the cause of the argument presented herself at the stage door and asked the doorman, "Would Miss Co-o-rnell see a stranger?" When word of this development circulated through the dressing rooms, something resembling pandemonium broke loose. Since the stranger had not given her name and since Miss Cornell was firmly convinced that she was the intended victim of a practical joke, she had her regrets conveyed to the caller. "Miss Co-o-rnell, I see, does not like strangers," the woman who had been kept waiting at the stage door for five or six minutes said, and walked away.

The minute she left the argument resumed, more intense and noisier than before, and continued the rest of the day and into the night. "Finally at about two o'clock I called the coast and asked if Garbo was in New York," Miss Cornell wrote. "The answer came back, quickly and emphatically, 'No.' Then we, and they, began checking, and it finally turned out that she *was* in New York and *had* been to see the *Barretts* on that afternoon. So I sent her a note, apologized for my rudeness, and asked her to come for supper at the house. This she did, about ten days later, and I can't remember ever having a pleasanter, more *gemütlich* evening. We all sat and talked, easily and comfortably, until about four o'clock in the morning. Miss Garbo turned out to be as delightful, as charming, as simple and as humorous a person as you could imagine."

Eventually, of course, the newspaper reporters got on to Garbo's presence in town, and her trail was dogged from then on. "I don't want publicity," she told reporters when they first accosted her in the lobby of the St. Moritz. "I just want to be alone. I am resting between my pictures. I will go back to Hollywood in a few days and start to work there again." Trying to avoid the newspapermen, she began using the employees' entrance to leave and return to the hotel. This ruse was soon discovered, and she was followed and pitilessly tracked almost everywhere—when she went shopping with her friend Lilyan Tashman as well as when she lunched with Berthold Viertel at the Voisin Restaurant.

Mata Hari (*above*) with Ramon Novarro

Garbo's struggle against the press for privacy and freedom became absurd, pathetic and usually unsuccessful. One bright morning early in January she set out for a walk in Central Park, across the street from her hotel. Wearing smoked glasses, low-heeled shoes and a tweed top-coat with a collar that reached to her ears, she descended from her suite to find the lobby congested with reporters and photographers. Weaving her way through them with the agility of an athlete, she dashed outside and into a taxi that sped off into the park. A stream of taxis carrying the newspaper folk followed. Approaching the Casino in the Park, Garbo ordered her taxi to halt, flung a bill at the driver, leaped from the machine and started to race across the greensward. The taxis bearing the newspapermen screamed to a stop, and the throng, alighting, took out after their quarry. Early morning strollers, seeing the group streaking across the park, spontaneously joined the chase. Now and then one of the crowd stumbled and fell but most rose again to resume the fantastic pursuit, the sportively mob-spirited hunters chasing the hunted. For some time the nimble-footed actress was able to outdistance her pursuers as she cut across the lawn at full speed. Finally she tired and turned to face the pack. "I can't say nothing," she panted. "I am not allowed to say nothing. I feel so sorry for you. You have such a—a tough job." Then she took off again. Hailing another taxi, she leaped in and lost the press bloodhounds in the maze of park byways.

After three weeks in New York, weeks that were hardly serene, Garbo entrained for the Coast. Word of her departure traveled ahead of her. In Chicago, where she was obliged to change trains, crowds gathered to watch as, in her customary disguise (now practically a sure identification), she walked with lanky stride through the LaSalle Street Station. Gasping fans and dogged reporters followed in her wake. She was asked the well-worn questions and tossed off answers on the run. "No, I am not in love," she said. "No, I am not ever to marry. No, I am not to stop playing in the movies. They are my life to me. I am happy to be far away from New York. They are so impolite in New York." She was asked if she was in love with Prince Sigvard. "No, I forget him," she replied. With whom, the reporters persisted, was she in love? "I love no one," Garbo said, desperately, and those were her final words.

Chapter Twenty-two

Garbo's contract with M-G-M, signed in 1927, expired in June, 1932. By that time she had made seventeen American films. During her seven years in Hollywood, her earnings from motion pictures had exceeded $1,300,000. (Her total income in 1932 alone amounted to $312,000.) The income-tax rates in effect during Garbo's early money-making years were comparatively low. Furthermore, her style of living had been notably modest. Thus, at the age of twenty-six, Garbo had become a millionaire.

It was no secret that she had tired of making American pictures. What would she do, now that she was freed of her contract and financially independent? Would she continue her career, or would she retire —that was the question. It was, as the New York *Herald Tribune* observed, "a question of incalculable importance to the American cinema fan."

To be sure, there were some other matters of importance before Americans in June, 1932. The country was sliding deeper into the Depression. Banks were closing, and unemployment was soaring. Bread lines were lengthening. Congress passed a relief bill, which President Hoover called a "pork barrel"; he said it would upset his plans for balancing the budget. The bonus marchers, some ten thousand strong, were converging on Washington. At Geneva, a disarmament conference was in its fifth month and getting nowhere. At Lausanne, a conference on reduction of war debts was deadlocked. In Germany, aging Von Hindenburg replaced Chancellor Bruening with the treacherous Franz von Papen, a fateful step that paved the way for Hitler's rise to power.

To Garbo's admirers, these developments were scarcely less distracting than the persistent rumors that she was headed for retirement. In articles bearing headlines such as "The Crisis! Will Garbo Come Back?" and "Whither Garbo?" the newspapers speculated at length on her plans. "For the moment," said one typical report, "the eyes of the entire industry are upon this exotic, silent actress, who has reached the extreme heights and now must decide—'Whither?' The paths are clear-cut. One leads to further acclaim and riches. The other to a life of ease among her own people with more money than she can spend; with opportunity to see Naples and Paris and all the wonder places of the Old World. When the name 'Garbo' no longer is on every tongue and her appearance not a signal for a mad rush of admirers, the mystery girl of pictures believes she may still live in the full sense of the word."

Two days before the expiration of Garbo's contract, her business manager issued the long-awaited announcement. Miss Garbo, he said, planned to leave Hollywood soon for "an indefinite stay in Sweden." That was all. As a going-away present, M-G-M gave Garbo a traveling bag. In return she gave the studio no positive word of her plans for the future.

After vacationing for a month in California, Garbo set out for New York, accompanied by Mercedes de Acosta. Giving the slip to Manhattan reporters, Garbo put up at the Gramatan Hotel in suburban Bronxville. When the press learned at last of her whereabouts, she posed obligingly for photographers but brushed off with noncommittal answers all the reporters' questions, except one. She was asked if she planned to marry while abroad. "No, no, no," she replied decisively.

On July 30, she sailed for home on the Swedish-American liner *Gripsholm*. She had taken more than her usual precautions to insure an unmolested departure. Besides arranging to have her name omitted from the ship's passenger list, she quietly slipped aboard the liner the night before it sailed. When, before sailing time, reporters discovered that Garbo was installed in Cabin No. 1 on A Deck, they trooped there in a body. The door of her cabin, they found, was guarded by two Burns detectives.

Still, Garbo had not won a complete victory in her desperate battle for privacy. The New York *Daily News,* a tabloid of notorious enterprise, had gone to the trouble of sending one of its reporters, Grace Robinson, on the *Gripsholm* to cover Garbo's crossing for the masses. "Miss Grace Robinson, famous reporter and magazine writer," the *News* proudly announced, "is sailing to Sweden with the enigma of movieland, Greta Garbo. From aboard the steamship *Gripsholm* she will radio daily stories of Miss Garbo's voyage to her homeland. Nobody knows Miss Garbo now—but you can if you read Miss Robinson's daily stories in the *News*." As it turned out, the *News* was wildly optimistic.

Garbo vacationed in Sweden for eight months. For the most part it was a restful time because she was able to stay out of public view and pursue her own kind of simple, undirected social existence. With her mother and her brother and his family she spent several weeks on an island in the Stockholm archipelago, where she swam, took sun baths and behaved much like other sun-hungry Swedes on their summer vacation. Returning to Stockholm in September, she rented a one-room furnished apartment and began seeing a few of her close Swedish friends. Also, Mercedes de Acosta paid a visit to Stockholm, and she and Garbo together occasionally attended the theatre and dined in fancy restaurants like the Operakällaren and the Cecil. Perhaps because Stockholmers began to regard Garbo as a native returned instead of a fabulous visitor, she was able, as time went on, to take her daily walks and go shopping without being followed or much bothered by autograph hunters. Once in a while she dropped into small, out-of-the-way movie theatres like the Bostock and Appollo that specialized in showing revivals of classic

As the ballerina Grusinskaya in Grand Hotel

films. However, when her own film, *Susan Lenox: Her Fall and Rise,* had its premiere in Stockholm, Garbo disappointed her countrymen by not attending, though her mother, brother and sister-in-law were in the capacity audience. Noting Garbo's absence and the probable reason for it, one of Stockholm's leading newspapers remarked with sympathy on "the tragedy of her popularity."

Aside from her brother, the only man Garbo spent much time with was a wealthy, self-made construction engineer named Max Gumpel, who enjoyed a reputation in Stockholm as a rather flashy man about town. Balding and monocled, Gumpel looked rather like a road-company version of Erich von Stroheim. Garbo and Gumpel had first met many years before, when she was a department store clerk. In his privately printed work, *Tales and Reality,* Gumpel has told how he was attracted to Garbo the instant he saw her and promptly invited her to dinner at his home. Artichokes were served on that occasion, Gumpel has recalled, and Garbo was somewhat dismayed, since she had never encountered that perplexing vegetable. After they had become friends, Gumpel presented Garbo with a gold ring set with a small diamond, "but she thought it was as beautiful," wrote Gumpel, "as a diamond in the English Royal Crown." A year or so later they parted amicably; he married, and she went on to a dramatic school.

It was not until the fall of 1932, after Gumpel had been divorced, that he heard from Garbo again. She telephoned him one day at his office and playfully asked him to guess who was calling. When she finally identified herself, Gumpel, like other people before him, thought somebody was playing a practical joke. He nevertheless sportingly invited the caller to dinner, which he said would be formal, at his home. Garbo replied that she didn't have an evening gown. Never mind, said Gumpel, just make yourself look as much like Garbo as you can. When she arrived, according to *Tales and Reality,* she was wearing only one piece of jewelry—the small diamond ring. "Then, thanks to her," the irrepressible Gumpel has recorded, "I also thought it looked like one of the British Crown Jewels."

After their poignant reunion, Garbo and Gumpel were seen together around Stockholm often enough to inspire rumors, with no

Grand Hotel

With John Barrymore in Grand Hotel

Grand Hotel

As You Desire Me, *with Erich von Stroheim*

foundation in fact, that they were planning to marry. Actually, Garbo had spent most of her time with Gumpel playing tennis; when their matches at the Tennis Stadion were discovered by the press, she stopped going there. Her friendship with Gumpel also had a practical slant. A shrewd businessman, he provided Garbo with useful counsel on the investment of some of her money in Sweden, particularly in Stockholm real estate.

Feminine companionship being apparently more to Garbo's liking, she passed much of her time in the company of the Countess Wacht-meister, with whom the actress had become acquainted on her previous visit to Sweden. A tall, vigorous woman, nine years older than Garbo, the Countess was a member of one of Sweden's most distinguished families, an accomplished horsewoman, expert skier, and, like Garbo, a great walker. Wearing hobnailed boots, trousers and other knock-about attire, she was fond of tramping over the grounds of the exten-sive Wachtmeister country estate, Tistad, southeast of Stockholm. During her Swedish sojourn, Garbo was often a guest in the seventy-five-

With Melvyn Douglas in As You Desire Me

room, sixteenth-century castle at Tistad, and, when the dismal Stockholm winter set in, she and the Countess took a holiday together in London and Paris.

Before coming to Sweden, Garbo had become greatly interested, through reading a biography recommended by Salka Viertel, in Queen Christina, the eccentric, seventeenth-century Swedish monarch who had a fancy for, among other things, wearing men's clothes. Though Christina's distaste for marriage was profound, she had swarms of lovers, domestic and imported. She rewarded her favorites lavishly with money, land and titles. During her ten-year reign as an adult she created seventeen new counts, forty-six barons and four hundred and seventy-five lesser nobles. She also gave away half of the crown lands. When her subjects began to find all this jollity a little excessive, Christina abdicated, at the age of twenty-eight. Attired in snappy breeches and doublet, she left the country, winding up in Rome, where she died in obscurity.

Both Garbo and Salka Viertel had decided that the life of Queen Christina, or some parts of it, would make an ideal screen vehicle for Garbo. With the constant encouragement of her friend, Mrs. Viertel and a collaborator undertook the writing of a dramatic work built around the character of the colorful queen. Garbo was so enthusiastic about the completed script, which was sent to her in Sweden, that she informed M-G-M she would sign a new contract on condition that she be allowed to portray Queen Christina on the screen. The studio readily agreed. With less alacrity, Metro also agreed to Garbo's other conditions: that she make only two pictures a year, at $250,000 apiece.

The business negotiations completed, Garbo departed for Hollywood, but she was in no hurry to get there. On March 26, 1933, she boarded the *Annie Johnson,* a five-thousand-ton freighter that carried four passengers besides Garbo and was headed for the West Coast of America by way of the Panama Canal. At dawn, thirty-four days later, the *Annie Johnson* docked at San Diego. Several scores of early-rising fans were on hand to greet the eminent passenger. She rewarded them with a wave of her hand. Tanned by the sun and wind during the long voyage, Garbo hurried ashore, where she was met by Salka Viertel. They motored off to Hollywood.

Chapter Twenty-three

Garbo astonished Hollywood and titillated her fans by picking John Gilbert to play the role of her lover in *Queen Christina*. The touching story circulated that she had selected Gilbert for the choice part to prop up his sagging career. There was no doubt that it needed support. Professionally, Gilbert had been on his uppers since appearing in his first talking picture, *His Glorious Night*. He had been done in primarily by his high, thin voice, which seemed incongruous in a personality built up on the screen as a great lover. When he first said, "I love you," in the talkies, audiences snickered; some laughed cruelly and uproariously. From then on, one of his friends has remarked, "He was worth less at the box office than a bag of popcorn." Probably no man in Hollywood, where obscurity has always been but a step from fame, ever fell so far so fast.

Garbo's selection of Gilbert was not, it would seem, a strictly sentimental gesture. She had previously given careful consideration to a number of other more likely contenders, including such disparate types as Franchot Tone, Nils Asther and Laurence Olivier. In fact, on the basis of screen tests of Olivier, Garbo had definitely decided on him, and the British actor had signed a contract. After rehearsing love scenes with him, however, Garbo announced that he wouldn't do. It was then that she decided to give Gilbert a chance. Physically, he was admirably suited to the role, that of a handsome young Spaniard, and the quality of his voice, Garbo had been assured, could be improved by newly developed sound techniques.

Gilbert and Garbo had not appeared in a film together since *A Woman of Affairs,* five years before. Meanwhile, Gilbert and Ina Claire had been divorced, and he had taken as his fourth wife twenty-one-year-old Virginia Bruce, who bore him a daughter a few days before the filming of *Queen Christina* began. The reunion of Garbo and Gilbert on the screen was the occasion for considerable publicity and recollections of what one fan magazine described as their "stormy, historic and

Queen Christina

With John Gilbert in Queen Christina

once-glorious romance." Garbo's attitude toward Gilbert on the set was friendly but professional. At one point the script called for a love scene of the more or less uninhibited kind that had done much to make Garbo and Gilbert famous. When they rehearsed the scene the first time, Gilbert responded with his old enthusiasm. Afterwards, according to another member of the cast, Garbo suggested to the director, Rouben Mamoulian, that the scene be played with somewhat less intensity. "Mr. Gilbert is a married man now, with a wife and baby," she remarked rather primly. "Backward, turn backward, O Time, in your flight," Gilbert said with a smile. The scene was played, as Garbo wished, in a lower emotional key.

During the filming of *Queen Christina,* Garbo developed a close friendship with Rouben Mamoulian, whom she had requested as the director of the picture. Born in Russia and schooled in Paris, Mamoulian was then a thirty-five-year-old, bushy-haired, bespectacled· bachelor, cultured, imaginative and one of the top-ranking men in his field. Garbo respected his talent and, when differences of opinion arose on the set, almost invariably deferred to his judgment. One of the most moving scenes in *Queen Christina,* in the opinion of many film scholars, comes at the finale when the queen, taking leave of her homeland after the death of her lover, stands gazing from the prow of the ship that is to bear her on what promises to be a long and lonely pilgrimage. Here, according to one student of the cinema, Garbo's performance was marked by "a symbolism touched with poetry," and the pose she struck had "the grace of a sensibility at last alive, at last willing to notice and to suffer." Garbo and Mamoulian worked on this scene with special intentness. It was shot again and again because Mamoulian was never quite satisfied with the expression captured on the queen's face. Finally, he told Garbo to make her mind a blank, completely vacant, a void, to think of nothing. Then the memorable scene was shot.

Garbo's friendship with Mamoulian was not confined to the studio. While *Queen Christina* was in production, Garbo frequently dined with her director at fashionable restaurants and even, on a couple of occasions, went dancing with him at a popular night club. When he bought a new

Queen Christina

home in Beverly Hills, gossip had it that he planned to take Garbo there as his bride. Rumors that they were planning to marry gained international currency when, shortly after completing *Queen Christina,* they left Hollywood together by automobile for a vacation at the Grand Canyon. They were spotted even before they had reached their destination. Their trail was thereafter so mercilessly dogged by reporters and scores of amateur sleuths that they turned around, two hours after reaching the Grand Canyon, and returned to Hollywood. Garbo and Mamoulian, according to their friends, were never close to marriage. Her romantic interest in the director, as in other men at that period, was typically casual and brief.

Queen Christina, in which Garbo returned to the screen after an absence of a year and a half, was a triumphant critical success. Even the exacting Mary Cass Canfield found no flaws; in this film, she said, Garbo "soared into the blue like some liberated bird." Though Garbo's performance naturally dominated the picture, everything else in the

Queen Christina

production—the scenario, direction, supporting cast—was also extravagantly praised, except the work of John Gilbert. Little attention was paid to him in the reviews; in some he was hardly mentioned. The knell for Gilbert, who only six years before had first electrified audiences with Garbo in *Flesh and the Devil,* was tolling. After *Queen Christina* he appeared in but one other film, an inconsequential work called *The Captain Hates the Sea.* Divorced by his fourth wife, his fortune depleted, Gilbert died of a heart attack in 1936, at the age of thirty-eight. It was reported, erroneously, that when Garbo was informed of his death she said, "What is that to me?" Actually, she was vacationing in Stockholm when Gilbert died, and was given the news by a Swedish reporter in the foyer of the Royal Dramatic Theatre during an intermission. She refused to make any comment; shortly afterward she left the theatre.

Garbo's personal opinion of *Queen Christina* was less admiring than the critics'. "I tried to be Swedish," she once remarked during an interview in Sweden, "but it's difficult in Hollywood to be allowed to try anything. It's all a terrible compromise. There is no time for art. All that matters is what they call box office."

While deploring Hollywood's lopsided respect for legal tender, Garbo was not grossly negligent in looking after her own purse. Before starting her next film, *The Painted Veil,* she managed, with the able assistance of Harry Edington, to raise her salary per picture from $250,000 to $270,000. At the same time Edington informed Louis B. Mayer that Garbo, already the highest-priced player in Hollywood, was forehandedly giving some thought to a new contract to go into effect after completion of *The Painted Veil;* the sum she had in mind for each picture after that was $300,000. Boosting Garbo's salary was opposed by some Metro executives, who pointed to the fact that while *Queen Christina* had pleased the critics it had fallen far short of being a box office hit. Perhaps, a few hardfisted M-G-M officials boldly suggested, the time had come to let their most expensive property seek her fortunes elsewhere. These dissidents were overruled by the Metro executives in New York who felt, according to *Variety,* "that Garbo's European standing had not been impaired by *Queen Christina,* and that for

Queen Christina (*above*) *with Lewis Stone*

prestige, if nothing else, she would continue to be a good will asset for the company."

Neither Garbo's prestige nor her studio's was enhanced by *The Painted Veil,* a commonplace melodrama adapted from Somerset Maugham's novel about a doctor, his wife and her lover who act out the routine triangle against an oriental background. Even such a confirmed Garbo addict as Alistair Cooke felt obliged to describe this piece of cinematic goods as "a very dreadful film." Herbert Marshall played Garbo's husband, the dedicated doctor, and George Brent was cast as the other point of the triangle. While the picture was in production, Garbo and Brent engaged in a brief, off-the-screen romantic interlude.

Since Garbo's return to Hollywood, Salka Viertel had become not only the actress' close friend but her professional adviser. She had assumed the handling of many of Garbo's contacts with the studio, suggested story ideas and, in collaboration with two other writers, produced the screen treatment of *The Painted Veil.* Mrs. Viertel was also instrumental in the selection of Garbo's next vehicle, *Anna Karenina,* and collaborated in writing the scenario. This was the second time that Garbo had undertaken the portrayal of Tolstoy's tragic heroine; eight years earlier, in the silent film called *Love,* she had played Anna opposite John Gilbert. The new version, given a strong supporting cast and a handsome and lavishly expensive production, turned out to be as signal a success as *The Painted Veil* had been a failure. For her work in *Anna Karenina* Garbo received the award of the New York Film Critics for the "best feminine performance" of the year, and the picture itself was judged, at the International Motion Picture Exposition held in Venice, the best foreign film of the year.

Whether dealing with material that was shoddy or sublime, Garbo approached her work with the serious, single-minded purpose of the true artist. She was a professional in every sense, with the professional's respect for her craft. "She was so completely thorough in her art," the director Richard Boleslawski has said, "that one found her almost as marvelous as the camera itself." It was not only Garbo's genius that inspired respect in every director she worked with; it was also her

The Painted Veil

With Herbert Marshall in The Painted Veil

Nordic efficiency. She unfailingly arrived on the set at nine o'clock, dressed, made up and letter-perfect in her lines. She had memorized as well the lines to be spoken by the other players who would appear with her; in addition, she had privately rehearsed the business of every scene—how she planned to sit in a chair, walk across a room—before reaching the studio. "She knew just what she had to do and how she expected to do it," Clarence Brown, who directed many of her pictures, has recalled. "If the director suggested changes, she listened respectfully, sometimes arguing quietly but never angrily. She always wanted to give the best she had. Everything was for the picture's sake." Garbo's other directors likewise made the pleasurable discovery that the most illustrious star in Hollywood was also professionally the least temperamental.

She had, to be sure, a few idiosyncrasies. For one thing, though the usual quitting time in Hollywood studios is six o'clock, Garbo refused to work a minute beyond five. At that hour, even if she was in the middle of a scene, she abruptly left the set. Working from nine to five, she explained when she first put her private rule into effect, was all she could physically endure. (Once, during the filming of *Anna*

Studio portrait, 1934

Karenina, Garbo worked until five twenty-five; the event was considered so noteworthy that the Associated Press sent out an item on it.) Despite her abbreviated working day, Garbo was one of the fastest workers in pictures. The actual shooting time on her films was considerably shorter than that of productions of comparable importance. Because of her painstaking preparation, retakes of her scenes were seldom necessary. Also, she saved time because she was not burdened with what Ernst Lubitsch called "a slavish devotion to the mirror," the most common failing, he once remarked, of women stars. "They are so much concerned about their looks," said Lubitsch, "that they exhaust their vitality powdering and making up. In the eight weeks that I worked with Garbo, she never looked into the mirror once unless I told her to do so. Nobody but the motion picture director can appreciate the significance of that fact."

Garbo allowed no visitors on the set when she was working. The ban was total and inflexible. When, on occasion, Louis B. Mayer felt obliged to escort friends or business associates to Garbo's set, she simply broke off the scene and retired to her dressing room, where she remained until her employer and his guests had departed. She had an uncanny ability to spot intruders. More than once, when doing scenes involving hundreds of extras, she stopped work to remark to the director, "There are people here who do not belong here." It would then be found that one or more Garbo admirers had mingled with the mob in the hope of seeing their heroine at work. During the shooting of *Grand Hotel,* John Barrymore invited his friend Arthur Brisbane, the famous editor, to visit him on the set. When he arrived, Barrymore and Garbo were in the middle of a scene. She stopped and courteously requested her eminent co-star to ask his friend to depart. The visitor departed. "I wasn't there when Brisbane came on the set and Garbo ordered him off," Lionel Barrymore, who also appeared in *Grand Hotel,* once remarked. "But it would have been the same had it been Jesus Christ. She didn't do it to be snotty. She was frightened."

There was another reason, as Garbo explained it, for her proscription of visitors. "Why do you mind people looking at you?" George Cukor, who directed Garbo in two pictures, once asked her. "When

Anna Karenina, *with Basil Rathbone*

With Fredric March and May Robson in Anna Karenina

people are watching," she replied, "I'm just a woman making faces for the camera. It destroys the illusion." To help her preserve the illusion, the sets on which she worked were always surrounded by black canvas screens. Only the people essential to making the scene were permitted within the screened area; they were given to understand that they had to avoid letting their eyes meet hers, for if they looked at her she was apt to become so disconcerted that she would have to stop and do the scene again from the beginning. Though directors often like to work in front of the camera, Garbo asked hers to work behind it. Not infrequently, when she was to do an important emotional scene, she went further and asked her director to stand outside the screened enclosure. Clarence Brown has recalled that he often found himself in the highly unusual situation of directing Garbo through a crack in a canvas screen.

Anna Karenina

Because of her fear of strangers, she insisted that the technical crews on all her pictures be made up of the same people. If one of the familiar electricians or property men was replaced, a good reason had to be given to Garbo. She also demanded the privilege of selecting her own cameraman. Her favorite was William Daniels, who photographed all but five of the pictures she made in America. Between Garbo and her talented cameraman there developed a great mutual fondness and professional respect. "The crews she worked with adored her," Daniels has said. "She called the electricians and prop men by their first names, and she was always giving presents to people." One of Daniels' most prized possessions is a gold cigarette case bearing the inscription, "To Bill Daniels, With Sincere Appreciation, Greta Garbo." Whenever possible, she wore an old pair of carpet slippers on the set for the sake of comfort. Before a scene was shot, she always asked Daniels, "Is the feet in?" If they were out of camera range, she kept the slippers on, regardless of what fabulous Adrian creation she was wearing.

Though Garbo was friendly with supporting players, gracious to the elderly extras and on occasion unbending enough to joke or pitch pennies with the crew members, she never invited anybody into her dressing room. She generally took her lunch there, alone. The only person who got inside her dressing room was her colored maid Ursula, who had the additional distinction of being the single individual on the Metro lot who possessed a photograph signed by Garbo. Between scenes she liked to exercise by walking around the lot, where she excited the same interest and curiosity as everywhere else. Other stars stopped to stare at her; secretaries and normally jaded publicity men gathered at their office windows to watch her pass. On her excursions around the Metro premises she rarely spoke to anyone, or was spoken to. She did, however, have one brief encounter with Harpo and Groucho Marx, who in high spirits entered an elevator in the M-G-M administration building one afternoon and found themselves standing next to a tall, slender woman whose face was concealed by a drooping hat. Groucho playfully lifted the brim, revealing the classic features of the Nordic star. "Excuse me," Groucho said. "I thought you were a fellow I knew in Pittsburgh." Garbo said nothing. Groucho didn't pursue it.

Chapter Twenty-four

One day in 1938 a Scottish youth was arrested for stealing a photograph of Greta Garbo from a movie theatre in Glasgow. When the offender was brought to court and the charge against him read, the magistrate, whose name was Robert Norman Macleod, asked, "Who is Greta Garbo?" By uttering those four words Robert Norman Macleod secured his little niche in history. His question was considered so incredible that stories about it were cabled to newspapers around the world. Not to know, in the fourth decade of the twentieth century, who Greta Garbo was automatically marked a civilized man a freak, and with reason. For Garbo was not only the best-known woman in the world; she had also become, as the perspicacious Alistair Cooke remarked at the time, "the unapproachable goddess of the most widespread and remarkable mythology in human history."

Garbo's fame as a goddess swelled fantastically as the thirties drew to a close. Her romantic attachments together with her celluloid triumphs made this period a kind of golden era for the millions who worshipped at her shrine. For the goddess herself it was a season, like all her seasons, more often melancholy than glad.

In *Camille,* released in 1937, Garbo gave what is widely regarded as her greatest performance. Out of the famous and flamboyant Dumas relic, a favorite vehicle of Bernhardt, Duse and numerous other actresses of genius through many generations, Garbo created a masterpiece. She had the benefit, to be sure, of the brilliant direction of George Cukor, a script skillfully adapted by Zöe Akins, Frances Marion and James Hilton, and a sound supporting cast that included Robert Taylor, Henry Daniell, Lionel Barrymore, Laura Hope Crews and Lenore Ulric. But it was Garbo's faultless performance that dominated the picture and made it an enchantingly beautiful and unforgettable film.

Through the magic of her acting Garbo transformed the essentially flimsy Dumas romance into a completely credible and moving love

Camille, *with Robert Taylor*

story. In the role of the errant, tragic Marguerite, she became a human being who really loved and suffered and died; the illusion was never marred. During the filming of the picture, she had taken pains to preserve the illusion by, among other things, adopting a rather special attitude toward Robert Taylor, then one of the newest notables in Hollywood, who played her youthful lover Armand. "While we were doing *Camille,*" George Cukor has recalled, "Garbo didn't talk much to Robert Taylor. She was polite, but distant. She had to tell herself that he was the ideal young man, and she knew if they became friendly she'd learn he was just another nice kid."

By playing the lady of the camellias, as the New York *Herald Tribune* observed in its review of the film, Garbo "challenged comparison with most of the great actresses of the last eighty years, but she can do so with triumphant assurance. Her sensitively thought-out and poignantly moving portrayal discloses the finest contemporary actress at the height of her power." The *Times,* paying tribute to her "perfect

Camille, with Lionel Barrymore

artistry" and "eloquent, tragic yet restrained performance," found Garbo "as incomparable in the role as legend tells us that Bernhardt was." Garbo's playing of the famous death scene called forth praise that was nothing short of ecstatic. "When she was dying," a British admirer remarked, "she had the appearance not merely of being ill, but of having lain in bed for months; in her weakness she could not smile, but retained the pride of a Bernini statue." And Mary Cass Canfield wondered "if a death scene has ever been played with such absence of bathos and such bitter truthfulness."

Garbo's memorable portrayal in *Camille* won her the award (for the second time) of the New York Film Critics for the "best feminine performance" of the year. She was also nominated in 1937 for the "best-actress award" of the Academy of Motion Picture Arts and Sciences. The Oscar that year was given instead to Luise Rainer for her work in *The Good Earth*. Strange are the ways of Hollywood. Garbo's countrymen were more appreciative. A few months earlier Sweden's King Gustaf V had conferred on Garbo the "Littris et Artibus" decoration, an ancient and highly prized award in recognition of literary and artistic merit. (Others who have been thus honored include Sarah Bernhardt, Jenny Lind, Ingrid Bergman and Marian Anderson.) The duty of delivering to Garbo the medal symbolizing the award was entrusted to the Swedish counsul general in San Francisco. He had hoped to make the presentation in person, but after trying in vain for many weeks to establish contact with the actress by telephone, telegraph and correspondence he at last gave up and forwarded the decoration to her by registered mail.

On Garbo's next picture, an ambitious work called *Conquest*, M-G-M spent $3,800,000. Purporting to tell the story of Napoleon and his favorite mistress, Countess Marie Walewska of Poland, *Conquest* had just about everything money could buy: expensive stars—Charles Boyer as Napoleon, Garbo as Walewska; a costly script by Salka Viertel, Samuel Hoffenstein and S. N. Behrman; a twelve-month production schedule; magnificent settings; a cast of hundreds; many photographic splendors, such as breath-taking Cossack raids and a glimpse of the retreat from Moscow; and so on. The picture turned out to be a

With Robert Taylor in Camille

shambling, episodic, pedestrian affair. Summing it up in his review, Frank S. Nugent remarked, "The company was overcharged."

To Garbo's great public, what she was doing on the screen at this time was of no greater interest than what she was doing away from it. According to reports coming out of Hollywood, she had at last found what the newspapers were pleased to call her "dream man." The character thus imaginatively described was the noted conductor, Leopold Stokowski. When *Conquest* was released, in the late fall of 1937, Stokowski's romance with Garbo was proceeding more or less according to what seemed to be the maestro's plan.

Stokowski had met Garbo in Hollywood some months before, not by chance. After having been the full-time conductor of the Philadelphia Orchestra for twenty-four years, he was then taking time out from his classical musical chores to work in the movies. A man who has always liked to keep up with the times, he had given his imprimatur to the newer art form by conducting and acting in *Big Broadcast of 1937* and *100 Men and a Girl.* Like a not inconsiderable number of other people, Stokowski cherished a desire to meet Greta Garbo. His fame and connections enabled him to do something about it. He looked up his old friend, Anita Loos, the witty writer best known as the author of *Gentlemen Prefer Blondes,* and beseeched her to arrange a meeting between him and the world's most famous blonde. Miss Loos, an experienced and influential Hollywood hand, had been casually acquainted with Garbo for several years; on her solitary walks along the beach the actress frequently stopped in at Miss Loos's house to pass the time of day. Obliging Stokowski, Miss Loos invited Garbo and one of her women friends to a small dinner party to meet the conductor.

"Stoky didn't waste much time on the overture," one of those who was present at the dinner and subsequently watched the development of the romance has said. "He got straight down to business, laying on the charm. He told Garbo they were destined to have a history-making romance, like Wagner's with Cosima. It was written in the stars. There was no use in their trying to escape it. The gods had made their decision. Mere mortals could only obey. It was the direct attack mixed with a little mystical stuff. Any kind of mystical stuff made quite a hit with Greta in those days."

Conquest (*above, right*) with Charles Boyer

Garbo was nevertheless at first somewhat taken aback by Stokowski's approach. Her practical Nordic mind bade her give the matter some thought. At that time, Stokowski, whose imposing appearance was distinguished by remarkably expressive hands, an ascetic-looking countenance and a mane of white hair, was fifty-five; Garbo was thirty-two. In conversation with friends she expressed bewilderment over the maestro's whirlwind courtship. "She was very cagey about everything," one of her friends has said, "but especially about money or the possibility that somebody would use her in some way. She seemed relieved to learn that Stoky was well off. Also, of course, they were both health cranks, so they had something in common to begin with. By and by Greta seemed to accept the idea that she was being swept into a world-shaking romance."

Once Garbo had become convinced that she and Stokowski could, in a manner of speaking, make beautiful music together, she appeared with him often at private social functions, where they gaily danced the rumba and seemed to enjoy themselves hugely. Reports of these goings-on naturally reached the gossip columns, which began carrying numerous items about how Garbo had "appeared on the Stokowski arm, as usual," at this or that social event and how she had "snuggled contentedly" in his arms "at many a private dancing party." The customary matrimonial rumors began to take shape. They became widespread when, in October, 1937, Stokowski's second wife established residence in Nevada and filed suit for divorce. A couple of days after this development became known, a reporter surprised Garbo as she was hurrying from her car into a friend's house and asked her when she and Stokowski planned to marry. "Such rumors are absurd," she said. "I will not deny that Mr. Stokowski and I are very good friends. But as far as marriage to him—no. That is out of the question." In early December, after his wife's divorce had been granted, Stokowski also denied that there was anything to the stories that he and Garbo were to marry. Later that month, however, when Garbo sailed for Sweden to spend Christmas with her relatives, it was duly noted that the maestro was on hand to bid her bon voyage. By that time, she had begun referring to Stokowski privately as "my boy friend."

The following February Stokowski also sailed for Europe. Arriving in Italy, he proceeded to the tiny, historic village of Ravello, where he had taken a month's lease on the ancient, handsome Villa Cimbrone, situated on a mountain perch commanding a magnificent view of the Mediterranean. Within a week he was joined by Garbo. She had traveled alone from Stockholm to Naples unnoticed by newspapermen. At Naples she was met by Stokowski, and together they motored in his car to Ravello, twenty-three miles away. When Garbo arrived at the Villa Cimbrone, one of the servants noted, she was wearing blue flannel trousers and a pair of sweaters. Her luggage consisted of one small suitcase much the worse for wear; no other luggage followed. She was, as usual, traveling light.

Their presence in Ravello undiscovered by journalists, Garbo and Stokowski were able to enjoy the first three or four days of their holiday in peace. They inspected the eleventh-century cathedral and took in the other sights in Ravello, motored about the countryside and sometimes had lunch at the Hotel Caruso, a local establishment. Since their villa lacked steam heat (as well as a telephone), they also dropped into the hotel for tea and for the purpose of getting warm. On her walks into the village Garbo attracted the attention of the peasants by her unusual dress. In addition to the blue trousers and two sweaters, she donned dark glasses and swathed her head in a variety of nondescript yellowish veils. The villagers had seen tourists in eccentric gigs before but never anything quite as rare as Garbo's. When, inevitably, it became known that "Greta" and "Stoky," as the tabloids referred to them with brash familiarity, were in residence at the Villa Cimbrone, correspondents of practically all nationalities descended on Ravello like an invading army. They began a monstrous journalistic siege, reports of which were daily dispatched to a gleefully curious world.

The attack began when reporters cornered Stokowski in the Hotel Caruso, where he had gone to make a telephone call. "Of course you may interview me," he told the newspapermen who surrounded him. "On what—art, music, anything you like. But, of course, not my private life. I never talk about personal things." Proceeding as if they had heard only his first sentence, the correspondents asked if his companion was Greta Garbo, if they were married, if they intended to be. "Who— Greta Garbo?" Stokowski replied archly. "Oh, you mean that film actress, I haven't the faintest notion where she is right now—certainly not with me." And with that he strode out of the hotel.

When newspapermen approached the Villa Cimbrone the following day, they found the gate locked and tacked onto it a large "keep out" sign; to add authority to the admonition, the gate was guarded by two carabinieri and three police dogs. Barred from the main theatre of operation, the hard-pressed correspondents were forced to compose their daily dispatches out of whatever little morsels they could pick up, or think up. The demand for news about Garbo and Stokowski was running so far ahead of the supply that even the shoddiest journalistic wares were eagerly sought. A typical story out of Ravello told how Garbo and "her white-haired musician friend strolled into the barnyard of the villa, where a cow named Emma was being milked. After stroking the cow's nose and murmuring a few Swedish endearments, Miss Garbo sat down on the stool, while Stokowski held the cow's head, and drew three quarts of milk." Other, and equally fanciful, newspaper tales had Stokowski "picking fresh white camellias and presenting them with conductorial bows to 'my lady of the camellias,'" and Garbo and Stokowski "strolling side by side and holding hands like puppy lovers." Into this welter of nonsense the staid London *Times* introduced one factual note when its correspondent cabled that "Miss Garbo has been obliged to have long curtains hung around the terrace to shield her from the attentions of the persistent photographers, who have not hesitated to climb trees and to lie in wait on the roofs of neighboring villas."

Virtual prisoners in their age-whitened retreat, Garbo and Stokowski managed to break out very early one morning and spend the day on the island of Capri. There, it was later discovered, they had tea at the residence of Dr. Axel Munthe, the well-known Swedish writer. The reporters, having been outwitted once, set up a twenty-four-hour guard around the Villa Cimbrone to make sure that its famous occupants did not make another successful dash for freedom.

Chapter Twenty-five

While a curious world wondered and speculated, Garbo and Stokowski were passing their days quietly, healthfully and decorously. Their existence at the Villa Cimbrone, an English gentleman having close connections with the villa and its servants later learned, was perhaps less exotic than millions of imaginative newspaper readers may have surmised. Still, with Garbo under its roof, the ancient structure was bound to become an enchanted place as well as the scene of a few mysteries and surprises.

The first surprise developed when Garbo's single, battered suitcase was unpacked by the villa's housekeeper, an elderly, French-speaking Swiss woman who had spent most of her life in service with the English aristocracy. (The previous year the villa had been rented by an English viscountess, a personage considered by the housekeeper to be a more suitable tenant than, as she expressed it, "a mere actress of no great lineage." Later on, the housekeeper was dumfounded to learn that the viscountess was so impressed that Garbo was living at the Villa Cimbrone that she almost wished she could exchange places with one of the servants.) Garbo's suitcase, the housekeeper discovered, lacked a single dress, a dressing gown or bedroom slippers. It did, however, contain a pair of blue espadrilles, several pairs of dark glasses, a bathing suit, one pair of coarse sleeping pajamas and, to the housekeeper's astonishment, several pots of jam.

Garbo instructed the maid to wash the pajamas every morning, iron them and return them to her room by evening. The jam Garbo guarded jealously. When she came down to breakfast each morning, she brought a pot of it with her. In addition to some kind of fruit; her breakfast consisted of cornflakes, covered with several spoonfuls of her special jam and over which she poured a cup of coffee. She apparently relished the soggy concoction, since she had it every morning. The Italian cook became curious about the ingredients of the jam, but she never had a chance to find out what kind of fruit it was made of; as soon as breakfast was over, Garbo took the jam with her and locked it in her bedroom.

Throughout their stay, the two health-minded vacationers followed a regimen of early to bed and early to rise, much exercising and sun-bathing and a careful diet. Upon arising at eight o'clock, Garbo and Stokowski appeared in bathing suits on the terrace, where they spent thirty minutes indulging in vigorous Swedish exercises. Garbo led the exercises, and was overheard one morning reprimanding the maestro, "One, two, one, two, Mis-ter Sto-kovf-ski, why can't you keep time, one, two." After breakfast and hiding the jam, Garbo joined Stokowski on the terrace for a sun bath or some reading. Sometimes they went for a stroll around the grounds.

Lunch was served promptly at noon, and the fare was never elaborate. It invariably consisted of raw carrots, but the repast was not without some variety, since two kinds of carrots were served, yellow and red. They were eaten straight, without salt, which was never allowed on the table. For a reason that mystified the servants Garbo ate her biggest meal at tea, which lasted from three-thirty to four-thirty. During this hour she plied herself with sandwiches, honey, jam, cookies, cake and other fattening delicacies. At dinner, which was served at seven, she reverted to her vegetarian diet, consuming only raw salad and fruit.

The day was over at eight o'clock, when Garbo went to bed. The mystery of the jam in the morning was matched by the mystery of the olive oil and salt at night. Upon retiring each night, Garbo took to her room a bottle of olive oil and a small saucer of salt. She had instructed the maid upon arriving that these items were to be prepared for her every evening, and each morning the maid found the bottle empty and the salt gone. The servants pondered what she did with the oil; one school held that she drank it, the other that she used it for complexion treatment. The mystery was never solved. As for the salt, the servants concluded she used that to brush her teeth.

The vacationers were somewhat inconvenienced by the fact that Garbo had neglected to bring any currency with her and had also failed to secure tourist lire checks, which travelers were required to have in order to obtain Italian money. Stokowski had provided himself with tourist lire checks, but the regulations allowed him to draw only three hundred lire per day, which was just about enough to enable one person to live decently. However, the famous pair were not living extravagantly. What with Garbo's having brought her own jam and her preference for carrots, she and her companion managed to make out.

Outside the Villa Cimbrone, public interest in the secluded residents was mounting dizzily. The local correspondents were maintaining their day and night vigil. Other reporters were scouring two continents in an effort to divine the celebrated couple's plans. It was widely reported that Stokowski, in a transatlantic telephone call to a friend in Philadelphia, had revealed that he planned to marry Garbo in Turin between March 15 and 17. When film actor Wallace Beery arrived in Naples on March 8, cables hummed with the word that he had come to serve as best man. A certain Lady Dunn, identified uncertainly by the New York *Daily Mirror* as an "English musician and friend of the conductor," was quoted as saying she had invited Garbo and Stokowski to visit her home in Canterbury, where "they would find the peace and dignity they seek for their nuptials." Mrs. E. T. Stotesbury, the dowager queen of Philadelphia and Palm Beach society, was also interviewed; amiable but not very helpful, she said she had not had "the pleasure of meeting Miss Garbo, but would like to very much."

Any item, however remotely it related to the drama at Ravello, made news. A reporter sought out the famous pianist Josef Hofmann, then sixty-two and the father of a seventeen-month-old son, and asked what he thought of "the romance between the fifty-five-year-old conductor and Greta Garbo." "I think they make a good couple," Hofmann replied with a smile. "Certainly there must be some attraction. And even a great musician gets bored with notes and bars and sharps and flats." Even Garbo's mother, according to the London *Daily Mirror,* was brought into the act. In the most unlikely story of all, the *Mirror,* quoting from what it ambiguously termed "a Paris dispatch," had Mrs. Gustafsson saying, "I would never consent to a marriage of my daughter with a man twenty-three years her senior who has been twice divorced and who has three children. What happiness could result from such a match?" So Garbo, according to the omniscient *Mirror,* had promised to call off the marriage.

Such was the situation after Garbo and Stokowski had been in residence at the Villa Cimbrone for three weeks. They were becoming restive in their confinement. In an effort to raise the journalistic siege, Stokowski, after conferring with Garbo, struck a bargain with representatives of the various large news agencies; in return for an interview with Garbo they agreed to call off their watch.

On the day of the ordeal, a delegation of correspondents was solemnly ushered into the library of the villa by Stokowski, who then left the room, rubbing his hands nervously. Garbo also appeared extremely agitated. The moment her interrogators entered the library she jumped from the sofa on which she had been seated and began pacing back and forth in front of the huge fireplace. She was wearing a blue gabardine suit with a Norfolk-style jacket, a yellow sweater, blue scarf and black gloves. She seemed to be suffering from a cold, and, as one of the correspondents noted, "her pale face, dusted faintly with powder but otherwise without makeup, was tight and unsmiling." Walking up and down in front of her natural enemies, she fingered and tugged at her gloves.

"Well," she said wearily, "what do you want?" A reporter asked whether stories that she intended to marry Stokowski were true. She shook her head. Another correspondent asked, "Are you married?" She shook her head again. Then, looking at the journalists and giving them a slight, cold smile, she said, "There are some people who want to get married, and there are others who do not. I never had any impulse to go to the altar." She spoke slowly, enunciating each word in her low, vibrant voice. There was a pause as Garbo looked briefly out the windows toward Amalfi Bay.

"I haven't many friends," she said suddenly. "I haven't seen much of the world, either. My friend, Mr. Stokowski, who has been very much to me, offered to take me around to see some beautiful things. I optimistically accepted." She hesitated for an instant, staring directly and unsmilingly at the newspapermen.

"I was naïve enough," she continued, "to think that I could travel without being discovered and without being hunted." Impatiently taking off her gloves, she said more rapidly, "Why can't we avoid being followed and examined? It is cruel to bother people who want to be left in peace. This kills beauty for me."

She then appealed to the newspapermen to leave her alone thereafter. They seemed in no hurry to depart, however, and one of them asked how many friends she did have. She replied that she had about a dozen, four or five in the United States, an equal number in Sweden, and two or three elsewhere.

"I live in a corner," she said. "I am typically alone, but there are so many beautiful things in the world I would like to see before they are destroyed." Even in Italy, she added, she had seen little because of the curious crowds, who had ruined her visit. "I wish I could be otherwise, but I cannot," she said with a throaty sigh. "I don't like this."

A reporter, returning to the main line of inquiry, asked Garbo if she had plans for marriage any time in the future. "Marriage?" she mused. "I wouldn't know. There seems to be a law that governs all our actions, so I never make plans." With that she indicated that the interview was over, smiled slightly as she thanked the newspapermen for their visit and bravely shook hands with several of them as they filed out.

The news agencies lived up to their bargain, but a number of free-lance photographers and reporters, who had declined or not been invited to the interview, continued to station themselves around the villa. During the final week of their stay, Garbo and Stokowski were thus beset with the customary harassment. Garbo had another vexing problem to deal with. Soon after it became known that she was residing at the Villa Cimbrone, she was deluged through the mails with letters, packages, manuscripts, plays, books, poems and paintings. Between fifty and seventy-five letters, along with half a dozen or more packages, were delivered at the villa in the course of an average day. Garbo instructed the Swiss housekeeper to burn everything that arrived without opening it. But the housekeeper's curiosity compelled her to open a few of the packages. One that slightly shocked her contained a brassiere and a note asking Miss Garbo to wear the piece of apparel, autograph it and return it to the sender.

Among the offerings that arrived a couple of days before Garbo and Stokowski left the villa was a package, addressed in strikingly beautiful handwriting, that the housekeeper also opened. In it she found two exquisite Spanish shawls, one white and one colored. Having noted Garbo's collection of veils, the housekeeper thought the actress might accept this gift and had the package left in her room. When she was preparing to leave, Garbo thanked the housekeeper for the package, said that she was keeping the colored shawl for herself and, owing perhaps to the fact that she had no money to tip, presented the white one to the housekeeper. After Garbo and Stokowski had driven away from the villa, the housekeeper took the white shawl from its package, and as she unfolded it a letter fluttered out. Written by a Sicilian baroness, the letter explained that the two shawls were the last valuable worldly possessions of her noble but impoverished family. Despite their circumstances, the baroness said, she had once been able to see Miss Garbo in a film and had always since thought of her as *una grande artista,* "as compassionate as she was talented." And now that the shawls had to be given up, the baroness concluded, it was her wish that they be offered to Miss Garbo, "at such price as her generous soul would elect." The housekeeper packed up the white shawl and returned it with a letter explaining as best she could that Miss Garbo had accepted the colored shawl and taken it with her to a destination unknown.

Upon leaving Ravello, Garbo and Stokowski motored to Rome, where they spent a week at the home of friends of the conductor, and then sailed for North Africa to do a couple of weeks' sightseeing. Returning to Italy, they motored leisurely across the Continent and arrived in Sweden early in May. Reports that they had married or planned to were still in wide circulation. The day they reached Sweden, Louella Parsons assured readers of her syndicated column that they need no longer speculate on Garbo's marrying Stokowski; it was already an accomplished fact, said Miss Parsons, with winning inaccuracy.

Garbo and Stokowski were together in Sweden for nearly three months. They made their headquarters at a country estate called Hårby, which Garbo had purchased in 1936, for the equivalent of fifty-five thousand dollars. (She sold it in 1939, shortly after the outbreak of war in Europe, at a profit.) Situated sixty miles south of Stockholm in

Garbo at a rare interview, aboard the Kungsholm *in 1938*

beautiful rolling country, Hårby comprised a thousand acres of farm-land and forest, a garden, a small park and a handsome, fifteen-room house, which commanded a fine view of Lake Sillen. Garbo and Stokowski had as much privacy as they desired on her estate. Soon after buying the property she had had all but one of the roads leading to it closed off. A barrier was erected at the entrance to the long driveway, and signs reading "Keep Out" and "Absolutely Private" were generously placed around the tract. In addition, though it was impossible to see anything at Hårby with the naked eye from across Lake Sillen, Garbo had also purchased a large tract of land on the opposite side of the lake from hers, evidently to preclude telescopic spying. Ensconced in her intruder-proof estate, Garbo and her guest settled down for a long rest. "We never saw them," one of the neighbors has recalled. "Somebody said she and the musician spent all their time doing Yoga exercises. We never really knew. As far as most of us were concerned, we really didn't care."

The mysterious couple did not, however, disappear completely from public view. One day they called at the local church, where, for reasons they did not explain to the clergyman, they consulted the so-called "central register" or church book, a repository of vital statistics about residents of the community. It was an uneventful visit aside from the fact that Stokowski's striking costume, consisting of sky-blue slacks and a colorful sports shirt, seemed to annoy the clergyman's dachshunds, who attacked with spirit. Occasionally, Garbo and her guest motored to the nearby village of Gnesta to do marketing. The famed actress was something less than a goddess to the tradesmen, who took exception to her habit of always complaining about prices. "Carrots cost too much," seemed to be her favorite expression, the local merchants recalled. "Gnesta soon lost interest," one resident has said. The fact that Garbo and Stokowski continued to subsist on their slender diet made for trouble among the help at Hårby, accustomed to hearty Swedish fare. "There was never anything coming out to the kitchen," was the laconic recollection of one of the maids, who left the estate because, she said later, she was always hungry there.

Along with numerous motor trips on which they took dietary picnic lunches, Garbo and Stokowski made a number of visits to Stockholm, where they attended the theatre and concerts and browsed among antique shops in the Old Town. In addition to being entertained by some of Garbo's friends in the city, they were also week-end guests at the country estate of Count and Countess Wachtmeister. At the end of July, their headline-haunted vacation over, Stokowski took leave of his companion and returned alone to the United States. Garbo arrived in New York a couple of months later and, to the surprise of the assembled newspapermen, granted a shipboard interview.

Naturally, she was asked, and in several different ways, about reports of her marriage to Stokowski. "I wish you wouldn't ask me that question," she said at last, after having parried others on the same subject. "I'm afraid if I were married, you would know all about it." Well, then, did she plan never to marry? "If I could find the right person to share my life with—perhaps I would marry," Garbo said. Did she think "single blessedness" was the proper state for a professional woman? "If you are blessed, you are blessed, whether you are married or single," Garbo replied.

Still the questions came and still Garbo did her best to please. A baby had been born on the liner during the voyage, said a reporter, and crew members had stated that Garbo visited the infant and mother daily in the ship's hospital. What about that? "Yes," said Garbo, "I spent some time with them. I am always very interested in babies. The birth of a baby is always a miracle." Would she like to have children of her own? Garbo shrugged and replied a bit harshly, "No. The world now seems much too difficult. I mean, partly because of danger of war in the world. I would not want to raise a son or any children to go to war. But I don't want to say any more about that. I don't know anything about politics." Had she enjoyed her vacation? Sighing huskily, she replied, "You cannot have a vacation without peace, and you cannot have peace unless you are left alone."

After spending a few days in New York, during which she was never seen with Stokowski, Garbo boarded a train for Hollywood. As

Garbo said he had promised, Stokowski had taken her around to see some beautiful things. Now, as her train rolled westward, another romance had ended.

Chapter Twenty-six

For thirteen years Garbo had enthralled audiences with her gift for beautifying illicit, tragic love. The peerless symbol of gorgeous tragedy, she had made her special province the portrayal of women who, judged by bourgeois morality, are so destructive of the established order that they do not deserve to end their days happily. Thus, in *Flesh and the Devil,* she drowned. In *A Woman of Affairs,* she crashed to death. In *Mata Hari,* she perished before a firing squad. In *Anna Karenina,* she threw herself under a train. In *Camille,* she was carried off by tuberculosis. And the finales of most of her other films had found her either in the shadow of death or in everlasting misery. Her métier was suffering, and Garbo, if not her audiences, had had enough of it.

Like most tragediennes, she had long nourished a desire to play comedy. Not since her appearance as a bathing beauty in *Peter the Tramp,* in 1922, had she had a chance to engage in antic make-believe. Though she had earnestly sought comedy roles, Metro executives had always been wary of risking their most valuable property in an experiment they considered so chancy. At last, by using her customary weapon of hinting broadly of a wish to retire, Garbo made her will prevail. Returning to Hollywood in the fall of 1938, after nine months abroad, she plunged into making *Ninotchka,* which proved her sure gift for comedy and turned out to be one of her best films.

A brilliant satire of Communism, *Ninotchka* was based on a mordant story by Melchior Lengyel and expertly adapted to the screen by Charles Brackett, Billy Wilder and Walter Reisch. The picture was further enhanced by the direction of Ernst Lubitsch, a great Garbo favorite, who had established a reputation as one of Hollywood's foremost directors in a series of films distinguished by sophistication, wit, elegance and nonchalance. Besides his masterly camera craftsmanship, Lubitsch possessed a rare ability to get the most out of his players. In working with Garbo he was a paragon of gallantry, thoughtfulness and charm. Arriving on the set in the morning, he called at Garbo's dressing room and formally paid his respects. Then he removed his coat and worked in shirt sleeves the rest of the day. At five o'clock, when work was over, Lubitsch again put on his coat and called at the star's dressing room, where he bade her a courtly good evening. This daily routine, as far as anyone could remember, was unprecedented on a Hollywood stage.

Now and again Lubitsch planned little tricks to keep his shy star in a gay frame of mind and create a light atmosphere on the set. One day when he was going over a scene with Garbo, she noticed on the arm of the director's chair a book titled *Parisian Nights.* She started to pick it up as Lubitsch, appearing elaborately oblivious of her interest, continued to chew thoughtfully on his cigar, but then she decided not to. They went on talking about how the scene should be played, Garbo meanwhile stealing glances at the book and Lubitsch pretending not to notice. The little game went on for several days. Finally, Garbo's curiosity could no longer be restrained. "I know it's a trick," she said, "but I've got to see what's in this thing." As she opened *Parisian Nights,* it went off, of course, with a bang, and everybody laughed, none harder than Garbo.

However elementary his joking routine with Garbo, Lubitsch considered it necessary because, he said later, "she is probably the most inhibited person I ever worked with. When you finally break through the inhibitions," he added, "and she really feels a scene, she's wonderful. But if you don't succeed in making her feel it, she can't do it cold-bloodedly on technique."

One of the memorable scenes in *Ninotchka* occurs when Garbo gets tipsy on champagne and, for the first time on the screen, really laughs. As the dedicated lady commissar sent to Paris to straighten out three erring comrades, she has been diverted from her grim mission by falling in with a Parisian man of the world (Melvyn Douglas), who shows her some of the pleasures of the capitalistic way of life, including good food and drink. Garbo was extremely apprehensive about the scene in which she gets gaily in her cups, particularly since it took place in what was supposed to be a public restaurant and so had to be done in

Ninotchka, *with Melvyn Douglas*

front of a number of extras. "I don't think I can play it," she told Lubitsch.

" 'Look here,' I said," Lubitsch once recalled, " 'I'll do anything you want. I'll change the script, the dialogue, anything, but this can't be changed. Too much depends on it. You must make up your mind that you'll have to play it.' So I waited two weeks before starting that particular scene. When we did get to it, she was very—afraid is too strong a word—timid. But I finally got her to relax completely by talking to her and being patient. I would go to her with a suggestion, saying, 'This

Ninotchka (*above*) *with the Moscow delegation* (*below*) *with Melvyn Douglas*

is how I see the scene. Now you go away and think it over.' And she would go into a corner, all by herself, and brood. Then she would do the scene again. If it still wasn't right, I'd say—just casually, passing by her—'Very good, but if you could just do . . .' Then I'd leave her alone again. Thus I gave her confidence, gradually, so that when she came to the drinking scene she was completely at ease. And she played it beautifully. So real. Not the routine of an actor who uses the customary tools. That's why it's so charming.''

Having shunned, as usual, looking at the rushes, Garbo did not see *Ninotchka* until after it had been cut and edited. Accompanied by Lubitsch, she attended a private showing of the picture at the studio. "Do you like yourself in it?" Lubitsch asked the star as the lights went up. "Even then," he said, "she didn't seem to know if she was bad or good." She was quite alone in her indecision, for Garbo's debut as a comedienne was unanimously hailed as a major screen event. The critics showed no restraint in acclaiming her as "a past mistress of comedy" and in describing how "the first lady of drama plays a dead-pan comedy role with the assurance of a Buster Keaton," the ultimate compliment. *Ninotchka* earned Garbo her second nomination for an Oscar, but it was Vivien Leigh who was chosen the best actress of 1939 for her performance in *Gone With the Wind*.

Throughout the filming of *Ninotchka,* Garbo was so uncommonly cheerful, when not involved in playing a scene, that people who had worked with her before were bewildered. She mixed easily with other members of the cast, joked with the crew, laughed at herself when, during the shooting of the drinking scene, she lost her balance and landed on the floor with a resounding bump, played one day in an impromptu noonday baseball game on the lot (revealing a good throwing arm—the result, she said, of youthful snowballing in Sweden), and gave what was believed to be her first autograph to a fan, a teen-aged girl who accosted Garbo as her car slowed down to pass through the studio gates. Never had she seemed so full of vigor and good spirits. One member of the cast wondered if his ears had deceived him when he heard Garbo say, "If you start to worry, it gets you down, especially in Hollywood."

All this unwonted geniality did not spring only from Garbo's pleasure, great as it was, in the opportunity to play comedy or from Lubitsch's gay pranks. Primarily accountable for her new and surprising public character was the dietitian, lecturer and writer, Gayelord (*Look Younger, Live Longer*) Hauser, under whose bubbly influence the actress had fallen.

Her acquaintance with the eupeptic dietitian began when she was taken by Mercedes de Acosta to a dinner party at Hauser's Beverly Hills estate, to which he had given the glad name Sunrise Hill. Garbo didn't like the party and left very early. Deeply disappointed and hurt, Hauser implored Miss de Acosta to persuade the actress to accept another invitation. Garbo at length relented, transmitting the information that she would come to dinner at Sunrise Hill on condition that no other guests would be present. Nothing could have pleased Hauser more. When Garbo made her solitary visit, Hauser served her one of his most tempting dishes—wild rice hamburgers. (These treats are made of wild rice and chopped hazelnuts or walnuts, with egg as the adhesive agent, and are fried in butter or peanut oil. Hauser later honored Garbo by dedicating the recipe for this dish to her in his cookbook.) For dessert Hauser served his guest broiled grapefruit, in the center of which had been dropped a soupçon of blackstrap molasses.

Garbo was much charmed by the food as well as by its ebullient creator. He was full of talk, energy and confidence, and he also made an impressive appearance, standing six feet three, handsome, broad-shouldered, black-haired and smartly and immaculately tailored. A man who had never married, Hauser was then forty-four, ten years older than Garbo, but he looked much younger than his years. Before long, the dashing dietitian had become Garbo's constant and exceedingly attentive escort.

Unlike Garbo, Hauser had no hesitancy in talking about himself, his career and his friends, who included, he once modestly acknowledged, "royalty, society leaders, stage and screen stars, statesmen, business executives, sportsmen, writers, philosophers, doctors, artists, scientists, teachers and preachers." Being something of a preacher himself, Hauser took pleasure in telling Garbo how he had found salvation through spinach and other healthful foods. At the age of sixteen, he had emigrated from his native Germany to the United States, where, after a few years, he contracted an ailment diagnosed as tuberculosis of the hip. Orthodox medical men gave him up, but a Dr. Benedict Lust, a so-called naturopath, persuaded him to try a regimen that included herb teas and special diets and sent him to a clinic in Europe to pursue the treatment. By eating only "living" foods, Hauser has said, he cured himself of his disease and determined to spend the rest of his life spreading the gospel of proper diet.

Back in the United States, he veered briefly from his objective by taking some courses at the Chicago College of Naprapathy, where he looked into the system of treating diseases by manipulating ligaments in the spine, pelvis and thorax, and by earning a diploma from the American School of Chiropractic. This scholarship may account for the fact that for many years the former student of bone and ligament pulling was popularly but incorrectly referred to as "Dr. Hauser," a bit of confusion that seemed to bother Hauser considerably less than it did the American Medical Association. ("I am a doctor," Hauser said, "not of medicine but of natural science.") His main interest being diet, Hauser opened a store in Chicago to dispense "natural foods," and the idea caught on. The business began to branch out after Hauser had made the acquaintance of Frey Brown, a young student at the Chicago Institute of Fine Arts, who saw possibilities that Hauser hadn't, such as starting diet classes at ten dollars a series and buying up the small company in Milwaukee that manufactured the foods Hauser sold. Brown became Hauser's business partner, and the two became inseparable companions.

Soon Hauser extended his operations, which now included lecturing and a correspondence course, to other dietetic trouble spots like Hollywood, where he converted Clara Bow, Laura La Plante, Billie Burke, Paulette Goddard and a number of other actresses. A superb showman who had developed an ingratiating platform manner that elderly women found irresistible, Hauser also had great success among the female winter residents of St. Petersburg, Florida. Then he carried the word to Europe. One of his American followers was Mrs. Ann Astaire, mother of Adele and Fred. Adele had married Lord Charles Cavendish and so was able, when Hauser arrived in England, to introduce him into what he has described as "London's most brilliant and influential circles." Through Lady Cavendish the doctor of natural science met Lady Mendl, who became probably his most devoted sponsor. She saw to it that he met a great many other members of the international set, including the Duke and Duchess of Windsor, Barbara Hutton, Lady Diana Manners, Archduke Franz Josef, Baron Philippe de Rothschild, and Mrs. Harrison Williams, most of whom became Hauser's disciples.

By the time Hauser began his courtship of Garbo, he was himself a member in good standing of the international set, a prosperous businessman and an established fixture of Beverly Hills society. Socially and temperamentally, he was well equipped to become her impresario. He began what resulted in a superficial metamorphosis by changing Garbo's eating habits. Taking her off a vegetarian diet, he prescribed one that included plenty of meat, particularly liver, as well as his "wonder foods," such as yogurt, dried skim milk, brewer's yeast, blackstrap molasses and vegetable juices. Garbo obediently downed this fare and, as far as her friends and associates could observe, thrived on it.

Dietary advice was only a part of Hauser's treatment. With it went his amateur but confident psychiatric counseling. A self-styled "minister of disturbance" who has said he delights in jogging people out of their "complacency and routine," Hauser essayed the task of making Garbo into a fun-loving social creature. Where others had failed, Hauser made some headway, at least for a while. Over and over again he told Garbo she had no reason to be melancholy and lonesome. For such feelings, said the doctor of natural science, she had nobody but herself to blame. What she had to do was let herself go, get out, mix with people, jump into the mainstream of life. Perpetually, he preached his doctrine that "fun is something that all human beings are entitled to, an essential, a must," and persuasively urged his repressed inamorata to follow him and have a fling at living.

If Garbo complained of a headache, she received scant sympathy from Hauser. Instead of commiserating (as Stokowski always had), the cheery minister of disturbance was apt to say, "Go put on your brown walking shoes. We'll get some fresh air. Best cure in the world for a headache." If she sighed that she was tired, Hauser suggested nothing so dull as a nap. Rather, he would mix her a bracing beverage, such as a "Sunshine Cocktail" (a mixture of the juice of oranges, carrots and celery) or perhaps put her in his car and drive to the Farmer's Market in Hollywood to partake of a big piece of revivifying yogurt pie. When Garbo opined that she was too weary to see a soul, Hauser was likely to collect a few friends and take her to a picnic on the beach. If she complained of insomnia, Hauser sternly forbade the use of barbiturates, recommending instead what he called "mental cocktails," a soporific compounded of beautiful thoughts.

Owing in large part to her natural longing to be led, Garbo submitted to Hauser's management with docility. She willingly accompanied him to private parties at the homes of his friends and also joined him in public excursions to the theatre, restaurants, concerts and galleries. Their developing friendship began to be the subject of much comment in the press. They were, Louella Parsons announced, "thataway." Into his lectures Hauser took to dropping clever little remarks, such as "I ain't a vegetarian, and Garbo does *not* have big feet," to the vast titillation of the ladies. Garbo didn't seem to mind. In fact, she even openly attended a few of Hauser's lectures. He had evidently convinced her that getting out in public in that way was good therapy. Of course, it wasn't bad for business, either.

On November 15, 1939, a few days after the premiere of *Ninotchka*, newspapers carried the information that Hauser had presented Garbo with a diamond ring and that she was wearing it on "the proper finger." Many people wondered how this select piece of intelligence reached the press; there seemed reason to doubt that Garbo had supplied it. However, there were no denials from either her or Hauser, and when they left Hollywood a few weeks later, with Frey Brown, for a vacation in the East, the gossip columnists confidently predicted that Garbo would soon be wed.

As Garbo's impresario, Hauser showed the actress New York as she had never seen it before. They had tea with Mrs. Cornelius Vanderbilt at her Fifth Avenue mansion and were entertained at dinner by many of Hauser's other celebrated friends. They had a box at the opera and attended the theatre and the ballet. They lunched at the Colony and dined at Twenty One and other fashionable restaurants. One night they were turned away from the dining room at the Algonquin Hotel because all the tables were filled—a circumstance that permitted Hauser to make the fictitious point to Garbo that she could, by continuing to be seen in public, be treated like any other visiting fireman. To make the visit complete, Hauser escorted Garbo to smart night clubs, and they even paid a visit early one morning to a hot jazz establishment on Fifty-second Street.

After this round of pleasure, Garbo and Hauser took off, early in February, for Palm Beach, where they put up at the fashionable White-hall Hotel and were continuously entertained by the dietitian's friends. Toward the middle of the month the vacationers, accompanied by Frey Brown, flew in a chartered plane to Nassau. There they boarded the fabulous yacht *Southern Cross,* owned by another of Hauser's friends, the wealthy, controversial Swedish industrialist, Axel Wenner-Gren. After cruising in waters around the Bahamas for a couple of weeks, the yacht put in at Miami, and Garbo's eventful sojourn with Hauser drew to a close.

For Hauser the vacation ended disappointingly. He had fully expected to return with Garbo as his wife. Before leaving for Florida he had confided to intimate friends in New York that he intended to marry the actress and had picked out the town in Florida where the nuptials would take place. He was so confident that he would make Garbo his bride that he had personally approved and left with a friend at International News Service a story of the wedding. As soon as the ceremony had been performed, Hauser promised, he would confirm the event by telephone, giving INS a news beat. The confirming call never came.

Though Hauser, like Stokowski, Gilbert and other hopeful suitors, failed to take Garbo to the altar, he continued to be her close friend and escort for many months after their return to Hollywood. Then, following the familiar pattern, Garbo gradually began to lose interest. At length she and Hauser drifted apart, but they remained on cordial terms. Like old soldiers, Garbo's romances never die—they just fade away.

Chapter Twenty-seven

The outbreak of the war in Europe presented Garbo with a new set of worries, both personal and professional. Fearing a German invasion of the Scandinavian countries, she had forehandedly arranged to bring her aged mother as well as her brother Sven and his family to the United States. Arriving in California at the end of December, 1939, they took up residence in a modest house in a secluded section of Inglewood. Garbo's relatives were, if anything, more reclusive than she. They kept strictly to themselves, and Garbo seldom spoke of them. Her mother died in California, but because of Garbo's almost morbid dislike of talking about personal matters, few people knew of the occurrence. When Garbo made her first trip to Sweden after the war, she visited a friend who remarked sympathetically about Mrs. Gustafsson's death. Garbo, who was standing at a window in her friend's apartment, replied, "What a lovely view from this window."

Garbo's career was more seriously affected by the spreading war than that of probably any other Hollywood actress because her pictures had always earned more money abroad than in the United States. In fact, few, if any, Garbo films ever returned their investment from exhibition in the United States alone. The knowledge that her lushly romantic, tragic roles had made her the idol of European audiences had always been an important factor in the selection of her vehicles. Now, in the middle of 1940, with the Continent embroiled in war, France in defeat and the rampaging German armies still on the march, the lucrative foreign market was all but gone. In these circumstances M-G-M was faced with the necessity of producing a Garbo film which, to make a profit, would have to appeal almost exclusively to American audiences.

After many high-level conferences, Metro executives came to the conclusion that the actress who had won her fame primarily by portraying lovely, world-weary women caught in the silken toils of ill-fated love had to be transformed into a vital, blooming American glamour girl. To this ill-advised enterprise Garbo gave her halfhearted consent. The vehicle selected for her debut as a sporting, fun-loving American type was called *Two-Faced Woman.* It was destined to be Greta Garbo's last moving picture.

Though the studio denied it at the time, *Two-Faced Woman* was a remake of a picture called *Her Sister from Paris,* originally filmed in 1925 and starring Constance Talmadge and Ronald Colman. Based on a dusty Hungarian play, *Two-Faced Woman* told the story of a plain wife who wins back her indifferent husband by impersonating her own glamorous twin sister. The theme was the familiar one of *The Guardsman,* with the roles of husband and wife reversed. However wispy the plot, Metro was not miserly in investing the picture with talent. The scenario was prepared by S. N. Behrman, Salka Viertel and George Oppenheimer; the cast included Melvyn Douglas, who had proved a perfect foil for Garbo in *Ninotchka,* Constance Bennett and Ruth Gordon; and the direction was entrusted to George Cukor, who had had such estimable success with Garbo in *Camille.*

As soon as *Two-Faced Woman* went into production, the Metro publicity department began an extensive campaign to prepare the American public for the emergence of "the new Garbo." In her next picture, it accordingly became known, she would appear, for the first time on the American screen, in a bathing suit—a brief one she had designed herself. Furthermore, she had cut her hair in a new short bob that the Metro publicity experts predicted would "set a style craze comparable to the long Garbo bob in 1932." In addition, it was announced that the hitherto inscrutable actress would be shown swimming, skiing, "wrestling with her man while clad in filmy finery" and joyously dancing a brand-new rumba called the "chica-choca." Metro's labors to Americanize Garbo in the public mind produced gratifying results. In an article about *Two-Faced Woman* published several weeks before the picture was released, *Life* described Garbo as "probably the greatest oomph girl of all time."

In contrast to the buoyant items distributed by the studio, Garbo was very moody and depressed while *Two-Faced Woman* was being

Two-Faced Woman (left) with Robert Sterling (right) with Melvyn Douglas

Two-Faced Woman (right) on M-G-M lot during filming

filmed. She didn't like the way things were going. There were clashes of temperament on the set, arguments and misunderstandings as well as frequent differences of opinion between the producer and the director. The tense, uncongenial atmosphere on the set, together with her own grave doubt about her role, gave her a deep sense of impending doom. She became so despondent that she confided to close friends her belief that there was actually a plot afoot at M-G-M to ruin her career. "They're trying to kill me," she often said darkly.

One person at M-G-M who shared Garbo's misgivings about her role was Adrian, the designer who had fashioned nearly all the star's costumes during her career at Metro. "It was because of Garbo that I left M-G-M," he said later. "In her last picture they wanted to make her a sweater girl, a real American type. I said, 'When the glamour ends for Garbo, it also ends for me. She has created a type. If you destroy that illusion, you destroy her.' When Garbo walked out of the studio, glamour went with her, and so did I."

Two-Faced Woman was released in November, 1941, and immediately ran into serious trouble. The National Legion of Decency promptly condemned the film as immoral. It was the first time in several years that leaders of the Catholic Church had put a blanket condemnation on a major Hollywood production. In a release to the press the Legion said the picture was offensive because of its "immoral and un-Christian attitude toward marriage and its obligations; imprudently suggestive scenes, dialogue and situations; suggestive costumes."

Other disapproving actions followed quickly. *Two-Faced Woman* was banned in Australia; the chief censor declined to state why. The Most Reverend Francis J. Spellman, Roman Catholic Archbishop of New York, asked pastors of Catholic churches to remind communicants that the Legion's rating of the Garbo comedy meant that "the picture is condemned as the occasion of sin and as dangerous to public morals." In Providence, Rhode Island, the police amusement inspector announced that he had forbidden the film to be shown there. The Catholic Interest Committee of the Knights of Columbus of Manhattan and the Bronx publicly denounced the film as "a challenge to every decent man and woman" and demanded that it be withdrawn immediately from distribution. Elsewhere other self-appointed censors turned up in force.

The furious attack on *Two-Faced Woman* astonished Garbo and deeply depressed her. She had always sought to avoid playing "bad womens," and now, it seemed, she had unwittingly made that very mistake. Her delusions of persecution became more intense. All the uproar the film had caused seemed to confirm her suspicion that she had been the victim of some dark intrigue. To her friends she said, "They've dug my grave."

Confronted with the Legion's action, M-G-M had to choose between ignoring the criticism—and thereby running the risk of the picture's financial failure—and altering the film in such a way as to suit the Legion—and thereby destroying whatever merit the picture possessed. Hollywood enterpreneurs, as everybody knows, have a deserved reputation for exercising good judgment when a dollar is at stake. M-G-M naturally did the sensible thing. Soon after the Legion voiced its objection, Metro quietly announced that *Two-Faced Woman* was being withdrawn for revision. The major change was the insertion of a scene in which the husband learns through a telephone call of his wife's intended deception. The heart of the plot was thus neatly cut out, with the result, as one of the reviewers later remarked, that "the romps of Melvyn Douglas and the wispily clad Miss Garbo across all sorts of upholstered furniture become a bewildering and pointless charade." For its pains M-G-M received the thanks of the Legion, which changed its classification of the film from "C" to "B." In other words, the picture was still, in the Legion's view, "objectionable in part." As it turned out, nobody won.

The purified version of *Two-Faced Woman* had its New York premiere on December 31, 1941. That being less than a month after Pearl Harbor, the timing was hardly fortunate. The critical reception was not auspicious. A few die-hard Garbo admirers, like Howard Barnes, valiantly recorded that the film was "captivating entertainment," but the praise was little enough. "Miss Garbo's current attempt to trip the light fantastic is one of the awkward exhibitions of the season," said the New York *Times,* and the film was otherwise condemned, on critical grounds, for its "shoddy workmanship" and as "a stale joke, repeated at length." Garbo's performance was found to be "gauche and stilted" and "one of the less propitious assignments of her career." The magazine *Time* described the picture as "an absurd vehicle for Greta Garbo," "a trick played on a beautiful, shy, profoundly feminine actress," and added: "Its embarrassing effect is not unlike seeing Sarah Bernhardt swatted with a bladder. It is almost as shocking as seeing your mother drunk."

The cruel Hollywood maxim—"You're only as good as your last picture"—applies less to Greta Garbo than to any other film actress in history. But, in however slight degree, it applies. She had been given mediocre scripts before, but always had been able to illumine them with the sorcery of her acting. *Two-Faced Woman* defied even Garbo's genius. M-G-M was disappointed by its distinct failure to make Garbo over into an oomph girl, and though the studio was willing to experiment further, Garbo wasn't.

Apprehensive of the transformative project to begin with, Garbo was made wretched by the censorship troubles *Two-Faced Woman* encountered, and plunged into despondency by the general apathy with which the picture was treated. In her own mind she was now firmly convinced that malevolent forces were at work to bring about her downfall. Her unreasonable but powerful fears, her recent professional setback, the effects of the war, the fact that she had all the money she needed, her natural laziness and lack of direction—all combined to make her lose interest in her career. Thirty-six and at the height of her dramatic power, Garbo made up her mind to withdraw from pictures until, she thought then, after the war. It was not the only irony of her life that she never returned.

Chapter Twenty-eight

For the past thirty years, Greta Garbo has been the world's most glamorous lady in retirement. She has been out of public sight, mostly, but not out of mind. Nor could she be, for Garbo is a legend, and a legend, unlike a mere mortal, cannot retire. Her years of seclusion, far from diminishing her baffling allure, have only enhanced it. This, too, was inevitable. All through the years that her celluloid image encircled the globe, Garbo was an enchanting figure with whom millions of movie fans felt intimate because of their sense of identification with her famous moody face on the screen. But because she was (besides a legend) a human being with an almost irrational feeling for privacy, she frustrated her admirers by refusing steadfastly to reveal herself to them. Garbo was never explained to the public (partly because she has never been able to explain herself to herself) and, retiring, she carried the mystery with her into the recesses of an even more private world, even further out of reach. As the mystery was compounded, so in direct ratio the fascination of her devout following increased. What they could no longer see at all became even more bewitching than what they had once been able to see occasionally by paying their money at a box office. So it is not only a mass form of unrequited love but the spell of an unsolved and ever deepening human mystery that has compelled Garbo's admirers to maintain their fanatic interest, to continue to speculate on her past, present and future and to treasure every snippet of news and bit of rumor that circulate about her. The mystery persists. One of Garbo's erudite worshippers has written, with a hint of despair, "Except physically, we know little more about Garbo than we know about Shakespeare."

Naturally and rightly, Garbo's abdication as the first lady of the screen has been widely lamented. One critic, in fact, has called it "unforgivable if only because it means that now we shall never see her as Masha in *The Three Sisters,* a part Chekhov might have written for her." Nor, as many other intelligent filmgoers had hoped, will she ever be seen as St. Joan or Hedda Gabler or in other roles that test the power of the great actress.

The filmgoers' loss has been the biographers' gain, for Garbo's retirement also means that she has stood still, like a sitter with infinite patience before a portrait painter, for three decades. She has, in effect, been suspended in time if not in place (she drifts between New York, Europe and various way stations) for almost half of her adult years. Her life all this while has not been obscured by important activity nor has her character been modified by important influences. On the contrary, so few outside forces of consequence have impinged upon her existence in retirement that this is the period in which her fundamental character has necessarily become, as far probably as it ever will, manifest.

The tragedy of Greta Garbo, it is now made clear, lies in the difference between what she really is and the aesthetic, romantic appeal she made and symbolized. The two entities, the woman and the legend, are at opposite poles, hopelessly irreconcilable. And yet, courageously, Garbo must live with both.

It is Garbo the symbol—"the divine symbol of discontent," the critic John Mosher called her—that has always fascinated the public, and still does. That is why, at sixty-five, she is still among the most sought-after actresses in the world. Every major studio in Hollywood has tried repeatedly to entice her into making another picture. Offers by the dozen have come from film companies in Britain, Germany, Italy, France and India. Scores of independent producers have attempted to make the coup of their lives by luring Garbo back to the screen. She has not turned a deaf ear to all these proposals because she had no intention, in the beginning, to make her retirement permanent.

Over the years she has listened to countless film ideas and read hundreds of scripts. At one time or another she has been reported ready to return to pictures in portrayals of Madame Bovary, Bernhardt, Duse, Modjeska, Cyrano de Bergerac and even St. Francis of Assisi, to name a few of the more disparate. Another and possibly more likely notion was submitted in the early 1950s by the director Clarence Brown, who visited Garbo in New York. "She was eager to have us start again,"

In Rome, 1949

George Schlee attempts to ward off photographer in Italy, 1949

Brown, who directed so many of her pictures that he became known as "Garbo's Man Friday," later said. "I had rather a good suggestion. Why not make *Flesh and the Devil* again? But then the company started talking about doing the picture in a Latin-American location with a cowboy as a lover. So, I just told them to forget about the whole thing." Garbo already had.

She was considerably more attracted by an idea for a film about a foreign correspondent and a beautiful lady spy, which was suggested by the late John Gunther, who, with his wife, was one of Garbo's good friends for many years. With her encouragement as well as that of Dore Schary, then production chief of M-G-M, Gunther went to work and wrote the scenario. After Garbo had read it, she said only, "I think it's a perfect part for Greer Garson," and that was the end of that.

Out of all the scripts she has read she has seriously considered only a half dozen or less. One of these was a film based on the life of George Sand, whose depiction on the screen had long been one of Garbo's cherished ambitions. In 1947 she agreed to play the part of the fabulous French novelist in a film to be produced by an independent firm and financed in a complicated manner by British, French and American capital. She was genuinely disappointed when this venture, which was also to have called for the services of Salka Viertel, George Cukor and Laurence Olivier, collapsed, primarily because of money troubles. A year later, she made another effort, her most determined one, to return to motion pictures. She actually signed a contract with independent producer Walter Wanger and accepted an advance payment of fifty thousand dollars to star in a picture based on Balzac's *La Duchesse de Langeais,* a florid tale of tragic love in which Garbo was to play the beautiful, worldly duchess who, after many a bittersweet romance, finally takes a nun's vows and dies at twenty-nine. Having made screen tests and learned the script, Garbo arrived, in the summer of 1949, in Rome, where the picture was to be filmed. However, one postponement followed another, caused by the producer's financial difficulties, and at length, through no fault of Garbo's, the project was reluctantly abandoned.

Since then, she has found no film idea to arouse her lasting enthusiasm, though she has been momentarily tempted. In 1952, Nunnally

In London, 1949

Johnson, one of Hollywood's wisest and wittiest producers, sent Garbo proofs of Daphne du Maurier's novel *My Cousin Rachel* and, with George Cukor (who, like Garbo, was in London at the time) acting as intermediary, invited her to undertake the title role in the film to be based on the book. After reading the novel, Garbo said yes, she would be delighted to play the part, and Cukor triumphantly cabled Johnson to draw up a contract. The next day, Garbo changed her mind. "I'm sorry," she told Cukor. "I can't go through with it. I don't have the courage ever to make another picture."

So it seems that Garbo the symbol, though hidden from public view, still exerts her peculiar magic. As one of her phrasemaking friends has said, "The ghost of Greta Garbo is everywhere."

The legendary Garbo, the one whose peerless image graced the screen, is the creation of imaginative people who, one of them said in a moment of disillusion, "turned a healthy peasant girl into an exotic spy." Not content to gaze upon the most fabulous face of the century, they invested its owner with mythical qualities that fascinated them and burdened her. They could not resist making up little stories about her. At one time the set on which she worked was plagued by a series of small fires and minor accidents, all seemingly inexplicable. So the mythmakers circulated the story that Garbo was at the root of it all. She was, they said deliciously, a poltergeist. They repeated to one another memorable remarks that added mystery to their ideal, such as that of the German director Ludwig Berger who once turned to Garbo after she had said something provocative (significantly, nobody remembers what) and sighed, "Ah, Greta, if you had been born in the sixteenth century, you would have been burned as a witch." Then there was the fiction that one of her admirers has said he half believed until he met her—"the old hilarious slander which whispered that she was a brilliant Swedish female impersonator." Garbo's intimates gossiped about her endlessly among themselves, and some of the facts and stories they related about her inevitably spread to outsiders ready to believe and pass on both facts and fancies. Thus the legend was spun and Garbo became in the minds of the imaginative millions the myth that had been fashioned by the few—a strange, hermetic goddess, a temple figure of beauty, secrecy and omniscience.

It may all have been, in the end, a great disservice, for the real Garbo was never able to live up to the myth. She has always been what she is today—a woman with a child's charming, tragic innocence. She is shrewd, selfish, willful, instinctive, completely self-absorbed. From her intimates she demands total attention and devotion; otherwise she sulks. She is secretive ("Greta would make a secret out of whether she had an egg for breakfast," a friend has said), and she has a child-like indifference to all desires but her own. One of her old and very good friends once came to her and explained that he was about to undertake a television program and, having had no experience before a camera, asked if she would give him a few pointers. Garbo declined, remarking wearily, "Oh, that is all in the past. I've forgotten all that." She is condemned to live in a small cloistered world because of her reluctance or inability to accept the responsibilities of adult friendship. A woman who has known Garbo for many years in both Hollywood and New York has said, "Greta is like the Mona Lisa—one of the great things in life. And as unattached to you as that."

An anomaly of Garbo's private life and her profession is that she was able to express emotions with such liberated clarity on the screen and yet away from it self-expression has always seemed an agonizing process. She is better at listening than talking; she enjoys hearing gossip (she is not at all given to saying malicious things herself); and she laughs appreciatively at uncomplicated jokes. Her private sense of humor is not excessively refined; she can be amused by a fairly exhausting story about a centipede taking off its shoes. Her conversational manner is inclined to be tentative; she often prefaces a comment with something to the effect that "I suppose this sounds silly, coming from me," or "You probably won't believe this, but . . ." Like a child who has moved into a new neighborhood, she is apt to attempt conversation with people she has just met (if she elects to pay them attention) by asking direct questions—"What do you do? Are you married? Do you have children?" and so on. When she made her first visit to the studio of a fashionable New York milliner, she dismayed the proprietor by asking, among other things, "Do you have a lover?"

It has always been Garbo's awful burden that because of her Sphinx-like air of omniscience people expect that she is constantly at the point of saying something of vast import. The few Garbo utterances that have made a lasting impression on her friends are notable less for profundity than mysteriousness. A traveling companion once found her sitting on the floor of her hotel room swathed from head to foot in blankets. Asked what she was doing, Garbo solemnly replied, "I am an unborn child." Another time she surprised a friend by saying, "I had an awful row with God this morning," a remark the more arcane because Garbo is not known to have strong religious inclinations. Nor have intellectual or literary pastimes claimed her attention. She thinks little about anything except what applies directly and immediately to her own life. Politics, literature, the state of the world interest her hardly at all. (She became an American citizen in 1951—"I am glad to become a citizen of the United States," was all she had to say on that occasion—but she seems never to have voted.) Her friends have given her books and been disappointed never to learn whether she has opened them. The fact that she was in earnest about her fantastic plan to try to talk Hitler into stopping the war indicates her rather tenuous grasp of world affairs. The war itself was a subject she preferred that her friends avoid discussing in her presence. It was too depressing, she said. Once at least the banned subject was brought up; the Russians were making their historic resistance at Stalingrad and friends at dinner were discussing the implications. During a break in the conversation, Garbo said, "Ooh, those Russian soldiers must be beautiful."

Garbo's preoccupation with herself and with the little things in life has on occasion momentarily vexed her friends, particularly the intellectuals who were instrumental in creating the legend. Even such an old friend and generous contributor to the legend as Cecil Beaton has evidently been so disappointed as to be moved, perhaps in a moment of pique, to record: "She is not interested in anything or anybody in particular, and she has become quite as difficult as an invalid and as selfish, quite unprepared to put herself out for anyone; she would be a trying companion, continuously sighing and full of tragic regrets; she is superstitious, suspicious and does not know the meaning of friendship; she is incapable of love." And he went on to wonder if "perhaps her magic is only a freak of nature which leads our imagination to make of her an ideal she can never be."

With Mrs. John Gunther (right) at Orly Field, Paris, 1951

Signing citizenship papers in Los Angeles, 1951

In 1954, more than a dozen years after making that pointed observation Beaton wrote about Garbo again. "The whole secret of her appeal seems to lie in an elusive and haunting sensitivity," he said, and this time went on to remark raptly on, among other things, her "inexhaustible spiritual assets." So it would seem that Garbo's magic, whether a freak of nature or whatever, endures and continues to entrance even those who may have been made keenly aware of her human weaknesses.

Today, at sixty-five, Garbo's power as an enchantress is intact. Old friends and new acquaintances, women as well as men—none, it seems, can resist her spell. "She may be as thoughtless as a spoiled child and just as difficult, but she is still the most vivid personality in my world," a famous actress has said. "Garbo is divine," artist and writer Fleur Cowles remarked in the 1950s. "She has a way of looking at you—and, well, you just can't take it. She was our guest one evening and was seated at dinner next to the Brazilian Ambassador. When he left, he thanked me quite emotionally. 'I will never forget you,' he said, 'because you gave me Garbo.'" A New York publisher and man about town who met Garbo when she was in her early fifties at a party and danced with her was still transported when he said afterwards, "Everywhere I—shall we say—contacted her while dancing I was conscious of a vibrant strength. If while talking she inclines two degrees toward you, you feel that she's sitting in your lap. She reaches out, touches your arm lightly, and you feel you've been compromised. I'm kidding—but not much."

Perhaps the most affecting example of Garbo's occult influence was submitted by Truman Capote in the middle fifties. "It happened," Capote related, "that once I stopped by the apartment of a friend who previously that afternoon had entertained Garbo at tea. As I entered the room and started to sit down in an especially comfortable-looking chair piled with pillows, my friend, a very sane fellow, suddenly asked would I mind not using that particular chair. 'You see,' he said solemnly, '*she* sat there: the dent in the little red pillow, that's where her hand rested—I should like to keep it a while longer.' I understood him perfectly."

Chapter Twenty-nine

Back in the days when Garbo's sublime face was adorning movie screens around the globe there were few who doubted that the greatest beauty of her age was destined to take her place in history alongside Helen of Troy, Cleopatra, Salome, Madame Pompadour, Ninon de Lenclos and the other legendary Circes. A few dissidents there were, however. Among them was Clare Boothe, who was herself to give history something to think about as she became the wife of Henry R. Luce, and went on to become a playwright, actress, congresswoman and ambassador. In the early thirties, Clare Boothe, then an editor of *Vanity Fair,* evidently felt the need to devote her talents to a consideration of one of the most delightfully pressing questions of the day: how the future would reckon with Greta Garbo.

Speculating on the matter in 1932, Clare Boothe readily acknowledged that Garbo was the one and only beautiful woman produced by the twentieth century who might wind up in the company of Helen, Cleopatra and the other lively charmers. But as she peered into the future Clare Boothe saw a hitch. "The only way a woman can gloriously succeed in impressing herself upon her age—the way of love—Garbo has, until now, failed in," she wrote, and further observed: "History has never reserved a place for a beautiful woman who did not love, or who was not loved by at least one interesting, powerful or brilliant man. . . . When we speak of Helen, we speak in the next breath of Menelaus, of Paris. Pompadour reminds us of Louis Quinze. Salome would have mattered little but for John the Baptist. . . . Cleopatra had her Caesar, and Mark Antony had Cleopatra. Is the most magnetic woman of her generation, the greatest beauty of her era, to be remembered because her name was 'associated with' (to use a genteel euphemism worthy of Will Hays, but hardly of Garbo) John Gilbert's?"

During the nearly forty years that have passed since that question was posed, Garbo's name has been "associated with" a number of other men—Rouben Mamoulian, Leopold Stokowski, George Brent, Gaylord Hauser, George Schlee, a New York businessman, and Baron Erich Goldschmidt-Rothschild, a wealthy German refugee. Whether any of them has the stature of a Caesar or a Baptist, only history, perhaps, will reveal.

Of the friendships Garbo has formed during the years of her retirement the two that lasted longest and therefore perhaps meant most to her were those with George Schlee and Baron Rothschild. The Baron, a worldly man of extensive means, was some fifteen years older than Garbo, tall, white-haired and distinguished in appearance. He had impeccable manners, fastidious tastes and, like Garbo, total leisure. In New York, she and Rothschild used to take long walks together in Central Park, dine at expensive restaurants, go shopping, visit.art exhibitions and otherwise pleasantly while away the hours. In the summer of 1952 they made a motor trip together through Austria, accompanied by the Baron's former wife and her mother. At the Park Hotel in Bad Ischl, where the party sojourned for several days, Garbo registered as "Mrs. Harriet Brown" and disguised herself by discarding the dark glasses and regularly wearing a gray wig. Her identity thus concealed, she and the Baron spent many peaceful hours hiking, swimming and engaging in other healthful pursuits. When reporters finally penetrated the disguise, Garbo said—in words that rang like a familiar echo out of the past—"I don't want to talk to anyone. You must understand. The Baron is just a very good friend."

Under the tutelage of her very good friend, who was a connoisseur and owned an important art collection in Germany before Hitler came to power, Garbo developed a certain interest in art and invested in a few paintings, including a Renoir. It was no doubt partly because of this developing interest that she was taken one evening in the early 1950s, when she was in Paris, to the apartment of Alice B. Toklas by two old friends, Mercedes de Acosta and Cecil Beaton. To visit Miss Toklas was considered a great privilege not only because of herself but also because in her apartment hung some twenty-five Picassos from Gertrude Stein's early collection; among them were the famous

"Young Girl with Basket of Flowers" and the great, huge, startling "Nude with Clasped Hands." Looking at the pictures was a ceremony that appreciative callers indulged in by the hour. When Garbo arrived with her friends and had been seated, Miss Toklas asked, "Would you like to see the pictures?" and as it was late turned on the side lights. Without rising, Garbo glanced circularly around the room and said, "Thank you very much." There was no additional comment by the beautiful visitor, whom Miss Toklas subsequently referred to as "Mademoiselle Hamlet."

Gayelord Hauser was the unwitting matchmaker in bringing about Garbo's friendship with George Schlee, which was of considerably longer duration than her relationship with Rothschild. As part of his energetic program to make Garbo look younger and live longer and be happier and healthier, Hauser aroused her interest in clothes and arranged for a friend to accompany her to the salon of Valentina, the famous and expensive couturière, to select a wardrobe. Schlee was Valentina's husband and business partner. As a consequence of Garbo's visit, Valentina and Schlee became good friends with their new customer, and as time passed Garbo and Schlee became very good friends.

It is the notion of some of Garbo's Swedish friends, who met Schlee when he made a visit to Stockholm with her in the early years of their friendship, that she was attracted to him because, to her, he bore resemblances to Mauritz Stiller. There were, it is true, some similarities. Like Stiller, Schlee was of Russian blood (as is Valentina, whom he married in Europe when she was seventeen; they came to the United States in 1927) and he had, like Garbo's early mentor, rather gross features, large hands, a varied background that enabled him to talk easily on nearly any topic, and he was a man of the world. Schlee, who was a few years older than Garbo, also had had experience in the theatre, and was capable of giving Garbo directions, a faculty in a man she has always instinctively prized. Throughout their friendship she relied on Schlee's advice more than that of any other person's in all matters connected with her attempts to return to the screen. He was one of her few intimates who ever expressed the belief that Garbo might one day resume her career. "She reminds me of Duse, whom I first saw in St.

Garbo in New York, 1951

On Madison Avenue, New York, 1952

Petersburg," Schlee once remarked. "She had been in retirement eleven years and returned to greater triumphs than ever. This will happen to Garbo."

The design for living that Garbo, Schlee and Valentina worked out over a period of several years naturally commanded the admiring interest of their mutual friends. In the beginning of his friendship with Garbo, they said, Schlee told his wife with Continental aplomb, "I love her, but I'm quite sure she won't want to get married. And you and I have so much in common." Valentina was said privately to have considered the arrangement far short of ideal and, being Russian, to have spoken dramatically of entering a convent. However, thanks to her not inconsiderable talents as an actress, she managed to appear outwardly unruffled.

During the theatrical season, Schlee was known to appear at an opening one night with Garbo and at another opening the following night with Valentina. In a casual, European manner, the trio occasionally spent week ends together at the homes of friends, though more often Schlee and Garbo arrived by themselves. Once when Schlee was in the hospital, Garbo and Valentina sensibly spelled each other in providing him company; Garbo handled the afternoon visit, while Valentina was tending to her work, and she took over the evening stint. Garbo attended Valentina's collections, and Valentina continued to make many of Garbo's clothes. At least once, the two women, escorted by Schlee, arrived at a dinner party wearing identical costumes (dark blue handkerchief linen skirts and white blouses) that Valentina had designed. Since she bears a noticeable physical resemblance to Garbo and since the two on this occasion had combed their hair back severely from their foreheads and were even wearing the same kind of make-up, their appearance, and all things considered, made a lasting impression on the other guests.

When Garbo made her first postwar visit to Sweden, in 1946, Schlee accompanied her, and was referred to in the Swedish newspapers as her *kavaljer*, or escort. They were met at the Stockholm railroad station, along with a large crowd that gave Garbo the usual noisy welcome, by her old friend and suitor Max Gumpel, who graciously turned over his villa in the Stockholm archipelago to the visitors. In the years that followed, Garbo and Schlee frequently passed their summers together on the Continent. During this period, Valentina often made business trips to Europe during the summer, and the threesome were once or twice in Paris simultaneously if not always together. In 1953, Garbo bought an apartment in a building near the river on East Fifty-second Street in New York. Her new quarters were in the same building in which Schlee and Valentina also lived.

The highly civilized manner in which Garbo was accustomed to arrange her social affairs may be indicated to a certain extent by one of the summer visits she made to Europe during the 1950s. She flew to the Continent with Schlee, who delivered her to Cecil Beaton, with whom she spent three weeks in England. (The previous summer she had been Beaton's guest for six weeks and been treated to a social whirl that included a meeting with Princess Margaret, with whom, someone said, she got along "like a palace on fire.") Leaving Beaton, she spent a few days with Schlee in Paris, and then went on to Austria to join Baron Rothschild, his former wife and her mother. After their motor trip, Garbo rejoined Schlee and they passed the balance of the summer in the south of France. A couple of weeks after returning to New York, Garbo was asked by an old friend who met her at a party how her summer had been. Looking tragic, Garbo said, without elaborating, "It was awe-ful, simply awe-ful." Since Garbo's friends are aware that she is sometimes difficult to please, they would not interpret her doleful comment as in any way a reflection on Schlee or Beaton or Rothschild or even on the Baron's former wife or her aged mother.

Chapter Thirty

When Garbo returned from Europe in 1946, she was asked by reporters about her plans for the future. "I have no plans," she said, "not for the movies, not for the stage, not for anything, and I haven't even got a place to live. I'm sort of drifting." It was an astonishingly frank answer and pathetically honest. For it would be hard to find a phrase to describe Garbo's existence since leaving motion pictures more apt than "sort of drifting"—or more pensive.

Since her retirement she has made her headquarters mostly in New York. She lived first in a furnished, two-room apartment (the blinds of which were seldom raised) in the Ritz Tower Hotel on Park Avenue, then in a four-room, furnished apartment in Hampshire House (which she thriftily sublet, storing her few possessions in one closet, when she was away) and later in her own seven-room apartment overlooking the East River. "How do you spend your time in New York?" a European friend once asked Garbo. "Oh," she replied, "sometimes I put on my coat at ten in the morning and go out and follow people. I just go where they're going. I mill around."

For many years now she has often been seen milling around on Fifth Avenue or Park or Madison or on the side streets uptown. Mostly she window-shops and watches the people but occasionally she makes a purchase or performs an errand. "The high point of her day would be to go to Saks or Bonwit's to exchange a sweater," a friend has said. "Then she would go home and take a nap." In her dark and generally somber attire, wearing the customary low-heeled shoes, face-concealing hat but no dark glasses, she is frequently recognized but seldom accosted. Just seeing her, however, is a thrilling event in the lives of most who do. People never forget the time or the place where, to their amazement, her figure materializes—at the blouse counter at Lord & Taylor, under the IBM clock on the corner of Madison and Fifty-seventh, at the Rosenberg Gallery on Seventy-ninth, strolling near

Arriving in New York on the Queen Mary *with George Schlee, 1953*

the lake in Central Park, coming out of a movie house on Fifty-eighth. Wherever it occurs, the meeting, impersonal and fleeting though it usually is, is indelibly etched in the memory of the beholder.

Leaving his office on upper Madison Avenue at dusk one evening, a middle-aged lawyer was startled and enchanted to recognize Garbo standing in front of a small linen shop that was advertising a going-out-of-business sale. The lawyer, a loyal Garbo admirer since his college days, watched from a respectable distance as she peered for some five minutes at the display of conventional goods. He followed as she moved down the street, stopping here and there—in front of a jewelry store, a shop that sells children's apparel, an establishment that deals in optical goods—just random window-shopping. Finally, the lawyer watched as Garbo turned down a side street and strolled off into the night while he reluctantly hurried to catch his train to the suburbs, where he greeted his wife with "Guess who I saw on the street today?" It happens all the time.

Though Garbo's wanderings about New York during the forties and fifties followed no charted course, she had certain more or less regular ports of call. On an average of once a week she made a trip to the Parke-Bernet Galleries, where she leisurely inspected the furniture, silver and objets d'art that were offered for auction each Saturday. On these visits she was often accompanied by Baron Rothschild. Though they also often attended the Saturday auctions, she never, in the memory of one veteran member of the staff, bought anything, nor did the Baron. For Garbo, visiting the galleries was a way of being with people in pleasant, interesting and undemanding circumstances. She was conspicuously absent the day the art collection belonging to the singer Hildegarde and her manager Anna Sosenko was auctioned, undoubtedly because it included the original of the famous Covarrubias caricature of Garbo and Calvin Coolidge. However, George Schlee was present and, presumably acting for Garbo, bought the picture for two hundred and seventy dollars.

Garbo also became a not unfamiliar figure on Third Avenue, where she went to browse in the antique shops. She spent so much time there that she became friendly with several of the proprietors, who found her charming, unaffected, pleasant to everyone. The shopkeepers learned that she liked to be let alone as she wandered about by the hour, looking at this, picking up that and occasionally asking the price of something. Her purchases were extremely infrequent; for years, about all she ever bought were a few small ceramic, brass or wooden cupids; she later bought some eighteenth-century furniture for her apartment. One of the shops she frequented had an annex, where furniture and other antiques were restored and reconditioned. This place became a favorite Garbo haunt. Saying little, she would sit in the annex by the hour watching the workmen ply their craft.

On her strolls around the city she also frequently dropped in at Hammacher Schlemmer, the fashionable home furnishings-hardware-food emporium on Fifty-seventh Street. For quite some time, her visits were confined mainly to browsing, but after getting her own apartment, which generally presented the impersonal aspect of a public room, she started going to the store almost daily to purchase kitchen utensils,

In Italy with George Schlee, 1954

Tipping baggageman after disembarking from the Gripsholm *in New York, 1954*

glassware and other household items. On her buying expeditions she was often accompanied by Baron Rothschild or Gayelord Hauser, whose advice in making her selections she appeared to welcome. All her purchases at Hammacher Schlemmer were in the reasonable price range. However, at Wynne & Treanor, then a select Madison Avenue food store, she sometimes let herself go, splurging on fresh caviar at around thirty-two dollars a pound; she also indulged her rather singular taste for pressed caviar, which was offered, perhaps because of its resemblance in appearance to black shoe polish, at only twelve dollars a pound. Garbo's other luxuries in food included smoked salmon and pâté de foie gras. Sometimes when she called at Wynne & Treanor she made but a single purchase, such as one can of French soup.

When the weather was inclement, she occasionally passed part of the afternoon at the Plaza Theatre, a small movie house on East Fifty-eighth Street that often showed foreign films. "Garbo doesn't like to be fussed over," the theatre manager once remarked. "If the house is crowded and we offer her a box, she always says, 'Oh thank you,' in a surprised way. She never asks for a box or demands favors the way other actresses do who come here." Without exception, the shopkeepers and business people who have come into contact with Garbo over the years have nothing but admiration for her courtesy and consideration.

Her days were not always spent in a solitary manner. She frequently lunched at the Colony with George Schlee and the John Gunthers or with Baron Rothschild at Maud Chez Elle, a superb, very expensive restaurant then on Second Avenue. Once in a while in the afternoon she dropped in at the Museum of Modern Art to have tea with her bachelor friend Allen Porter. Or she stopped by the apartment of one of her women friends. She never called ahead of time (she has always been loath to make an appointment much more than an hour in advance), and she departed as abruptly as she arrived. A retired professional woman upon whom Garbo used to call every once in a while described her visits by saying, "It's like being friends with a hummingbird. She lights on your hand, and there is this vivid creature, and then she flies away."

During this period, Schlee, Rothschild, Hauser or some other admirer usually took Garbo to dinner, escorting her to a restaurant or to the home of a friend. She generally avoided popular, showy eating places, like Twenty One, where she was likely to be stared at by columnists, expense-account diners and tourists. She had a fondness for two restaurants in the East Fifties—the Viennese Room, which she visited with the Baron about once a week, and Semon's, an establishment that specialized in Brazilian food, where she went about as frequently with Schlee. Always she was a quiet, unobtrusive guest, drinking vodka and wine but only moderately, shyly complimenting the proprietor on the preparation of one of her favorite dishes, such as avocado stuffed with shrimp and crab meat, and demanding no special attention beyond asking please that all the fat be trimmed off the lamb chops.

With Schlee or Rothschild as her escort Garbo went out a good deal socially in the evenings, sufficiently often so that a man who met her at three different parties within a period of two weeks was prompted to describe her as "a hermit about town." At large social affairs, such, for example, as those she attended in the city and country homes of Fleur and Gardner Cowles and Maud and Eustace Seligman, Garbo usually gave the appearance of being at ease and even of enjoying herself. Most of the other guests at such functions she had met before; also, being mainly people of affairs or celebrities, they were not likely to pay her so much attention as to make her uncomfortable. There seemed, in fact, to be a spontaneous conspiracy to pretend that she was just another guest, a considerate idea but impossible, of course, to realize. No matter what Garbo did or said—or didn't do or didn't say—a special radiance surrounded her. "It is about as easy to relax in her presence," a woman who often saw her socially remarked, "as it is with royalty."

Other social acquaintances of that era observed that Garbo could carry on a conversation, especially on an uncomplicated subject like travel, without showing the intense discomfiture that was known to have plagued her in earlier years, but she participated very little in general conversation among a number of people. The few remarks she made were confined as a rule to very brief side comments on the subject under discussion. These utterances, which often seemed to stem from free association of ideas, sometimes made a considerable impression and had an effect perhaps different from what Garbo had intended. She once attended a dinner party at which another guest was Mrs. Henry Ginsberg, wife of a motion picture executive, who came to the party alone because her husband was out of town on business. During dinner, Albert Einstein was being discussed in some connection. "Speaking of Mr. Einstein," Garbo said in a conversational lull, "where is Mr. Ginsberg?" For some reason, this was taken as a hilarious bon mot. The other guests were convulsed. Garbo laughed a little too.

Though Garbo was often seen during the forties and fifties playing the part of a guest, nobody saw her in the role of a hostess. She never entertained. The only person who ever got into her house in Hollywood, according to a standard joke among her friends, was a burglar. (Garbo escaped the intruder by agilely climbing out of her second-story bedroom window and sliding down a drainpipe.) In New York, too, she showed a remarkable consistency in dealing with the problem of social reciprocation by simply avoiding it. Her friends often speculated on why she never entertained. Was it because of her unwillingness to put herself out for anybody, or was it because she didn't know how? Whatever the reason, it mattered little. There were always plenty of people to entertain Garbo.

Thus the decades passed and Garbo drifted and her friends deplored her prodigal squandering of the precious hours on her tiny, unmeaningful pursuits. "There is not enough time for anyone to fulfill the purpose of one's life," a venerable actress said at the time. "But Greta does nothing. She just throws away her days. She always talks about her last picture as her grave, and that is so foolish. Every artist is bound to have successes and failures. One success out of three is a good record. And she had but one failure in her whole life. It is almost criminal. She could have been doing such beautiful things all these years." Garbo knew that, too, of course, and it was one of the reasons for her enduring private melancholy. Her efforts to resume her career were frustrated, like so much else in her existence, and in later years she had no Stiller to fight for her and make things come out right. Alice B. Toklas with her uncanny acumen may have summed it up when she characterized Garbo as "Mademoiselle Hamlet."

Garbo (with sunglasses) on Capri, 1955

The script of Garbo's life would have had a different, though perhaps no happier, finale if she could have allowed herself to be molded into the standardized Hollywood product, sharing her life with the crowd, endorsing soaps and cigarettes, showing herself in public to drum up trade for her pictures and giving interviews to ears that longed only to hear serialized love confessions. Garbo did none of that. She did nothing that was second-rate. She had dignity and nobility, and she had genius. Like so many great actresses, she may never have possessed a particle of intellectual power, but she had genius before the camera because she was guided by a secret, sublime, infallible instinct to do the right thing in the right way. So unerring was her instinct that it produced the illusion of a most subtle intelligence. She was a true artist and she practiced her art, to the extent she was permitted, as she has always lived her life, with a fine indifference to the opinion of the herd. "She is brave, poor Garbo," one of her oldest European friends has said. "She has the braveness to be herself."

Epilogue

Through all the changing scenes of the past decade and a half, Garbo has remained mysteriously and marvelously intact, both as a woman and as a legend. Even her beauty has been but slightly impaired by the ravages of time. Today, at sixty-five, she is still a stunning international ornament. Inevitably, fine lines have begun to appear around her mouth and around her matchless, navy-blue eyes. But the sheen of her hair, the fresh texture of her skin, the litheness of her figure, the vigorous cadence of her walk, the arresting resonance of her voice—all suggest a woman in her very early fifties. "She is so beautiful, *so* beautiful it's incredible," the novelist Irwin Shaw said after dining with her recently. That's the way people were talking about Garbo forty years ago. Her beauty is ageless.

So is her legend. It prospers with every passing year. She does nothing to nourish it, except to go on being her elusive self, which seems to be quite enough. Photographers with long-lens cameras continue to lie in wait on the streets, at airports, and on Mediterranean beaches in the hope of snapping the face of the century. On the rare occasions when they succeed, the results are published around the world. Any news relating, however remotely, to what the critic Richard Whitehall has called "the cinema's most beautiful memory" is duly reported in the press. In 1967, the Stockholm apartment house in which Garbo grew up was demolished to make way for a road improvement; American and European newspapers conscientiously informed their readers of this momentous event.

The news stories in which Garbo continues to figure most often involve her rumored return to the screen. Though she hasn't made a picture in thirty years—and almost certainly will never make another —movie producers on three continents have never ceased trying to entice her out of retirement. During the past fifteen years, she has been reported to be interested in starring in no less than a dozen films. As recently as February, 1971, widespread publicity was given to reports that she had indirectly approached Luchino Visconti, the Italian film director, to express her interest in playing the role of the Queen of Naples in Visconti's production of Proust's *A la Recherche du Temps Perdu.* As usual, nothing further developed. Garbo's decision to remain in retirement has been a wise one, in the opinion of James Mason, who was to have played opposite her in a film version of Balzac's *La Duchesse de Langeais,* the ill-fated project that most nearly succeeded, in 1948, in bringing Garbo back to the screen. "I think she would have to be ever so dotty to make another film," Mason told a friend in London recently. "Her memory is so gorgeous. Her last picture—that concoction called *Two-Faced Woman*—may have been unfortunate, appearing in a bathing suit and so on. Nevertheless, there is hardly a foot of her film that is not beautiful, and so it should remain." Garbo evidently agrees. Nowadays, when anyone suggests that she ought to make another film, she habitually replies, with seeming modesty, "What can you do with an old actress?" Her friends have heard this often. "It's just a throwaway line," one of them has said. "Actually, she is very conscious indeed of her position and her fame and her legendary situation, but she uses that stock response because it puts an end to the discussion, which is what she wants."

During the past decade and a half, Garbo's fame, far from fading, has flourished. The 1960s, in particular, were vintage years for the Garbo legend. It was during this period that she was, in a professional sense, quite miraculously reborn. Through the widespread showing of her films on television and at "Garbo Festivals" both here and abroad, she became a star to a whole new generation—"the generation," as *Vogue* put it, "that Never Knew."

The revival began in the summer of 1963, when the Empire Theatre, in London, put on a five-week season of Garbo films. They set a box-office record for the theatre. "I've never been so flabbergasted," the manager told reporters. "At my age—fifty-three—you can't help being a Garbo fan. But three out of four of the customers seeing these films are young people pulled in by curiosity. They come out raving about Garbo."

The same year, the State-subsidized television network in Italy showed *Anna Karenina, Camille,* and three other Garbo films on five successive Sunday evenings. The films were watched by some ten million people—nearly the maximum Italian television audience. The country's movie houses were suddenly quite empty on Sunday nights, usually their busiest night in the week. The drop in business was so precipitous that the movie exhibitors in Rome closed their theatres for twenty-four hours in what was called an "anti-Garbo-on-TV" strike. Meanwhile, the Italian newspapers had taken up the Garbo phenomenon. "The Fascination of Garbo Is Unchanged While All Around Her Has Crumpled," said one. "Why Garbo Still Bewitches the Public," headlined another in red type over a full-page story. The noted Italian movie director, Michelangelo Antonioni, also essayed the timeless task of trying to analyze Garbo's bewitchment. Basically, he decided, it came down to the fact that we "are intrigued to discover the enduring validity of female beauty amidst the moral chaos of our era."

As the decade moved on, this intriguing discovery was made by other millions who flocked to Garbo festivals from Paris to Los Angeles and in many points between. The most ambitious revival was staged in 1968 by the Museum of Modern Art, in New York, which put on a unique and, except for *The Divine Woman* (a print of which could not, for some unexplained reason, be found), complete retrospective of Garbo's film career. The program included twenty-six feature films. Within four days of the announcement of the festival, all of the twelve thousand tickets had been sold. Even so, long queues waited outside the auditorium before every performance in the hope that a seat would somehow become available. In 1969, *two* theatres in London's fashionable West End presented Garbo festivals simultaneously, thus bringing to a fitting crescendo a renaissance without parallel in the history of motion pictures.

It was not only the public that gave the returning Garbo a triumphant welcome. The movie critics—an entirely new generation of them—also celebrated her remarkable resurgence. With few exceptions, their critical reactions ranged all the way from praise to breathless praise. Like their predecessors in the thirties, the younger critics vied with one another in celebrating Garbo's beauty, especially her face —"the furthest stage to which the human face could progress," said one British critic, "the nth degree of structural refinement, complexity, mystery, and strength," while an American critic found Garbo's face "the synthesis of all desires—straight nose, articulating nostrils, the wide, soft mouth, the eyes flashing every frequency from infra-red to ultra-violet, the palpable cheeks that are subtle breasts for the body of her face, the curve of her chin and jaw that closes off the whole form with a ravishing flourish of authority." The neck, according to another of the younger American critics, was also rather special, being "somewhere between a swan's and a goose's, a flight in the air as of doves." To which an English movie reviewer, himself taking wing, added that the effect "when she undulates her swan neck and dips and lifts her sumptuous, milky shoulders rising from the lace of a sweepingly low-cut corsage is sheer intoxication, evoking that tear-pricking, lump-in-the-throat, low, joyous gasp of gratitude that here could be a creature so divinely *right*."

It was left to Jack Kroll, writing in *Newsweek,* to explain why Garbo still unhinges people this way. "Her genius," he wrote at the time of the Modern Museum's festival, "was to be all possible objects of desire—innocence, experience, strength, passivity, tenderness, cruelty . . . Garbo was something that the male of the species never expected to encounter in this world; but when he did, he realized in his bowels that without possessing this creature he would never be complete. When Plato spoke of the desire and pursuit of the whole, he was talking about Garbo. She was Woman—the beginning and end and all of the middles."

If Garbo read Mr. Kroll's rhapsody or any of the other recent paeans, she has never let on. In fact, people who see her frequently have never heard her utter a word about any aspect of the fantastic revival. One friend, unable to restrain himself, did bring up the subject over drinks one afternoon a while ago, saying something about how thrilling it must be once again to be the toast of the cinematic world. Garbo's reply was brief. "I don't get a penny out of it," she said.

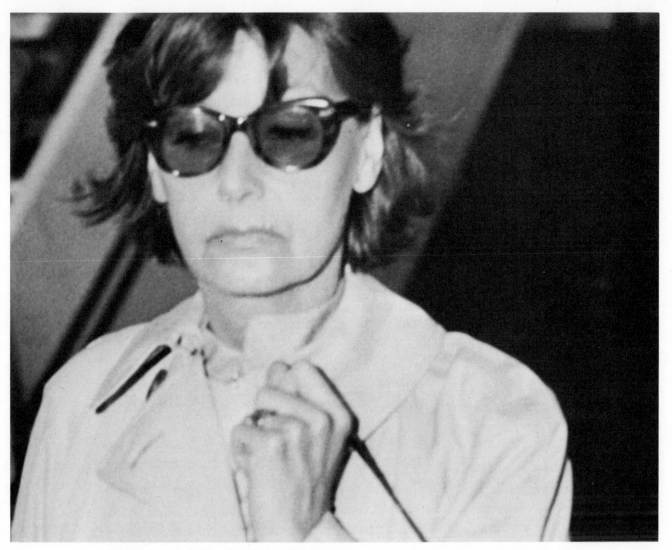

Boarding plane at New York airport, 1956

"Le Roc" (foreground)

In her personal life, no less than in her continued aloofness to her professional career, Garbo has remained remarkably consistent during the past fifteen years. Her existence remains as supremely self-centered, as aimless, and as filled with trivialities as it has been since she began her retirement. She is still, as she said of herself years ago, "sort of drifting." She spends a good deal of her time traveling. To judge by her itineraries, she has only a modicum of interest in seeing new places. Her trips usually take her back to the same places in Europe—the Riviera and Paris, less occasionally to London, and rarely to Sweden —that she has been going to ever since she elected the life of total leisure. Until the fall of 1964, she was generally accompanied on her travels by George Schlee, whose wife, Valentina, continued to remain, from all outward appearances, admirably serene about the arrangement.

As a rule, Garbo and Schlee spent most of the summer at Cap-d'Ail, on the Riviera, living in a villa aptly named "Le Roc." Bleakly situated at the tip of a peninsula of sheer rock, the square-shaped building looked quite unattractive from the outside, but Valentina had decorated the interior with great charm and style. Though the villa was generally referred to in the neighborhood as "Garbo's house," it had been bought and was owned by Schlee. Garbo and Schlee kept to themselves, pointedly avoiding their neighbors, and never, as far as they happened to notice, entertaining any guests. Residents nearby were aware that Garbo usually took an early morning swim, after a maid had reconnoitered the area to make sure that it was clear of prowling photographers. Doffing a white terry-cloth robe, Garbo, clad only in rather long swimming trunks, would plunge into the water. She also preferred to be topless when sunning near the villa.

Besides idling about "Le Roc," Garbo and Schlee often went cruising on yachts belonging to various friends, including Aristotle Onassis (in the late fifties, Winston Churchill was also frequently among the other guests), Ricardo Sicre, a Spanish financier, and Sam Spiegel, the movie producer. "Schlee was like a manager," one of the seafaring hosts has recalled. "He had absolute control. When he didn't want to do something, they didn't do it, no matter how she felt about it. On the boat, she was always very pleasant, very gay, very amusing.

She didn't talk a great deal. You might have thought that she was in the clouds, not really listening, and then she would make some comment that would show she had been following it all right along. She liked very much to get compliments from men. This made Schlee very upset. He was as jealous as the devil. I don't think he could tolerate having her exposed to other people, especially to interesting or attractive men. Whenever that happened—and it happened several times—he would invent some excuse for cutting the trip short. He'd say he'd forgotten about having to get back to meet a lawyer or a banker from New York, or something of the sort. So, we would put into a port, and he would hire a car to take them back to their place. She never objected, never spoke a contrary word. Schlee dominated her completely."

During the first week of October, 1964, Garbo and Schlee arrived in Paris from the Riviera, and checked into adjoining rooms at the Crillon Hotel. The following day, Schlee, who had not been in good health for a couple of years, died suddenly of a heart attack. "I'm afraid Garbo didn't cope very well," a friend has since remarked. "She packed her bags and fled to a friend's place." Valentina, escorted by a pair of New York bachelors, flew to Paris to claim her husband's body and accompany it back to New York. She let it be known that Garbo would not be welcome on the same plane or at the funeral. "Valentina doesn't feel she has to put on a show any longer," a friend has said. "First, she rid the villa of photographs and mementoes and all other relics of Garbo. Then she put the place up for sale. Not only that. She called in a Greek Orthodox priest to exorcise Garbo's presence from her—Valentina's—New York apartment. I understand the exorcising was very complete, including even the refrigerator. Apparently Garbo was in the habit of looking in there for snacks." Though Valentina and Garbo continue to live in the same apartment building, they both now take elaborate precautions to avoid meeting in the lobby or in the elevator.

Garbo was deeply affected by Schlee's death, so much so that she was, as one of her friends put it, "in deep mourning." The depth of her grief surprised some people who had known her for a great many years. It was the first time they had seen her weep. "If she loved him, she didn't realize it until afterwards," one of her old but less reverent friends has said. "My personal opinion is that she isn't capable of love. What she probably missed was the companionship and sense of protection he provided. She has always needed a sort of Big Daddy in the background."

Left without her special friend and protector, Garbo has taken up with some of her companions of earlier days, including Gayelord Hauser, the lively dietitian who once pursued the improbable goal of making Garbo his wife. Thanks, apparently, to his continued intake of blackstrap molasses, yogurt, and other "living" foods, Hauser, at seventy-five and still a bachelor, remains full of bounce, and is noticeably pleased to resume the role of occasional escort. Garbo spent the summer following Schlee's death cruising among the Greek islands with two other old friends, Cecil Beaton and Baroness Cecile de Roths-

With George Schlee in Paris, 1956

child, on the latter's yacht. The Baroness, a daughter of a French banker, is a white-haired, self-assured, cosmopolitan woman, who has made a reputation as a connoisseur of objets d'art and of people. Being the kind of person who is accustomed to taking command, she was the one to whom Garbo turned when Schlee was stricken, and it was to her Paris residence that Garbo repaired.

The Baroness is among the select few who visit Garbo in her apartment, and are entrusted with her private telephone number. Possession of the number does not, however, guarantee getting through to its owner. As often as not, Garbo will answer the phone, and even if the caller's voice is as instantly recognizable as, for example, Cecil Beaton's, she will reply in the impersonal tone of a maid, "Miss Garbo isn't in. Is there a message?" Not all of her friends find this little conceit amusing.

In the past few years, Garbo has also resumed her friendship with Salka Viertel, the Polish-born actress and writer, who was probably Garbo's closest confidant and adviser during her years in Hollywood. Mrs. Viertel now lives in Klosters, the famous ski resort in Switzerland, where her son, Peter, a writer, and his wife, Deborah Kerr, and their family also make their residence. Garbo now customarily spends several weeks in Klosters during the fall. At that season, the village is virtually deserted of visitors; she can accordingly move about freely without attracting attention, and thus probably behave more naturally than she can anywhere else. But what really attracts Garbo to Klosters is, of course, the presence of Mrs. Viertel. Now in her early eighties, small, white-haired and elegant, she remains a woman of great charm, dignity and generosity. "For Garbo, Salka is like a nanny," a friend who sees them often in Klosters has said. "She looks after her. In a way, it's like a daughter coming home."

When Garbo first started sojourning in Klosters, Mrs. Viertel, who lives very modestly in a small chalet, arranged for Garbo to use the apartment belonging to Anatole Litvak, the movie director. He later sold his place to Gore Vidal, the novelist, and since he, like Garbo, also enjoys being in Klosters in the fall, Mrs. Viertel was obliged to find other quarters for her. She called several friends who have apartments or chalets in the village, and asked if Garbo "could have" one of them for a few weeks. The matter of rent wasn't mentioned. At length, Mrs. Viertel made arrangements for Garbo to use the apartment owned by Comte Frederic Chandon de Briailles, familiarly known as Freddy, who is vice president of the Moet & Chandon champagne firm and a friend of Peter Viertel. The apartment of "F. Chandon," as the nameplate reads, is one of four in a two-story chalet that is about a ten-minute walk from the center of the village. The building looks toward the public tennis courts, where Garbo occasionally plays tennis with one of Mrs. Viertel's granddaughters.

In addition to finding pleasant living quarters on ideal terms, Mrs. Viertel also provides the kind of social setting that Garbo finds agreeable, one that is interesting, circumspect and untaxing. She has the chance to meet all kinds of people—writers, artists, musicians—who come to visit Mrs. Viertel as well as her and the Peter Viertels' friends who maintain residences in the village—among them, Gore Vidal, Robert Parrish, the film director, and his wife, and Irwin Shaw. Garbo appears to be at ease with all of them, especially with Shaw. "Irwin has a very good way with her," one of the Klosters group has said. "He's jolly and a little bit flirty, and she likes that." Shaw occasionally takes Garbo and Mrs. Viertel to lunch at the Chesa Grischuna, the most fashionable hotel in Klosters, and Garbo has also often been among the dinner guests at his chalet. "One night when she was leaving, I kidded her," Shaw has recalled. "I said, 'Look, Greta, I've entertained you umpteen times at my house. Now it's time for you to entertain me.' You know what? She did—in style. She gave a dinner party for twelve of us in the bar at the Chesa. And she was such a conscientious hostess that she arrived there at six o'clock and hovered about to make sure everything was exactly right."

Normally, Garbo's life in Klosters is as uneventful as it usually is anywhere else. She rises early, and eats a light breakfast. She whiles away the early morning reading the newspapers, though she almost never speaks of anything she has seen in them. About ten-thirty, she sets off for her daily walk into town. As she strode toward the village one crisp morning not long ago, she was wearing rather large dark

On the Riviera with Aristotle Onassis, 1957

glasses, a black pea jacket, a white turtleneck sweater, beige slacks, and soft-soled shoes. Over her shoulder she carried a brown-leather bag. Her light-brown hair, worn slightly less than shoulder length, was combed back and held by a black ribbon. Smaller in stature and thinner in the face than one remembers her from the films, she looked as chic as ever.

Reaching the main street, she stopped to look in the window of a boutique called Zimba, which specializes in sports clothes, and then went inside. She looked at sweaters, scarves and other things on display. Speaking in a very soft and pleasant voice, she asked the clerk to see some wool stockings. She bought one pair. As a rule, she doesn't act with such haste in making a purchase. When, the year before, she decided to buy a parka, Mrs. Viertel went with her to every clothes shop in town, not once but several times, before Garbo finally made up her mind.

Back on the street, she looked in the windows of a couple of other shops, and then stopped in the Speiss butcher shop, as is her daily custom, and bought one small steak. A half block away, she entered a tobacconist-newspaper shop, bought a couple of newspapers and thanked the proprietress. (Garbo's friends continue to be impressed by her unfailing courtesy to clerks, servants and others in similar positions.) Outside again, she headed toward home, passing the Cinema Rex, which she has never been known to attend, and onto a walk through an open field where beginners' ski classes are held in winter. Her day's work was finished.

Though Garbo is occasionally invited out to lunch, she normally takes it at home alone, eating her steak. She relaxes for a while, and then goes for a walk, always alone, on one of the mountain paths. On the afternoon walks, she strides even more vigorously than she does on the morning outings. Like an athlete, she often carries an extra sweater or two, putting them on and taking them off when she moves from the shade to the sun and back again. She prefers the lower and safer, if less scenic, paths; this is sensible, since the purpose of her walk is not sightseeing but exercise, which she considers a daily must. As always, she takes very good care of herself, except for rather heavy cigarette smoking, a lifelong habit that she apparently doesn't intend to change. To the best of her friends' knowledge, the only time she has suffered any serious physical ailment was in 1962, when, for a period of time, she had twice-weekly treatments for arthritis at New York University's Medical Center. Though she now seems to be in excellent health, she is, as one of her friends has said, "wildly hypochondriacal," and never tires of discussing her ailments, real or imagined, often with childish frankness.

After her walk in the mountains, Garbo takes a short nap, and in the late afternoon goes to Mrs. Viertel's chalet for tea. This is the high spot of Garbo's day. There are usually other guests, often film or literary friends of Mrs. Viertel. If they are strangers to Garbo, she doesn't seem to enjoy herself as much as she does when only Mrs. Viertel and some of her local women friends are present. On these days, Garbo is relaxed and quite talkative. "It's just sort of girl talk," one of the guests has said. "I remember once she said that she never wears a brassiere. I guess that makes her pretty up to date, come to think of it. There's a little giggling and chatter. One day she said that on her walk in the mountains a man had chased her or waved at her with a cane. It wasn't quite clear what had happened, but she made quite a production of it. 'Oh, it's ruined everything,' she said, looking very sad. Another time, she told us that on her walk she had met a woman with a mustache. She said, 'She was one of the most beautiful women I have ever seen.' We didn't know whether this was supposed to be a joke, or what. Nobody laughed."

Garbo doesn't usually enliven the teas with such interesting contributions. Her conversation is normally concerned with less exciting matters, such as her plans to buy a new sweater, her satisfaction with a new pair of walking shoes, or where she plans to hike the following day. "She talks only about herself, but she doesn't talk about herself at all," one of her tea companions has said. "In other words, she talks almost exclusively about things that relate to herself but only in an impersonal way—her walks, her shopping plans and so forth—but never a word about her thoughts or ideas or hopes or anything else that would be self-revealing in any way."

Garbo's day usually ends when the tea ends, though she may once in a while attend a small party, such as the champagne-and-caviar do that Gore Vidal laid on after buying his Klosters residence. Since champagne and caviar happen to be two of Garbo's favorites, she didn't stint herself on the refreshments. Becoming very merry, she laughed and made little jokes in her rather heavy-handed way. "She was much struck by Gore," one of the other guests has said. "She was all giggles and flirting like a schoolgirl." She invited Vidal to sit by her near a front window, and talked about the days when she had lived in the same apartment. "This is where I used to curl up every night and have a whisky and watch the people of Klosters," she said, casually striking a pose as memorable as something from one of her films. That the scene from the window embraced nothing more memorable than a grocery store and a tobacco shop only added to the poignancy of the line.

Though obviously enjoying herself, Garbo left the party shortly after nine, and walked home alone in the late twilight. She likes to get to bed not later than nine-thirty. She once puzzled a friend in Klosters by remarking that she didn't know where any of the light switches were located in Chandon's apartment. It was one of her typically offhand remarks that don't require a reply, but it stuck in her friend's mind. She

On the Riviera, 1958

subsequently concluded that the reason Garbo didn't know the location of the switches was that she was always in bed before it was dark, and so had no need for artificial light. "I suppose it's some kind of index to the life she leads," the friend said.

When the skiing season approaches and Klosters begins to fill with people, Garbo returns to New York, and melts into what she considers its agreeable anonymity. She still lives in the same seven-room cooperative apartment, at 450 East Fifty-second Street ("I had a hard time getting this apartment," she once told a friend. "They don't like actresses in this building"), which she has occupied for nearly twenty years. The living room has been made more attractive in recent years, thanks in part to her acquisition of some additional very good paintings, including a Modigliani. The other rooms retain their spare, rather institutional look—"Swedish Impersonal," as one visitor has described their decor. Garbo doesn't like having servants about, and gets along with the services of a cleaning woman who comes in twice a week. On the rare, though in recent years slightly more frequent, occasions when Garbo invites one or more of her friends for drinks or what passes for a meal (usually something from a delicatessen), she manages the uncomplicated hostess tasks herself. The fact that it's cheaper that way is only an incidental consideration, but still a consideration. Though she is several times a millionairess, she is disinclined to spend money unnecessarily, except occasionally on herself. Once, after she had purchased a pair of very expensive sweaters at Sulka, she remarked to her shopping companion, "And I am supposed to be so mean." What seems to be her constitutional inability to give money, either publicly or privately, or time, of which she has an abundance, to help anybody or any charitable organization continues to be a source of nagging concern to some of her less retentive friends. "My God!" one of them exclaimed when the subject came up not long ago. "Doesn't she *ever* think of anybody but herself?" None of her circle has a clue to her plans, if any, for bequeathing her fortune.

For many New Yorkers, the possibility of seeing Garbo on the street ranks high among the city's dwindling public attractions. The chances of catching a glimpse of "the most famous solitary of the century," as one of her phrase-making admirers has described her, are as good today as they ever were, for she is still in the habit of taking a daily midtown walk. It varies in length from about two to four miles, depending on the weather and her mood. She follows no fixed route, though she generally nowadays stays within a rectangle bounded by Seventy-ninth and Forty-second Streets on north and south and First and Fifth Avenues on east and west. Her favorites are Third, Fifth and Madison. Except for occasional purchases at a health-food store, she doesn't buy much, but she pauses frequently to look in the windows of shops, especially those displaying antiques and paintings. Actually, almost anything, from a poster in the window of a travel bureau to a booklet on inflation in a bank window, will momentarily engage her attention. Her visits to the Parke-Bernet Galleries, once an almost regular weekly ritual, have become less frequent, probably because she likes to have a companion when she goes there, and there are fewer of them now.

On her random walks about the city these days, Garbo customarily wears conventional street clothes—a dress, a coat or jacket, a modified face-concealing hat (or in warm weather, a kerchief), low-heeled shoes and plain dark glasses—that are intended to make her unobtrusive. To a certain extent, they do, because the world has now caught up with the casual style that has been hers since the thirties. She not only fits the contemporary scene, she did much to create it. Trousers, turtleneck sweaters, dark glasses, see-through blouses—she was wearing them all decades ago. Despite her intentionally plain everyday clothes, there is something about Garbo's ambiance that causes her to be recognized by passersby. They react to the experience in different ways. Jackson Pollock, the noted abstract painter, was walking with friends on Third Avenue one spring afternoon when Garbo strode past. Without a word, Pollock abruptly turned around and followed her; his friends didn't see him again that day. The responses to a Garbo encounter are generally less dramatic, usually ranging from a look of wide-eyed surprise to an audible gasp and perhaps the whispering of her name. However the shock of recognition manifests itself, Garbo pretends not to notice, and goes on her silent way.

Garbo's days are not always spent alone. She may lunch at the Colony with Jane Gunther, the widow of the late writer, or have a healthful snack with Gayelord Hauser or go to to some small, fashionable restaurant with the Baroness Rothschild, if she happens to be in town. With her walk, an occasional lunch and other scattered but time-filling pursuits, Garbo manages the daylight hours, but the evenings, without Schlee, are more difficult. As a consequence, she appears on the New York social scene much less frequently at present than she did when he was her escort. Many of her evenings are now spent at home alone watching television. However, if she is no longer a hermit about town, she has by no means become a recluse. She still goes out for drinks or dinner at the homes of old friends, and she enjoys an impromptu outing when she's in the mood for it. One of her friends, an artist, telephoned her on a beautiful Sunday in autumn, and asked if she'd like to take a

On a recent vacation in Europe

drive with him around downtown New York, which, he explained, is quite picturesque and practically deserted on weekends.

"Do you think I should?" she asked.

"Yes, I think you should. It would be good for you."

"All right," Garbo said. "I will walk past your apartment in half an hour."

The artist met her on the street, and they spent a leisurely afternoon visiting Trinity Church and other sights of interest in Lower Manhattan, including a street market, where vendors were selling clothes and a variety of other goods. Garbo bought herself some woolen underwear, and they walked around for a while, looking at the other merchandise as well as at the old buildings in the area before driving back uptown. "It was a very nice little expedition," the artist has said. "She can make the time pass very pleasantly and be very good company indeed. The basic thing about her is the integrity. You're aware of that always. Also, of course, you're always sensitive about her anonymity, and that makes you a little self-conscious. This is too bad, because she can be very human. The trouble is that she isn't allowed to be, at least in our own minds."

One of Garbo's idiosyncracies that still tries the patience of even her most devoted friends is her habit of vacillating about accepting social invitations that are not strictly impromptu. This practice has now developed to the place where it can unnerve the coolest hostess in town. When Garbo receives an invitation, she may accept at once, call up later and decline, change her mind again and perhaps even once again and, finally, appear or not, depending apparently on her mood at the last minute. "She can drive you right up the wall," a New York hostess with much Garbo experience has said. "But once she arrives at the party, you know it's been worth all the agony. She always looks stunning, and when she wishes, she really puts herself out to be pleasant and agreeable." One of the people for whom Garbo put herself out much more than usual was Jacqueline Kennedy, whom she met at a dinner party before Mrs. Kennedy's marriage to Onassis. Though Garbo has never expressed any interest in politics, she did respond to the Kennedy charisma. "She seemed to have very affectionate feelings toward both Jack and Jackie," a friend has said. "I think she admired them the way she would admire highly professional theatrical people." At the dinner party, Garbo was at her most amiable and charming, and the two women seemed to get along very well. Rather early in the evening, Garbo rose and said, jokingly, to the hostess, "I must go. I am getting intoxicated." After she had left, Mrs. Kennedy, who was obviously not attuned to Garbo's rather simple notion of humor, said, "I think she was."

However limited her own repertoire of drawing room wit and humor, Garbo responds quickly to funny stories and anecdotes told by others. Though not prudish, she is visibly offended by coarse language. At a dinner party not long ago, she sat opposite a famous author who had drunk well but not wisely and whose conversation had become rather gamey. Garbo turned him off by ceasing to pay him any attention, pretending, in effect, that he didn't exist. She is very much aware that she continues to be a priceless addition to any social gathering, and has long since become accustomed to being recognized instantly by everyone

In England, 1965

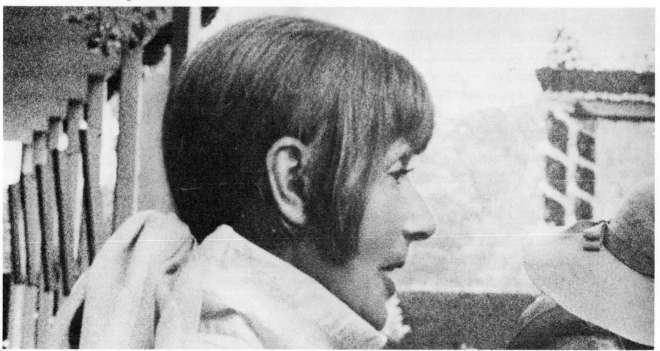

At a wedding in France, 1970

present. She is genuinely surprised if, as happened at a party in New York a couple of years ago, someone doesn't. "You know," she said to the hostess afterwards, "that man didn't even know who I was." Nowadays, Garbo usually arrives at parties alone and leaves alone. "Many times, I have asked if I could take her home," a man who frequently attends the same affairs has said. "She always says, 'Oh, thank you so much. I can manage.' You often wonder how she gets home."

That isn't the only thing that people who have known Garbo for a long time still wonder about. One recent afternoon, she was having a drink with a friend on the terrace of his New York apartment and chatting, as usual, about small, impersonal matters. There came a gap in the conversation. The silence was broken when Garbo, apropos of nothing that had been touched upon before, said, "I am a lonely man circling the earth."

Her host, a man of notable directness, said, "What do you mean by that?"

Garbo took a sip of her vodka. "Someday," she said, "I will tell you how it is with me." She smiled briefly, and changed the subject.

None of Garbo's friends would think of urging her to explain the teasing, arcane remarks that she sometimes makes any more readily than they would consider inquiring about her habit of referring to herself in the masculine gender. "You know," Garbo is apt to say, excusing her early departure from a party, "he's got to be in bed by nine-thirty." Speaking of smoking, she often says, "I have been smoking since I was a small boy." She seems amused at times by the effect of quips like these on people she is with. "She says something like that, and then sort of laughs," one of her New York escorts has said.

What George Cukor, who was probably Garbo's favorite director, recently called "Garbo's own brand of eroticism" came through strongly to the younger generation of critics. Penelope Gilliatt, reflecting on the matter, wrote: "She always seems miles beyond the boundaries of sex, equally and pityingly remote from the men who are in love with her and the women who are vying with her . . . She droops like a girl, strides like a man, has the concave chest of an English schoolboy, and carries her beautiful shoulders as though they were a yoke of milk

Garbo walks alone in Klosters on her sixty-fifth birthday

pails. She looks ravishing in Camille's ball-dresses and heroic in long boots, but only moderately at home in any clothes at all." In a word, Garbo has always been an original, on the screen or off.

In spite of a few small revelations from time to time, Garbo's inner life remains as essentially private at sixty-five as it was at twenty-five. ("One almost feels grateful to Garbo for keeping herself so resolutely to herself, for leaving us a little mystery," Joan Crawford recently remarked.) To this day, it is doubtful that anybody really understands how Garbo's mind works or what she thinks about fundamental matters, if indeed she thinks about them at all. "She has the native intelligence typical of a peasant," Marlene Dietrich once observed, in what may not be remembered as the most dispassionate judgment ever made. Even Garbo's close friends can, at times, find her behavior less attractively mystifying than mildly exasperating. "She never does anything that's bad or unruly or very interesting," one of her oldest New York friends said recently. "You might think she was more like a well-trained child. But then you see her, and you realize all over again that there's just nothing on earth like her."

Ultimately, of course, how Garbo stands in the opinion of her friends, what she thinks, how she spends her days and nights—such matters are of no importance. What matters is her uniqueness as an actress. Her legacy is the artistry preserved in her films, and they, as recent events have amply proved, will endure. "She is the true immortal," David Robinson, one of the perceptive younger critics, wrote in 1969. "Other legends and other goddesses crumble and fade into loveable or laughable antiques; but Garbo miraculously remains."

The Films of Greta Garbo

European

1. COMMERCIAL FILMS

In 1921, Greta Garbo made her first appearance before a motion picture camera in an advertising film made for Paul U. Bergström's department store, in Stockholm; the picture was produced by Hasse W. Tullbergs and directed by Captain Ragnar Ring. In 1922, Greta Garbo appeared in another commercial film, this one to advertise the products of the Consumers' Cooperative Association of Stockholm; the picture was produced by Fribergs Filmbryå and directed by Captain Ragnar Ring.

2. LUFFAR-PETTER (PETER THE TRAMP)

A comedy written, directed and produced by Erik A. Petschler. Premiere: Odeon Theatre, Stockholm, December 26, 1922.

Fire Lieutenant Erik Silverjälm	Erik A. Petschler
Max August Petterson (alias Luffar-Petter)	
Greta	Greta Gustafsson (Greta Garbo)
Artillery Captain	Helmer Larsson
Police Officer	Fredrik Olsson
Tyra	Tyra Ryman
Mayor's Wife	Gucken Cederborg

3. GÖSTA BERLING'S SAGA

Adapted from the novel by Selma Lagerlöf. Scenario by Mauritz Stiller and Ragnar Hyltén-Cavallius. Camera, Julius Jaenzon. Produced by Svensk Filmindustri. Directed by Mauritz Stiller. Premiere: Röda Kvarn, Stockholm, March 10, 1924.

Gösta Berling	Lars Hanson
Majorskan Samzelius	Gerda Lundeqvist
Major Samzelius	Otto Elg-Lundberg

Melchior Sinclaire	Sixten Malmerfelt
Gustafva Sinclaire	Karin Swanström
Marianne Sinclaire	Jenny Hasselqvist
Countess Martha Dohna	Ellen Cederström
Countess Ebba Dohna	Mona Mårtenson
Count Henrik Dohna	Torsten Hammeren
Countess Elisabeth Dohna	Greta Garbo

4. DIE FREUDLOSE GASSE

(Shown in the United States as THE STREET OF SORROW; in England as THE JOYLESS STREET)

Adapted from the novel by Hugo Bettauer. Scenario by Willy Haas. Camera, Guido Seeber. Produced by Sofar-Film. Directed by G. W. Pabst. Premiere: Mozartsaal, Berlin, May 18, 1925.

Councillor Franz Rumfort	Jaro Furth
Butcher of Merchior Street	Werner Krauss
Maria Lechner	Asta Nielsen
Greta Rumfort	Greta Garbo
Frau Greifer	Valeska Gert
Lieutenant Davy	Einar Hanson
Regina Rosenow	Agnes Esterhazy
Rosa Rumfort	Loni Nest

American

Note: All of Greta Garbo's American films were produced by Metro-Goldwyn-Mayer.

1. THE TORRENT

Adapted from the novel by Blasco-Ibáñez. Scenario by Dorothy Farnum. Camera, William Daniels. Directed by Monta Bell. New York Premiere: Capitol Theater, February 21, 1926.

Leonora	Greta Garbo
Don Rafael Brull	Ricardo Cortez

Remedios	Gertrude Olmstead
Pedro Moreno	Edward Connelly
Cupido	Lucien Littlefield
Doña Bernarda Brull	Martha Mattox
Doña Pepa	Lucy Beaumont
Don Andreas	Tully Marshall

2. THE TEMPTRESS

Adapted from the novel by Blasco-Ibáñez. Scenario by Dorothy Farnum.
Camera, Tony Gaudio. Directed in part by Mauritz Stiller and completed by
Fred Niblo. New York Premiere: Capitol Theater, October 10, 1926.

Elena	Greta Garbo
Robledo	Antonio Moreno
Manos Duros	Roy D'Arcy
M. Fontenoy	Marc McDermott
Canterac	Lionel Barrymore
Celinda	Virginia Brown Faire
Torre Blanca	Armand Kaliz
Josephine	Alys Murrell

3. FLESH AND THE DEVIL

Adapted from Hermann Sudermann's novel, *The Undying Past*. Scenario by
Benjamin Glazer. Film Editor, Lloyd Nosler. Camera, William Daniels.
Directed by Clarence Brown. New York Premiere: Capitol Theater, January 9,
1927.

Felicitas Van Kletzingk	Greta Garbo
Leo Von Sellinthin	John Gilbert
Ulrich Von Kletzingk	Lars Hanson
Hertha Prochvitz	Barbara Kent
Uncle Kutowski	William Orlamond
Pastor Breckenburg	George Fawcett
Leo's Mother	Eugenie Besserer
Count Von Rhaden	Marc McDermott

4. LOVE

Adapted from Leo Tolstoy's novel, *Anna Karenina*. Scenario by Frances Marion. Film Editor, Hugh Wynn. Camera, William Daniels. Directed by Edmund Goulding. New York Premiere: Embassy Theater, November 29, 1927.

Anna Karenina	Greta Garbo
Vronsky	John Gilbert
Grand Duke	George Fawcett
Grand Duchess	Emily Fitzroy
Karenin	Brandon Hurst
Seresha	Philippe de Lacy

5. THE DIVINE WOMAN

Adapted from Gladys Unger's play, *Starlight*. Scenario by Dorothy Farnum. Film Editor, Conrad Nervig. Camera, Oliver Marsh. Directed by Victor Seastrom. New York Premiere: Capitol Theater, January 14, 1928.

Marianne	Greta Garbo
Lucien	Lars Hanson
M. Legrande	Lowell Sherman
Mme. Pigonier	Polly Moran
Mme. Zizi Rouck	Dorothy Cumming
Jean Lery	John Mack Brown
Gigi	Cesare Gravina
Paulette	Paulette Duval

6. THE MYSTERIOUS LADY

Adapted from Ludwig Wolff's novel, *War in the Dark*. Scenario by Bess Meredyth. Film Editor, Margaret Booth. Camera, William Daniels. Directed by Fred Niblo. New York Premiere: Capitol Theater, August 4, 1928.

Tania	Greta Garbo
Karl	Conrad Nagel
General Alexandroff	Gustav von Seyffertitz
Colonel Von Raden	Edward Connelly
Max	Albert Pollet
General's Aide	Richard Alexander

7. A WOMAN OF AFFAIRS

Adapted from Michael Arlen's novel, *The Green Hat*. Scenario by Bess
Meredyth. Film Editor, Hugh Wynn. Camera, William Daniels. Directed by
Clarence Brown. New York Premiere: Capitol Theater, January 19, 1929.

Diana	Greta Garbo
Neville	John Gilbert
Hugh	Lewis Stone
David	John Mack Brown
Geoffrey	Douglas Fairbanks, Jr.
Sir Montague	Hobart Bosworth
Constance	Dorothy Sebastian

8. WILD ORCHIDS

Adapted from an original screen story by John Colton. Scenario by Hans Kraly,
Richard Schayer and Willis Goldbeck. Film Editor, Conrad Nervig. Camera,
William Daniels. Directed by Sidney Franklin. New York Premiere: Capitol
Theater, March 30, 1929.

Lillie Sterling	Greta Garbo
John Sterling	Lewis Stone
Prince De Gace	Nils Asther

9. THE SINGLE STANDARD

Adapted from the novel by Adela Rogers St. Johns. Scenario by Josephine
Lovett. Film Editor, Blanche Sewell. Camera, Oliver Marsh. Directed by John S.
Robertson. New York Premiere: Capitol Theater, July 27, 1929.

Arden Stuart	Greta Garbo
Packy Cannon	Nils Asther
Tommy Hewlett	John Mack Brown
Mercedes	Dorothy Sebastian
Ding Stuart	Lane Chandler
Anthony Kendall	Robert Castle
Mr. Glendenning	Mahlon Hamilton
Mrs. Glendenning	Kathlyn Williams

10. THE KISS

Adapted from an original screen story by George M. Saville. Scenario by Hans Kraly. Film Editor, Ben Lewis. Camera, William Daniels. Directed by Jacques Feyder. New York Premiere: Capitol Theater, November 15, 1929.

Mme. Irène Guarry	Greta Garbo
André	Conrad Nagel
M. Guarry	Anders Randolf
Lassalle	Holmes Herbert
Pierre	Lew Ayres
Durant	George Davis

11. ANNA CHRISTIE

Adapted from Eugene O'Neill's play. Scenario by Frances Marion. Film Editor, Hugh Wynn. Camera, William Daniels. Directed by Clarence Brown. New York Premiere: Capitol Theater, March 14, 1930.

Anna	Greta Garbo
Matt Burke	Charles Bickford
Marthy	Marie Dressler
Chris	George F. Marion
Johnny the Priest	James T. Mack
Larry	Lee Phelps

12. ROMANCE

Adapted from Edward Sheldon's play. Scenario by Bess Meredyth and Edwin Justus Mayer. Film Editors, Hugh Wynn and Leslie F. Wilder. Camera, William Daniels. Directed by Clarence Brown. New York Premiere: Capitol Theater, August 22, 1930.

Rita Cavallini	Greta Garbo
Cornelius Van Tuyl	Lewis Stone
Tom Armstrong	Gavin Gordon
Harry	Elliott Nugent
Susan Van Tuyl	Florence Lake
Miss Armstrong	Clara Blandick
Beppo	Henry Armetta

13. INSPIRATION

Original screen story and scenario by Gene Markey. Film Editor, Conrad A. Nervig. Camera: William Daniels. Directed by Clarence Brown. New York Premiere: Capitol Theater, February 6, 1931.

Yvonne	Greta Garbo
André	Robert Montgomery
Delval	Lewis Stone
Lulu	Marjorie Rambeau
Odette	Judith Vosselli
Marthe	Beryl Mercer
Coutant	John Miljan
Julian Montell	Edwin Maxwell

14. SUSAN LENOX: HER FALL AND RISE

Adapted from the novel by David Graham Phillips. Scenario by Wanda Tuchock. Film Editor, Margaret Booth. Camera, William Daniels. Directed by Robert Z. Leonard. New York Premiere: Capitol Theater, October 16, 1931.

Susan Lenox	Greta Garbo
Rodney	Clark Gable
Ohlin	Jean Hersholt
Burlingham	John Miljan
Mondstrum	Alan Hale
Mike Kelly	Hale Hamilton
Astrid	Hilda Vaughn
Doctor	Russell Simpson

15. MATA HARI

Original screen story and scenario by Benjamin Glazer and Leo Birinski. Film Editor, Frank Sullivan. Camera, William Daniels. Directed by George Fitzmaurice. New York Premiere: Capitol Theater, December 31, 1931.

Mata Hari	Greta Garbo
Lt. Alexis Rosanoff	Ramon Navarro
General Shubin	Lionel Barrymore

Adriani	Lewis Stone
Dubois	C. Henry Gordon
Carlotta	Karen Morley
Caros	Alec B. Francis
Sister Angelica	Blanche Frederici

16. GRAND HOTEL

Adapted from Vicki Baum's play. Scenario by William A. Drake. Film Editor, Blanche Sewell. Camera, William Daniels. Directed by Edmund Goulding. New York Premiere: Astor Theatre, April 12, 1932.

Gursinskaya	Greta Garbo
Baron von Gaigern	John Barrymore
Flaemmchen	Joan Crawford
Preysing	Wallace Beery
Otto Kringelein	Lionel Barrymore
Senf	Jean Hersholt
Meierheim	Robert McWade
Zinnowitz	Purnell B. Pratt

17. AS YOU DESIRE ME

Adapted from Luigi Pirandello's play. Scenario by Gene Markey. Film Editor, George Hively. Camera, William Daniels. Directed by George Fitzmaurice. New York Premiere: Capitol Theater, June 2, 1932.

Maria (Zara)	Greta Garbo
Count Bruno Varelli	Melvyn Douglas
Carl Salter	Erich von Stroheim
Tony Boffie	Owen Moore
Mme. Mantari	Hedda Hopper
Lena	Rafaela Ottiano
Baron	Warburton Gamble
Captain	Albert Conti

18. QUEEN CHRISTINA

Original screen story by Salka Viertel and Margaret F. Levine. Scenario by Salka Viertel and H. M. Harwood. Dialogue by S. N. Behrman. Film Editor,

Blanche Sewell. Camera, William Daniels. Directed by Rouben Mamoulian.
New York Premiere: Astor Theatre, December 26, 1933.

Queen Christina	Greta Garbo
Don Antonio de la Prada	John Gilbert
Magnus	Ian Keith
Chancellor Oxenstierna	Lewis Stone
Ebba	Elizabeth Young
Aage	C. Aubrey Smith
Prince Palatine Charles Gustavus	Reginald Owen
French Ambassador	Georges Renevent

19. THE PAINTED VEIL

Adapted from W. Somerset Maugham's novel. Scenario by John Meehan, Salka Viertel and Edith Fitzgerald. Film Editor, Hugh Wynn. Camera, William Daniels. Directed by Richard Boleslawski. New York Premiere: Capitol Theater, December 7, 1934.

Katrin	Greta Garbo
Walter Fane	Herbert Marshall
Jack Townsend	George Brent
General Yu	Warner Oland
Herr Koerber	Jean Hersholt
Frau Koerber	Beulah Bondi
Mrs. Townsend	Katherine Alexander
Olga	Cecilia Parker

20. ANNA KARENINA

Adapted from Leo Tolstoy's novel. Scenario by Clemence Dane, Salka Viertel and S. N. Behrman. Film Editor, Robert J. Kern. Camera, William Daniels. Directed by Clarence Brown. New York Premiere: Capitol Theater, August 30, 1935.

Anna Karenina	Greta Garbo
Vronsky	Fredric March
Sergei	Freddie Batholomew
Kitty	Maureen O'Sullivan

Countess Vronsky	May Robson
Karenin	Basil Rathbone
Stiva	Reginald Owen
Yashvin	Reginald Denny

21. CAMILLE

Adapted from Alexander Dumas' novel and drama. Scenario by Zoë Akins, Frances Marion and James Hilton. Film Editor, Margaret Booth. Camera, William Daniels. Directed by George Cukor. New York Premiere: Capitol Theater, January 22, 1937.

Marguerite	Greta Garbo
Armand	Robert Taylor
Monsieur Duval	Lionel Barrymore
Nichette	Elizabeth Allan
Nanine	Jessie Ralph
Baron de Varville	Henry Daniell
Olympe	Lenore Ulric
Prudence	Laura Hope Crews
Gaston	Rex O'Malley

22. CONQUEST

Adapted from the novel *Pani Walewska* by Waclaw Gasiorowski and a dramatization by Helen Jerome. Scenario by Samuel Hoffenstein, Salka Viertel and S. N. Behrman. Film Editor, Tom Held. Camera, Karl Freund. Directed by Clarence Brown. New York Premiere: Capitol Theater, November 4, 1937.

Marie Walewska	Greta Garbo
Napoleon	Charles Boyer
Talleyrand	Reginald Owen
Captain d'Ornano	Alan Marshal
Count Walewska	Henry Stephenson
Paul Lachinski	Leif Erickson
Laetitia Bonaparte	Dame May Whitty
Prince Poniatowski	C. Henry Gordon
Countess Pelagia	Maria Ouspenskaya

23. NINOTCHKA

Adapted from an original screen story by Melchior Lengyel. Scenario by Charles Brackett, Billy Wilder and Walter Reisch. Film Editor, Gene Ruggiero. Camera, William Daniels. Directed by Ernst Lubitsch. New York Premiere: Radio City Music Hall, November 9, 1939.

Ninotchka	Greta Garbo
Count Leon d'Algout	Melvyn Douglas
Duchess Swana	Ina Claire
Iranoff	Sig Rumann
Buljanoff	Felix Bressart
Kopalski	Alexander Granach
Commissar Razinin	Bela Lugosi
Count Rakonin	Gregory Gaye

24. TWO-FACED WOMAN

Adapted from a play by Ludwig Fulda. Scenario by S. N. Behrman, Salka Viertel and George Oppenheimer. Film Editor, George Boemler. Camera, Joseph Ruttenberg. Directed by George Cukor. New York Premiere: Capitol Theater, December 31, 1941.

Karin	Greta Garbo
Larry Blake	Melvyn Douglas
Griselda Vaughn	Constance Bennett
O. O. Miller	Roland Young
Dick Williams	Robert Sterling
Miss Ellis	Ruth Gordon
Miss Dunbar	Frances Carson
Dancer	Bob Alton

Index

Page numbers in bold refer to photographs in text.